AGRICULTURAL FUTURES AND OPTIONS

Agricultural futures and options

A GUIDE TO USING NORTH AMERICAN AND EUROPEAN MARKETS

Edited by Richard Duncan

WOODHEAD PUBLISHING LIMITED

Cambridge, England

Published by Woodhead Publishing Ltd,
Abington Hall, Abington,
Cambridge CB1 6AH, England

First published 1992

British Library Cataloguing in Publication Data
A catalogue record for this book is available from the British Library.

ISBN 1 85573 075 8

Designed by Andrew Jones (text) and Chris Feely (jacket).
Typeset by BookEns Ltd, Baldock, Herts.
Printed by Galliard (Printers) Ltd, Great Yarmouth.

Contents

Preface

This book has been written primarily for potential or actual users of agricultural futures markets. It should also provide a useful introduction to more academic students.

In attempting to cover the world's agricultural markets we needed to be flexible about what to include and what to leave out. In the former category we have included coffee, cocoa and sugar, as they are all so much a part of the world's traditional commodity trading and futures markets. In the latter category you will find no further reference to Japanese or South American markets because we see them as solely of domestic interest. Australia and New Zealand have had meat and wool markets respectively but these are now moribund. The same can be said for potatoes in New York and eggs in Chicago. Success in this area of commercial endeavour is just as elusive and uncertain as in any other. There is no magic formula although there are some obvious ingredients and negatives to avoid.

Several knowledgeable contributors were involved to accommodate the variety and geographical spread of the agricultural commodities included. These are duly acknowledged elsewhere but let me take this opportunity to thank them for contributing in a kindly and enthusiastic manner. While, naturally, the United States markets occupy the majority of the pages because of their age, sheer volume and what they can tell us, we wanted to give ample cover to their European equivalents. The oft mentioned '1992' has come. Eastern Europe (a major area of agricultural production) is looking towards various forms of free market forces for salvation. If our experience and historical perspective tell us anything, it is that a freeing up of the European markets will require somewhere to lay off price risk and seek price discovery. The European markets we have today will have to evolve and devolve some to satisfy these needs. In seeing what exists we can perhaps better prepare for the future. During the course of preparing this book dramatic changes have been taking place in Eastern Europe and there is much talk about those countries establishing their own exchange. Time as usual will tell.

We use a lot of jargon and have a particular definition for a lot of quite common words in the futures industry so I commend an early scan of the glossary (Appendix I). It is as well you start early becoming familiar with our vocabulary. I make no apology for the use of repetition as different contributors describe the various agricultural futures and options and remind us what a seemingly strange or common word or phrase means in this context.

The glossary was kindly provided by the Chicago Board of Trade. We have added a few English definitions or additions where necessary and removed references to words or terms not directly concerned with agricultural futures and options.

Richard Duncan

Contributors

John Adcroft A senior commodity futures floor trader for GNI Ltd (a major United Kingdom futures and options brokerage house) and Vice-Chairman of the London Fox Potato Market Management Committee.

Clive Baxter A director of Muirpace Ltd (a major United Kingdom futures and options brokerage house) and Vice-Chairman of the Soyabean Meal Futures Association.

Alan Blair A former senior international grain trader for Tradax and Cargill and Vice-President of Cargill Investor Service Inc, and now an independent consultant on futures and options and commodity futures funds.

Peter Boswell Formerly with a leading private meat trader and Vice-Chairman of the London Meat Futures Exchange. Now concerned with meat exporting for the United Kingdom Meat and Live Stock Commission.

James Davison A senior futures and options broker for Cargill Investor Services Ltd in London.

Richard Duncan Joined Cargill Inc in Minneapolis, Minnesota, USA as a trainee grain trader in 1959 having graduated from Cambridge, England. Apart from just over two years between 1971 and 1973 when he was Director of Wheat Sales for the Canadian Wheat Board he spent his working life with the Cargill Group until July 1988.

Michael Engelbach Managing Director of Ferruzzi Trading (UK) Ltd, a leading international grain exporter from the United Kingdom, and Chairman of the London Grain Futures Market.

Donald Spence Longtime London coffee and sugar trader, formerly head of research for Man International and now an independent futures and options consultant.

Acknowledgements

In addition to the contributors mentioned on the previous page I would like to thank the following:

British Cereal Exports and Stephen Hawes of Harper Graphics, St Ives, Cambridgeshire for permission to reproduce the United Kingdom crop information contained in Chapter 9.

Cargill Investor Services Inc (CIS), Chicago for extensive use of their Insight material when referring to the Chicago Mercantile Exchange meat futures.

Chicago Board of Trade for various statistics and much of the glossary. Also, together with the Chicago Mercantile Exchange, for their assistance in the preparation of the early chapters.

Commodities Corporation of Princeton, USA for permitting the quote about Fundamentals versus Technicals in Chapter 4.

Commodity Research Bureau for allowing the reproduction of their agricultural futures charts included in Chapter 1.

Grain and Feed Trade Association (Clearing House), Home Grown Cereals

Authority, Stephen Carter of London Fox, and Gordon Wood for their help in the production of Chapter 9.

London Fox for the Paris Market statistics.

E D & F Man for their charts included with Chapter 6 and Chapter 8.

New York Coffee, Sugar and Cocoa Exchange for allowing us the use of the Euro-Differential trading example in Chapter 6.

Public Ledger for allowing me to quote extensively from its Golden Jubilee edition of Broomhall's Corn Trade News.

Winnipeg Commodity Exchange for the canola and other Canadian agricultural statistics.

Introduction

To the general public futures, and even more so options on futures, are still a scarcely known, even suspect, subject. Yet, did they but know it, the general public is a major beneficiary from the use of futures and, to a much lesser extent, options. We shall come to the history of agricultural futures shortly, but, suffice it to say now, that most major agricultural commodities, many metals, the main oil and oil products, and financial instruments, are traded by the principal players using futures as a hedge or insurance mechanism. Without the facility to lay off or limit price risk these players would not or could not enter into the scale of forward commitments we take for granted.

Given the time it takes to grow, ship and process the raw materials for common household products such as breakfast cereals, flour, sugar, coffee, potatoes and meat - and given the often unpredictable movement of prices of those raw materials - how is it that retailers can buy what they want when they want for our shopping convenience and without generally undue price fluctuation? Some of the answer is in wise purchasing and stocking but no pipeline is large nor long enough to make much of an impact in the food sector. The main answer for all the above agricultural commodities and several more is by matching expected forward needs with flexible pricing. Futures have provided the flexibility for the major producers, traders and users of raw agricultural materials for many years (in some cases over a century).

It is no coincidence that the world's leading agricultural commodity trading companies remain privately owned over several or more generations. They use futures as a commodity and as insurance whenever they feel the price risk needs limiting or offsetting. Agriculture, and the resulting agribusiness, is a high risk business – wars, weather, 'weevils', and worldwide bureaucracy make for price uncertainty. Yet in an area so politically sensitive and commercially important as food production and marketing there is a need for price and supply reliability. Futures have played and continue to play a major part in providing price transparency and stability.

Birth of exchange

The history of modern futures trading began on the Midwestern frontier in the early 1800s. It was tied closely to the development of commerce in Chicago and grain trade in the Midwest. Chicago's strategic location at the base of the Great Lakes, close to the fertile farmlands of the Midwest, contributed to the city's rapid growth and development as a grain terminal. Problems of supply and demand, transportation and storage, however, led to a chaotic marketing situation, which resulted in the local development of futures markets.

The city had no central trading facility and farmers had to go from merchant to merchant seeking the best price for their crops. At harvest, the streets teemed with farmers' freight wagons and the abundant supply sent prices plummeting. Disappointed farmers often found no buyers at all and chose to dump the grain in Lake Michigan. By spring, supplies were depleted and prices shot up. With prices fluctuating so wildly, disputes between buyers and sellers were common.

As grain trade expanded, a centralized marketplace – the Chicago Board of Trade – was formed in 1848 by 82 merchants. Their purpose was to promote commerce in the city by providing a place where buyers and sellers could meet to exchange commodities. What made the CBOT increasingly popular as a centralized marketplace was the growing use of contracts 'to arrive'. These contracts allowed buyers and sellers of agricultural commodities to specify delivery of a particular commodity at a predetermined price and date.

These early forward contracts in corn were first used by river merchants who received corn from farmers in the late fall and early winter. But the merchants had to store the corn until it reached a low enough moisture content to ship and the river and canal were free of ice.

Seeking to reduce the price risk of storing corn through the winter, these river merchants would travel to Chicago, where they would enter into contracts with processors for delivery of grain at an agreed upon price in the spring. In this way, they assured themselves a buyer and a price for grain. The earliest recorded forward contract in corn was made on March 13, 1851, for 3000 bushels of corn to be delivered in June.

Cash forward contracts did have their drawbacks. They were not standardized according to quality and delivery time, and merchants and traders often did not fulfil their forward commitments. In 1865, the Chicago Board of Trade took a step to formalize grain trading by developing standardized agreements called futures contracts. Futures contracts, in contrast to forward contracts, were standardized as to quality, quantity, and time and location of delivery for the commodity being traded. The only variable was price - discovered through an auction-like process on the trading floor of an organized exchange.

In the same year the Chicago Board of Trade introduced futures contracts, it initiated a *margining system* to eliminate the problems of buyers and sellers not fulfilling their contracts. (A margining system requires traders to deposit funds with the exchange or an exchange representative to guarantee contract performance.) Although early records were lost in the Great Chicago Fire of 1871, it has been quite accurately established that, by 1865, most of the basic principles of futures trading as we know them today were in place. But no one could have guessed how this infant industry would change and develop in the next century and beyond.

Growth in futures trading increased in the late 19th and early 20th centuries as more and more businesses adopted futures trading into their business plans.

As the following list of the world's agricultural futures markets shows the oldest existing exchange outside North America was established in Brazil in 1917 and remains today trading live cattle, arabica coffee and cotton. The oldest existing European exchange was originally established in London in 1929 to trade grain.

Non-US exchanges which trade futures and futures options

Country	Exchange name	Start year*	Status
Brazil	Bolsa de Mercadorias de Sao Paulo	1917	Active
	Bolsa Mercantil & de Futuros	1986	Active
Canada	Winnipeg Commodity Exchange	1909	Active
France	Marche a Terme Int'l de France	1989	Merged with Paris Commodity Exchange in 1989
Hong Kong	Hong Kong Futures Exchange	1979	Active
Japan	Hokkaido Grain Exchange	1951	Active
	Kanmon Commodity Exchange	1953	Active
	Kobe Grain Exchange	1952	Active
	Kobe Raw Silk Exchange	1951	Active
	Kobe Rubber Exchange	1952	Active
	Maebashi Dried Cocoon Exchange	1952	Active
	Nagoya Grain and Sugar Exchange	1956	Active
	Osaka Grain Exchange	1952	Active
	Osaka Sugar Exchange	1952	Active
	Tokyo Commodity Exchange	1951	Active
	Tokyo Grain Exchange	1952	Active
	Tokyo Sugar Exchange	1952	Active
	Toyohashi Dried Cocoon Exchange	1951	Active
	Yokohama Raw Silk Exchange	1951	Active
Malaysia	Kuala Lumpur Commodity Exchange	1980	Active
Netherlands	Amsterdam Potato Futures Market	1959	Active
United Kingdom	Baltic Futures Exchange	1929	Active } merged 1991
	London Futures and Options Exchange	1982	Former London Commodity } merged 1991

* Year in which trading in futures and futures-options began.

The history of grain futures markets

Futures Trading is not new as the next few pages will show, being taken directly from George Broomhall's Corn Trade News Golden Jubilee Edition published in 1938.

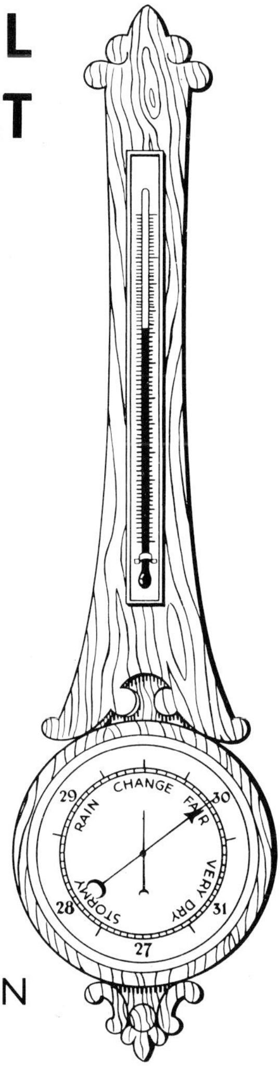

CHANGE
RAIN
FAIR
STORMY
VERY DRY
27
28
29
30
31

MODERN GRAIN FUTURES TRADING

By JAMES E. BOYLE
(*Professor of Rural Economy*).

EACH business day of the year, the world prices of grains are registered in the great futures markets of Liverpool, Winnipeg, Chicago, Buenos Aires and Rotterdam. They are also registered in a dozen or so lesser markets. The futures market is now recognized by business and financial interests as the one most correct and most dependable barometer of grain values.

In ancient Greece and Rome and in the Italian, French, Hanseatic, Dutch and English commercial centres of the Middle Ages, there was a vast grain trade carried on, both domestic and foreign. Yet these earlier business men never did develop future trading as we know this commercial institution to-day. Future trading in grain contracts, as we know and practice it, was actually born about eighty years ago. Yet feeble beginnings of it were visible many centuries earlier.

Future trading is an evolution. But why was it so slow? Why did it take 2,000 years to grow up? Some interesting evidence will throw light on this question.

GRAIN TRADING—THREE TYPES.

Speaking the language of to-day, we can say that in all its long centuries of history, the grain trade has had only three types of trading, namely, the actual, visible grain on the spot, which we call cash grain; specific lots of grain bought for deferred shipment, which we call To Arrive grain; and a contract calling for a definite amount and grade of grain for a specified price and specified place and time of delivery, which contract is legally fulfillable in two ways—by delivery of the grain or by delivery of another contract offsetting the first one. Obviously, in the To Arrive business, the emphasis is on a specific lot of grain, which is finally delivered to settle the contract. In dealing in futures, the emphasis is shifted to the contract, and any lot of grain meeting the grade and place requirements can be delivered on the contract, or, in actual practice, this first contract is almost always offset by a second contract. According to the United States Supreme Court, such offset has the legal effect of delivery.

The difference between To Arrive and Future Trading can be easily illustrated by the case of the flour millers. In the first half of the nineteenth century, American flour millers were the principal users of the To Arrive method of purchase. Making a contract to sell flour and making another contract (often with farmers) to buy wheat, the miller was hedged. In the past fifty years, however, the larger flour mills did their hedging chiefly in the futures market, and since they have no intention of taking delivery of the grade specified in the futures contract, they must and do almost universally settle these futures contracts by offset. Meantime, they buy the particular wheat they need for their blend, some on the spot market, some on the To Arrive market.

FUTURE TRADING—SEVEN FOUNDATION STONES.

The slow development of future trading is better understood if we keep in mind the seven foundation stones or principles on which our current system rests. They are simple and obvious. Yet I must enumerate them here, just to put them in their proper setting. I am speaking here of a futures system whose legality is beyond question, and which is reasonably free from ecclesiastical and political attacks.

1.—TRANSPORTATION. First of all, we must have a system of transportation that can move grain swiftly, cheaply, long distances. We have that. For instance, at the time of the French Revolution, it cost as much to move a bushel of grain fifty miles as it now costs to move it five thousand miles.

2.—COMMUNICATION. In the next place, we must have rapid and accurate communication with all other grain regions and markets of the world. We have that now. An order can be sent from Liverpool to New York, be executed and confirmed, all in less than one minute. One hundred years ago, the usual basis of business in wheat and cotton between Liverpool and New York was either by consignment or on To Arrive terms, two months being the period allowed for arrival.

3.—STORAGE. There must, of course, be ample storage facilities at delivery points or future trading in grain would be an impossibility.

4.—GRADING. Certainly one of the greatest forward steps in developing future trading is an accurate system of standards and grades. Future trading as we know it to-day would be clearly impossible without our scientific grades. In the field of State grain grading, the principal credit must go to Canada's Grain Act of 1912 and to the United States Grain Standards Act of 1916. Before these dates, however, there were several decades of scientific and efficient commercial grades.

5.—WAREHOUSE RECEIPT. A legal and negotiable warehouse receipt is another essential of modern future trading. Out of the bill of lading as a negotiable symbol of property, there developed our present storage documents. Both legally and commercially, these two documents had their real evolution in Great Britain. The Dock Warrant was developed in connexion with the East India Trade at London and the metal trade of Glasgow. During the Middle Ages, of course, the theory prevailed that only goods could be bought and sold—visible, tangible goods present at the market. Thus it was that the famous iron warrants of Glasgow were precursors of the present futures contracts in grain.

6.—NEW VIEW OF SPECULATION. Obviously future trading can have no safe political standing in a country until the lawmakers recognize that speculation is inevitable and necessary.

7.—NEW UNDERSTANDING OF BUSINESS. There must be frank recognition of the two types of temperament in business men :—there is one type who want to speculate—assume risks in hope of profit ; there is another type who do not want to speculate. The organized futures market sets the stage for these two classes. It thereby harnesses that force called speculation and puts it to work in moving the grain from producer to consumer at an admittedly low margin of cost.

BIRTH OF FUTURE TRADING.

We know now, as a positive fact, that future trading was evolved from To Arrive dealings. Scattered examples of To Arrive contracts are to be found as far back as our historical records go. But To Arrive, as a system of grain trading had its birth in connexion with the maritime trade of London and Amsterdam. Cargoes still at sea were sold, delivery on contract to be made upon arrival of the vessel. In England, during the eighteenth century, this form of To Arrive business was slowly and soundly developed, and its basis made secure, legally, by reason of the development of the bill of lading as a negotiable symbol of property.

The To Arrive business, however, was on a firm economic and legal basis at least one hundred years, before it gave birth to the lusty infant known as future trading.

The available records indicate that our modern future trading was actually born in the City of Chicago sometime in the decade following 1850. This was a period of tremendous and rapid expansion in Chicago's grain trade. According to the eighth census of the United States, the value in dollars of U.S. grain exports increased as follows : In the decade 1833-1843, by 8 per cent. over the preceding decade ; during 1843-1853, the increase was 171 per cent. ; during 1853-1863, the increase was 158 per cent. Grain came into Chicago by wagon road, by canal, and by rail. It left Chicago by the Lake. Schooners competed for cargoes. In 1850, Chicago dealers were buying a large portion of their grain To Arrive. To Arrive contracts were frequently sold, and passed through a number of hands before the actual grain arrived.

One day a new thing happened. The master of a schooner, anxious to be certain of a cargo on time for an early sailing, entered into a contract with a dealer for the purchase of this grain. It looked like an ordinary To Arrive deal ; it was not—the merchant did not have the grain. In other words, he had sold short.

This short sale, this *marché à découvert* as the French call it, was the actual birth of modern futures. Final proof is lacking as to the name of the individual who made this first short sale. Evidence now available, however, indicates that it was Mr. J. H. Dole, of 158 South Water Street.

Soon many Chicago dealers were selling short. Soon there developed a lively trade in these contracts. Still, it was not till October 13th, 1865, that the Chicago Board of Trade adopted its first rule on the subject of future trading.

SOME EARLY ATTEMPTS AT FUTURE TRADING.

At this point, we may pause and take a long backward look over economic history, noting particularly the strenuous opposition to any and all development of the grain trade.

It is the clear teaching of all history that wheat should be considered a matter of commerce and not a matter of administration.

Early attempts at future trading failed, chiefly because of ecclesiastical and political opposition. Back of this opposition, of course, was the heavy mass pressure of popular ignorance and prejudice.

Transport of grain, during one thousand years of Europe's history, was blocked by petty customs and police regulations. Thus, at the time of the French Revolution, on the Loire river, between Orleans and Nantes (200 miles), there were twenty-eight custom-houses.

Storage by private dealers was either forbidden entirely or disrupted by the " Ever Normal Granaries " that each Continental country or each large city set up for itself. These granaries had two very marked effects : (1) They made prices fluctuate violently, by adding to all the known economic risks the further unknown political risk. (Parenthetically, I may say, that on February 16th, 1938, the United States passed a law providing for making this granary experiment all over again.)

The decrees of emperors and the laws of States forbade any form of future trading. As early as Charlemagne's day, the French farmer, hard up for cash, would sell his growing crop for future delivery upon payment of a little " earnest money." Charlemagne issued a decree against this type of future trading. This prohibition against buying or selling grain *en vert* was renewed from time to time in France for the next seven hundred years.

The Germanic States had similar prohibitions against selling grain *auf dem Halm.*

It is true that these French and German prohibitions were rarely enforced. Economic attrition finally wore away these useless police measures.

While England escaped the follies of the Ever Normal Granary, yet she did greatly hamper all wholesale and retail trade in grain by her laws on forestalling, regrating, and engrossing. These emotional statutes were enforced in a half-hearted way for several centuries ; then economic attrition wiped out these well-intended but harmful measures.

Mention has been made of ecclesiastical opposition to speculation in all its forms and to future trading in its crude early form. In the year 1565, the learned and potent Bishop of Ghent preached a powerful sermon against the sins of his day, including buying or selling for future delivery. This sermon was printed in pamphlet form, and four or five copies have come down to our time ; one is before me as I write these words. It is only one document out of several hundred I have on this same general subject. Truly may we say that the way of the grain dealer was hard and it still is.

APPROACHING FUTURE TRADING.

Where commerce thrived the most, there the grain traders approached the nearest to future trading exactly as we know it to-day. Two examples :

The Hansa towns, during their last century of full bloom, developed the futures contract in a truly remarkable degree in that form we now call To Arrive. They stopped at that point. In other words, they did not develop short selling, and so they failed to create a real futures market.

The Amsterdam grain dealers, during the sixteenth and seventeenth centuries and early part of the eighteenth century, led all others. In 1493, a rudimentary grain exchange was set up in Amsterdam. In 1617 a modern grain exchange was instituted. At first most of this Dutch trade was on a To Arrive basis. Grain came in from Poland, Danzig, and the " Whole East," and moved South and West. No accurate and reliable grading system was developed, although samples of grain were kept in a cupboard. Under these crude conditions, short selling actually began in Amsterdam as early as 1617. But the contract was too speculative, not merely as to price changes but as to grade risks. The Dutch Government, alarmed at the " unbridled speculation," took drastic steps to curtail or end it. Short selling was prohibited. During the year 1647-1648, the city itself went into the grain business, erecting four large granaries. The city did this to bring down the price and quiet the clamour of the people. A little later, the city was furnishing cheap bread to the people.

Holland's commercial and political peak was passed about 1650.

SUMMARY.

Looking back over all this chequered record, two points at least stand out clear in the present : (1) Future trading has reduced the risks in handling grain. (2) Thereby it has lowered the costs.

This article was written specially for this Jubilee Number by Professor Boyle several months before his death, which took place on 18th September, 1938.

GRAIN EXCHANGES OF THE WORLD

UNITED KINGDOM :

Liverpool (Futures).

London Baltic Exchange (Futures)
Mark Lane Exchange (Spot)

Bristol Channel and West of England.

Hull.

Glasgow.

Leith.

UNITED STATES :

New York.
Chicago (Futures)
Minneapolis (,,)
Kansas City (,,)
Duluth (,,)
St. Louis (,,)

CANADA :

Winnipeg (Futures)
Vancouver.

ARGENTINA :

Buenos Aires (Futures)
Rosario (,,)

CONTINENTAL :

Rotterdam (Futures)
Amsterdam.
Antwerp (Futures)
Marseilles (,,)
Le Havre (,,)
Paris (,,)
Budapest (,,)

AUSTRALIA :

There is a grain exchange at Melbourne and probably also at Sydney, but no futures markets exist in Australia.

PART

1

The North American markets

While a brief mention will be made about the Winnipeg Commodity Exchange, Part 1 is primarily concerned with the futures and options exchanges in Chicago and New York. They are pre-eminent in virtually every agricultural commodity whilst also providing facilities for many non-agricultural futures and options markets to operate. Naturally enough they have been at the forefront of the futures industry's evolution and with their increasingly international approach, particularly from Chicago, are likely to remain so. As the Chicago markets are the world's main agricultural futures fora it is primarily in relation to them that this book deals with the workings and uses of agricultural futures markets as a whole.

CHAPTER

1

Introduction to the Chicago agricultural futures markets

The exchanges

There are in Chicago the two largest futures exchanges in the world: the Chicago Board of Trade (CBOT) and the Chicago Mercantile Exchange (CME), the latter often being referred to as 'the Merc'. There is a third, much smaller exchange in Chicago, the MidAmerica Commodity Exchange ('MidAm'). In the international context, this only needs to be mentioned for the sake of completeness. There are also relatively minor futures exchanges in Kansas City and in Minneapolis, where wheat futures are traded. These will be mentioned towards the end of Chapter 3, together with Chicago wheat futures.

Scale of operations

In the futures industry, it is usual to define the size and importance of an exchange by reference to the number of transactions made during a given

Table 1.1 Transaction volume in the principal US agricultural futures markets, other than those in New York

		1990	1989	1988
Chicago Board of Trade				
Corn		11 423 027	9 270 784	11 105 516
Soyabeans		10 301 905	9 634 802	12 497 096
Soyabean meal		4 904 471	4 486 865	5 313 081
Soyabean oil		4 658 302	4 300 797	4 896 194
Wheat		2 876 270	3 237 709	3 377 738
Oats		433 567	349 836	354 578
Sub-total		34 597 542	31 280 793	37 544 203
Chicago Mercantile Exchange				
Live cattle		3 797 376	4 265 710	5 477 205
Live hogs		2 241 272	1 891 905	2 008 750
Pork bellies		1 303 129	1 310 976	1 186 599
Feeder cattle		391 308	465 274	702 438
Sub-total		7 733 085	7 933 865	9 374 992
Kansas City	Wheat	1 136 234	1 236 084	1 338 711
Minneapolis	Wheat	477 043	413 073	423 542
Sub-total		1 613 277	1 649 157	1 762 253
Grand total		43 943 904	40 863 815	48 681 448

period, i.e. the number of contracts traded. In 1990 the total volume on the eleven licensed futures exchanges in the United States was 276.5 million. Rather more than 75% of this total transacted volume was on the three Chicago exchanges already mentioned. However, both on the CBOT and on the CME, the greater part of the total volume is in the financial futures sector, whereas this book is concerned only with agricultural markets. Within the total US futures volume, including the New York Exchanges, agricultural commodity futures in 1989 and again in 1990 represented about 20%. In 1988, however, a serious drought in the US Midwest caused unusual volatility and nervousness in the prices of agricultural commodities; and in that year agri-futures accounted for 24.6% of the total US volume.

For practical purposes, one can say that any US futures market on which the annual volume is less than 500 000 transactions, i.e. about 2000 per trading day, is clearly a minor market and can be disregarded in a serious study such as the present work, which does not seek to be exhaustive.

The transaction volume 1988–1990, in the principal US agricultural futures markets other than those in New York, is shown in Table 1.1. This table demonstrates that these three years have seen fairly steady volume; 1988 was a particularly active year as a result of price volatility, caused by the very serious drought in that year, which has already been mentioned. In 1986, the grand total volume on the same 12 markets was just below 30 million contracts, that being a period of very large grain and soya stocks in the US and relatively low price volatility as a result. Thus there was a 62% leap in volume between 1986 and 1988.

The MidAm exchange exists for the very small trader: its contracts for wheat, corn, soyabeans and soyabean meal cover quantities one-fifth the size of those at the CBOT; the MidAm cattle and hog contracts are one-half the size of those at the CME. If one converts all the MidAm volume in these commodities to the size of the contracts at the major exchanges, the total MidAm volume in 1990 (in these six markets taken together) would have amounted to less than 500 000 lots. The MidAm will therefore be disregarded in the present study.

What is a futures contract and what is a futures exchange?

Each futures exchange in the US is somewhat comparable with a stock exchange. Its role is to provide a closely regulated trading place, where many market participants can meet and transact business, according to well-defined rules, with the prices of all transactions being almost instantly relayed to other interested parties all over the world. When the concepts of futures markets are being discussed, one often hears the valid and important observation that, because of their transparent openness and because of the diversity of interest on the part of the many participants, futures serve above all as a 'price discovery mechanism'. Major price movements occur first in the futures marketplace and then in the physical dealings, rather than vice versa.

Agricultural futures markets were the earliest type of futures in the US. Certain CBOT grain futures were active even before the First World War, along essentially the same lines as today. It is true that financial futures are now traded (in the US and elsewhere) in much larger volume than agricultural futures. Nevertheless, financial futures did not exist in 1970; and they were a minor sector of the futures industry even in 1980. The history of today's agri-futures contracts on the CME is much shorter than that of the CBOT grains: it begins with pork bellies in 1961, followed by live cattle in 1964.

Table 1.2 shows the historical development of the transaction volume in the six CBOT agricultural contracts. It will be seen that, from 1980 to 1989, there were six years with a total volume between 31 and 38 million contracts and four quieter years with a volume between 20 and 28

Table 1.2 CBOT contract volume, '000 contracts

Year	Corn	Soyabeans	SB meal	SB oil	Wheat	Oats	Total
1965	794	3 565	325	594	684	90	6 052
1970	2 140	2 031	868	1 907	560	92	7 599
1975	4 839	3 914	791	1 490	2 263	155	13 451
1980	11 956	11 768	3 219	3 168	5 428	321	35 860
1981	10 675	10 490	3 040	3 047	4 512	370	32 134
1982	7 951	9 165	2 840	2 994	3 881	425	27 255
1983	11 925	13 680	3 876	3 855	3 887	360	37 583
1984	9 109	11 363	3 822	4 010	2 975	155	31 434
1985	6 393	7 392	3 339	3 647	2 128	99	22 998
1986	6 160	6 134	3 049	3 183	2 090	141	20 756
1987	7 253	7 379	3 798	3 912	1 929	291	24 563
1988	11 106	12 497	5 313	4 896	3 378	355	37 545
1989	9 271	9 635	4 487	4 301	3 238	350	31 281
1990	11 423	10 302	4 904	4 658	2 876	434	34 598

Note: It will be noted that in 1965 soyabeans alone accounted for almost 60% of the entire volume of these six commodities. Wheat volume in 1975 was four times that of 1970. 1972 was the year of the so-called 'great grain robbery': this was the summer when the USSR pounced on unprecedented quantities of US grain, principally wheat, in what the then Secretary of Agriculture called 'the greatest grain transaction in the history of the world'. It will also be noted that, between 1970 and 1980, the futures volume in both corn and soyabeans increased more than five-fold.

million. In a longer perspective it will be noted that even 1985's 'quiet' volume of 23 million was three times that of 1970. But it should also be remembered that the size of the US corn crop in 1970 was only 4.1 billion bushels, whereas that of 1985 exceeded 8.8 billion bushels, an increase of 116%. Similarly the US soyabean crop in 1985, 2.1 billion bushels, was 85% greater than the 1970 figure of 1.14 billion. These remarkable increases in the scale of US production have been brought about more through improved yields per acre than by significant increases in the acreage harvested.

These figures for futures volume are inevitably rather dry and meaningless statistics on first sight. They can take on more meaning when one relates them to the size of the key crops which are actually physically produced in the US in a given year. In the drought year of 1988, CBOT corn futures volume was just over 11 million contracts, each of 5000 bushels; so this volume entailed 55 billion bushels or about 1.4 billion tonnes. The corn crop of the US, harvested in the last quarter of 1988 and thus drastically affected by the drought, was about 4.9 billion bushels. So the entire crop for that year only just exceeded the average *monthly* volume of the CBOT transactions. The pattern is even more startling when one looks at soyabeans for 1990, a fairly normal year. Futures volume of 10.3 million contracts, just over 50 billion bushels or 1.35 billion tonnes, was *twenty-five* times greater than the 1990 soyabean crop produced in the US.

A futures market allows for standardised contracts to be traded at high volume for low cost. What is meant by 'standardised'? Every contract of CBOT corn futures, for example, is for exactly the same quantity of 5000 bushels per contract unit (about 127 tonnes); it covers a standard quality; it calls for delivery on certain standardised dates in the recognised delivery months (March, May, July, September, December); and such delivery must occur in a certified warehouse in either Chicago or Toledo (Ohio). As all these elements are invariable in CBOT corn futures transactions, the only points to be settled between two market participants in the frenzy of the market place are the number of contracts, the delivery month and most importantly the price.

The standardised features of the futures contracts listed above are shown in Table 1.3.

Table 1.3 Standardised features of futures contracts

Commodity	Contract unit	Contract months	Daily limit
CBOT			
Wheat	5000 bushels	Mar, May, July, Sept, Dec	20 cents/bushel
Corn	5000 bushels	Mar, May, July, Sept, Dec	10 cents/bushel
Oats	5000 bushels	Mar, May, July, Sept, Dec	10 cents/bushel
Soyabeans	5000 bushels	Jan, Mar, May, July, Aug, Sept, Nov	30 cents/bushel
Soyabean oil	60 000 lb	Jan, Mar, May, July, Aug, Sept, Oct, Dec	1 cent/lb
Soyabean meal	100 short tons	Jan, Mar, May, July, Aug, Sept, Oct, Dec	$10 per short ton
Minneapolis Grain Exchange			
Wheat	All data the same as for Chicago wheat		
Kansas City Board of Trade			
Wheat	5000 bushels	Same as Chicago	25 cents/bushel
CME			
Feeder cattle	44 000 lb	Jan, Mar, Apr, May, Aug, Sept, Oct, Nov	1.5 cents/lb
Live cattle	40 000 lb	Feb, Apr, June, Aug, Oct, Dec	1.5 cents/lb
Live hogs	40 000 lb	Feb, Apr, June, July, Aug, Oct, Dec	1.5 cents/lb
Pork bellies	40 000 lb	Feb, Mar, May, July, Aug	2 cents/lb

Note: A bushel, the unit of trading grain in the US, is a measure of volume rather than of weight. The metric tonne equivalents of the 5000 bushel contract units on the CBOT are:

- Corn: 127 t
- Wheat and soyabeans: 136 t
- Oats: 72.57 t.

The hours during which futures trading is authorised are as follows, basis local Chicago time:

All CBOT agricultural contracts + the other two wheat markets:	09.30–13.15
CME: Live and feeder cattle:	09.05–13.00
Live hogs and pork bellies:	09.10–13.00

What is meant by 'high volume'?

On a fairly active but not exceptional day, during the 3 hours and 45 minutes in which trading is permitted, the volume of trades in the CBOT corn futures will be over 60 000 contracts. That represents over 7.5 million tonnes; and, since there has to be a buyer and a seller on each transaction, one can say that 15 million tonnes of trading activity have been involved during less than four hours. That is indeed a high volume.

What is meant by 'low cost'?

A brokerage commission is charged on each futures transaction (except in the case of 'locals' - see below). This is a matter of negotiation between principal and broker; but a fairly large market participant will pay less than \$7.50 for each one-sided transaction (i.e. each purchase or sale). Contract values fluctuate considerably. For example, with a value for soyabeans of \$6.00 per bushel, i.e. \$30 000 for a standard contract of 5000 bushels, this commission represents one fortieth of one percent of the value of the goods. That is indeed a low transaction cost.

Who uses the agricultural futures markets and why?

An over-simplified view divides the users of any futures market into two categories:

(a) Hedgers, who have a commercial involvement in the handling and trading of the commodity in question, e.g. corn or cattle. They use the mechanism of the futures market to eliminate from their business activity the greatest part of the hazards implicit in price fluctuations, which (as will be seen) can be substantial in agricultural commodities;

(b) Speculators, who come to the futures markets with the deliberate objective of assuming the risks of the price fluctuations. They are confident that they will be right more often than not in their judgement of price direction; and that they will therefore come away with considerable net profits at the end of the year, as their reward for accepting market risk.

A hedger may be a farmer, a distributor of agricultural commodities or a processor, who makes flour from wheat, or vegetable oil from soyabeans, or chicken-feed from corn and soyabean meal. The commercial hedger (as opposed to the farmer) may be in Iowa or in Italy or in Korea. He is usually in a fiercely competitive business, where potential profit margins are extremely slim. He cannot tolerate the risk of a major price swing against him in his raw material; he is willing to forgo the possibility of a windfall profit from a favourable price swing. The futures are a necessary but secondary element in his business.

A speculator, on the other hand, by definition has no involvement in physical commodity handling. The futures market itself gives the raison d'être for his participation.

In reality this distinction is not watertight. Commercial hedgers should theoretically use the futures at all times for 100% of their exposure to price fluctuation. In practice, to a greater or lesser extent, they deviate from this rule. From time to time, they will 'take a view on the market' and choose to remain uncovered on a portion of their exposure. Their intimate professional grasp of events in their commodity business will sometimes lead them to become 'well-informed speculators'. In the same way, large commercial banks would never boast of speculating. But in reality, in their foreign currency dealing room, they will routinely 'stay uncovered' or 'run a book' on a portion of their dealings. This is only speculation under a different name.

Within the 'pure speculator' category, one must distinguish three subspecies. There are thousands of private individuals, especially in the US but also elsewhere in the world, who are lured into a speculative trade in the futures market by the excitement and by the potential (remote, alas) of 'making a killing'. This is the sort of person who enjoys a visit to a gambling casino or to a greyhound stadium. The professionals in the industry are convinced that the so-called 'small spec' always loses all his money sooner or later - and probably sooner.

On the trading floors of the large US futures exchanges, there are hundreds of professional futures traders, known in the jargon as 'locals'. They form an important group of speculators. In most cases they are self-employed independents; and they play a double role. On the one hand, many of them will act as a 'broker's broker', executing orders from large brokerage houses and receiving a small commission for doing so. On the other hand, they will make frequent trades for their own account and risk. In doing so, they take on speculative risk; but they may do so for only a minute or two, on the basis of their special 'feel' of a given market at a given moment in the day. This can only come from being right on the spot, while the hundreds of orders flow into the exchange. A local will typically sell at 10.14 am and buy back at 10.17 am. It is very unusual for a local to hold any position at the end of the trading day. These locals play an important role in providing liquidity to the markets during quiet moments in the day. They act as 'market makers'.

The third sub-group within the category of speculators consists of professional portfolio managers for outside clients, known as Commodity Trading Advisors or CTAs. Collectively they have great financial power within certain futures markets. Hedgers are examined in more detail in Chapter 3 and CTAs in Chapter 4. Enough has already been said above on the subject of small specs and locals.

Futures market prices each day are the result of the interaction of the needs and the market opinions of many hundreds of dealers, speculators and floor brokers. No one of these and no group of these can control or manipulate or even influence price levels, except in a very short time-frame.

A study of the price charts in Fig. 1.1 illustrates the degree of price fluctuations within the main agricultural commodites. In three cases out of four (the exception being live cattle) one can see an instance, during the years 1987 to 1990, of a price movement within a twelve month period of between 60 and 80% from low to high.

Going long and short in a futures market

A Long is a trader who has bought contracts which he has not yet resold. A Short is a trader who has sold contracts and has not yet bought them in. Here an important basic feature of futures markets must be stressed, which is not applicable to other markets such as stock exchanges. It is just as easy and as usual, and it is no more hazardous or speculative, for any market participant (whether a hedger or not) to enter the market with a short position, by selling contracts, knowing that he will need to

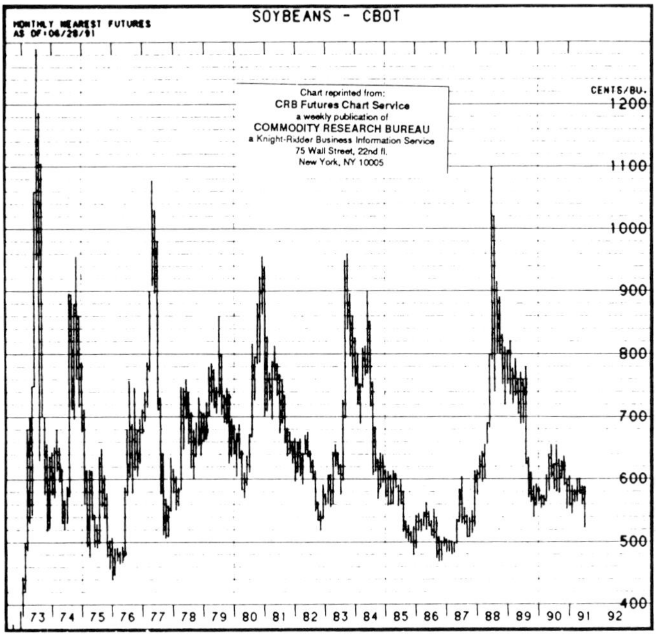

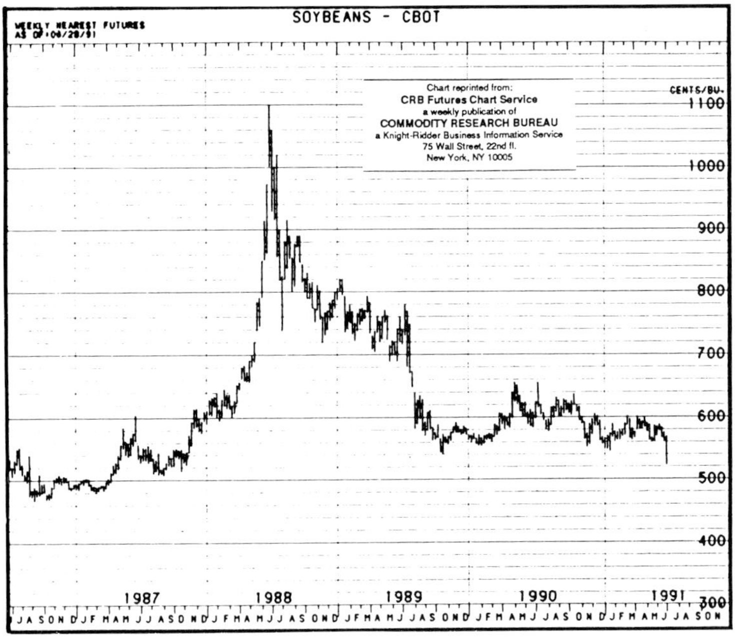

1.1 Price charts for soyabeans, corn, live hogs and live cattle traded on the Chicago Board of Trade.

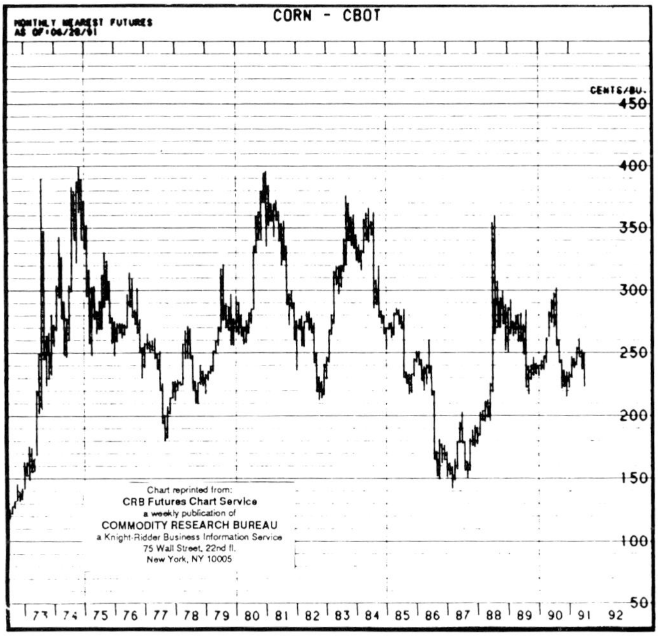
CORN - CBOT
CENTS/BU.
450
400
350
300
250
200
150
100
50
73 74 75 76 77 78 79 80 81 82 83 84 85 86 87 88 89 90 91 92
Chart reprinted from:
CRB Futures Chart Service
a weekly publication of
COMMODITY RESEARCH BUREAU
a Knight-Ridder Business Information Service
75 Wall Street, 22nd fl.
New York, NY 10005

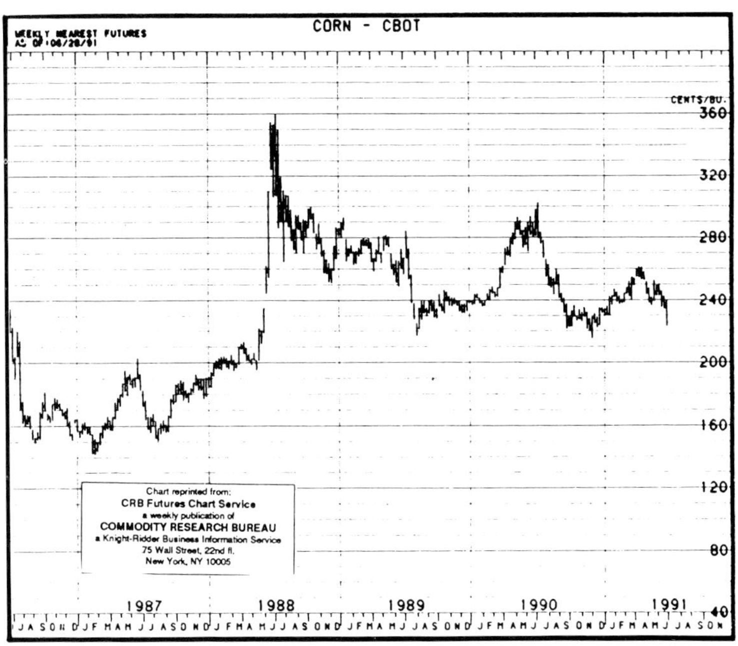
CORN - CBOT
CENTS/BU.
360
320
280
240
200
160
120
80
40
1987
1988
1989
1990
1991
Chart reprinted from:
CRB Futures Chart Service
a weekly publication of
COMMODITY RESEARCH BUREAU
a Knight-Ridder Business Information Service
75 Wall Street, 22nd fl.
New York, NY 10005

1.1 cont'd

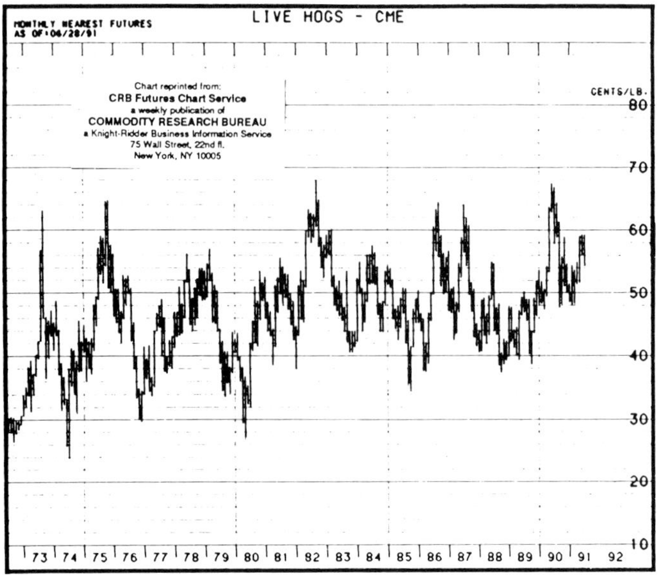
LIVE HOGS - CME
Chart reprinted from:
CRB Futures Chart Service
a weekly publication of
COMMODITY RESEARCH BUREAU
a Knight-Ridder Business Information Service
75 Wall Street, 22nd fl.
New York, NY 10005
CENTS/LB.
80
70
60
50
40
30
20
10
73 74 75 76 77 78 79 80 81 82 83 84 85 86 87 88 89 90 91 92

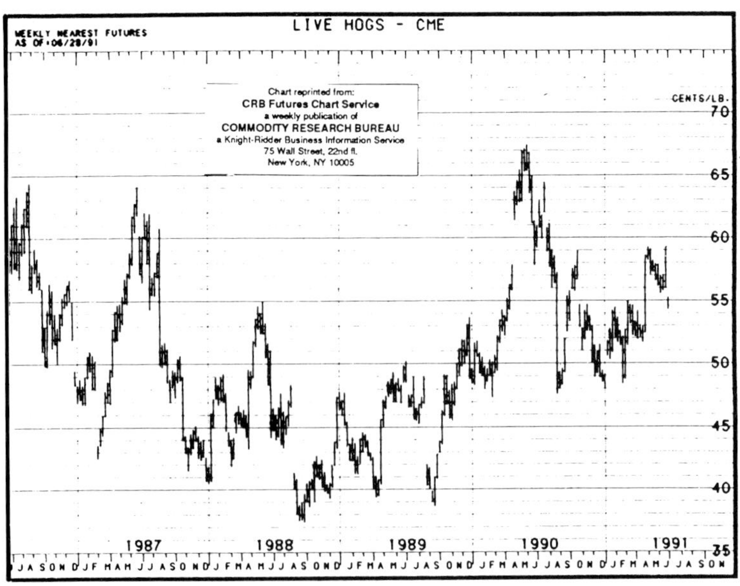
LIVE HOGS - CME
Chart reprinted from:
CRB Futures Chart Service
a weekly publication of
COMMODITY RESEARCH BUREAU
a Knight-Ridder Business Information Service
75 Wall Street, 22nd fl.
New York, NY 10005
CENTS/LB.
70
65
60
55
50
45
40
35
1987 1988 1989 1990 1991

1.1 cont'd

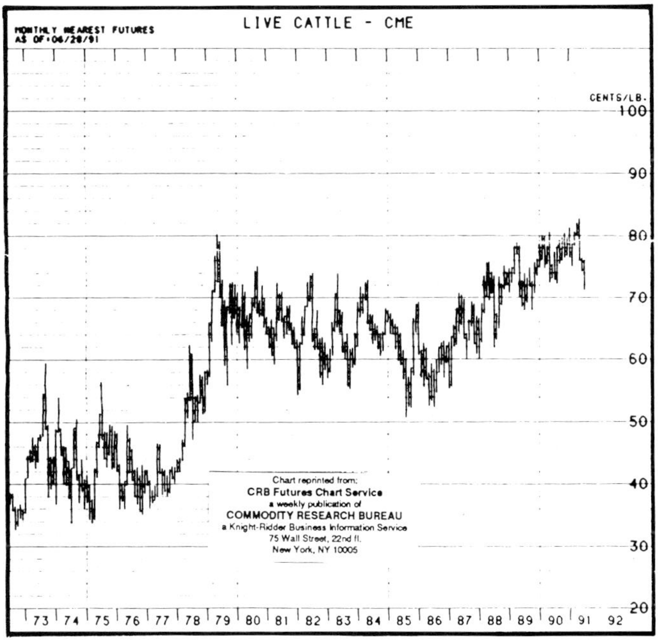
MONTHLY NEAREST FUTURES
AS OF 06/28/91
LIVE CATTLE - CME
CENTS/LB.
100
90
80
70
60
50
40
30
20
Chart reprinted from:
CRB Futures Chart Service
a weekly publication of
COMMODITY RESEARCH BUREAU
a Knight-Ridder Business Information Service
75 Wall Street, 22nd fl.
New York, NY 10005
73 74 75 76 77 78 79 80 81 82 83 84 85 86 87 88 89 90 91 92

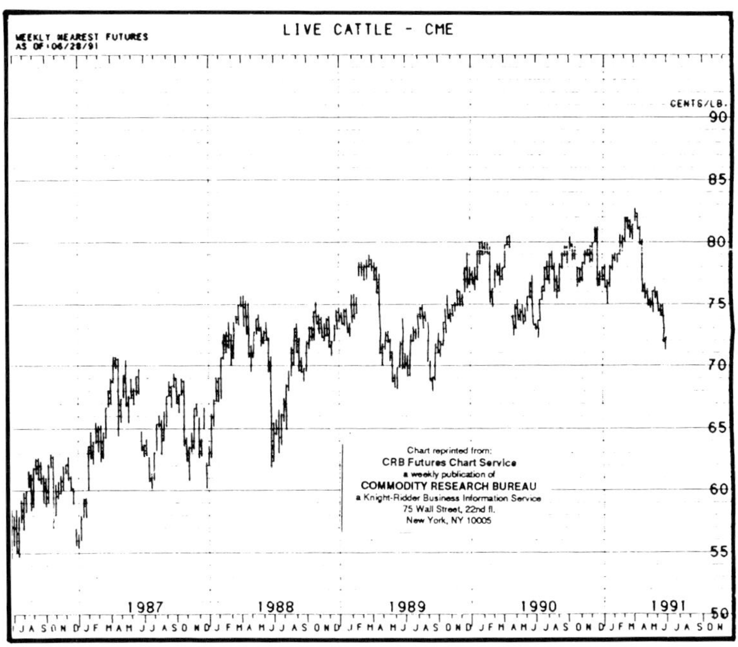
WEEKLY NEAREST FUTURES
AS OF 06/28/91
LIVE CATTLE - CME
CENTS/LB.
90
85
80
75
70
65
60
55
50
Chart reprinted from:
CRB Futures Chart Service
a weekly publication of
COMMODITY RESEARCH BUREAU
a Knight-Ridder Business Information Service
75 Wall Street, 22nd fl.
New York, NY 10005
1987 1988 1989 1990 1991
J A S O N D J F M A M J J A S O N D J F M A M J J A S O N D J F M A M J J A S O N D J F M A M J J A S O N D J F M A M J J A S O N

1.1 cont'd

cover or buy back his commitment at a later date, as it is to 'go long' by buying futures contracts which he will later have to liquidate or resell. It is not easy for the uninitiated to grasp this point; but they must do so.

This brings us to a very important, but paradoxical, fact of life in the futures markets. All agricultural futures markets (with the exception of the CME feeder cattle contract, see below) are geared to the clear understanding that, upon maturity of the contracts in each established delivery month (as already mentioned, for corn these are March, May, July, September and December), physical delivery of the goods *can* take place, as prescribed in the contract specification. When trading stops in a given delivery month, all remaining shorts must stand ready to make a physical delivery; and all remaining longs must accept physical delivery and start paying warehousing and other charges accordingly. However (and herein lies the paradox), in reality physical delivery occurs on only a very small scale (normally less than 2% of all the positions that have at some time been held by traders during the trading life of the contract). Over 98% of futures positions entered are 'offset' before maturity, i.e. those who have bought (longs) will subsequently resell their contracts before the date for possible physical delivery arrives; and those who have sold short will buy back their contracts (whether at a profit or at a loss is immaterial) before the date arrives on which they might be required to make a physical delivery.

The reasons for this paradox are twofold. Firstly, the awareness of possible physical delivery must always be present, if the contract is to be meaningful for the hedgers. Otherwise the speculative element might get carried away from time to time; and the futures prices would have a life of their own which was in no way linked to the realities of the value of the underlying commodity. But, secondly, the true role of the futures markets is to provide price 'discovery' and price protection for hedgers, as will be seen in more detail later, and is not to provide a mechanism for gaining access to physical goods nor for disposing of them.

Some statistics on physical deliveries on the CBOT agri-futures are shown in Table 1.3. It will be seen that the volume of deliveries, year in year out and across the full spectrum of the CBOT agri-futures, is less than 1% of the year's total volume of transactions. Nevertheless, from time to time, the quantities delivered against one particular maturing contract can be substantial. Almost 140 million bushels were delivered against the November 1990 soyabean contract. This equates to 3.8 million tonnes and is over 20% of the expected US soyabean exports for the whole crop-year 1990–1991. However, this does not mean that such a large quantity of soyabeans were actually in Chicago's enormous grain silos. Any market participant who is long 'spot' futures at the beginning of a delivery month knows that he may receive from the clearing house a delivery notice coming from one of the shorts who plans to make physical delivery. The party who is long may be content to take physical delivery and pay for the goods which he has thus acquired via the futures market. But in many cases it does not suit him to do so. In that case he sells his futures and informs the clearing house that he wishes to 'redeliver' the physical goods which have been tendered to him. Thus the same warehouse receipts, giving title to physical grain, frequently circulate several times among different 'owners', each one keeping his ownership only for a few hours. Futures professionals will watch to see whether delivery receipts come into 'strong' or 'weak' hands, as this can have considerable impact on the nearby futures price and on the carrying charge from the spot to the next delivery month.

As already mentioned, the practice of (possible) physical delivery at the maturity of a futures contract applies to all the agri-futures in Chicago except feeder cattle on the CME. For the first 15 years of the existence of this contract, physical delivery was potentially involved with feeder cattle. But experience showed that this led to an unacceptable number of problems and disputes owing to the wide range of grades, weights and locations which were permitted under the CME delivery rules. Therefore, with effect from the September contract in 1986, the CME introduced 'cash settlement' on feeder cattle futures, for those who had not sold out their longs or covered in their short positions before the last day for trading. This important procedural change has been well received in the trade. The average annual number of 'deliveries' (i.e. cash settled contracts) in feeder cattle in the four years following the change has been over 7500 contracts, whereas in 1984 and 1985 it was less than 2500.

In 1991 the CME introduced a new futures and options contract on broiler chickens; and here again the futures upon maturity are to be settled not with a physical delivery but with cash, on the basis of a USDA (United States Department of Agriculture) survey of average broiler prices in 12 major US cities. At the time this book was written, it was too early to determine whether this new CME broiler contract will prove to be a viable and successful venture for the exchange.

How is business conducted on the futures markets?

Anyone who visits the CBOT or CME for the first time, especially at the time when an exchange official rings a bell to signal the start of the day's trading, can be forgiven if he comes away convinced that he has witnessed unadulterated bedlam. At various places on the floor area of the huge trading room have been installed the various 'pits' for the different commodities which are to be traded. Each pit is octagonal, with several steps leading up from the floor to a raised octagonal platform and then further steps down from this platform to an inner space back at floor level. Seen from the top step, this inner space at a lower level looks slightly like a pit, but really not enough to justify the name. Crowded on the steps of each of the active pits are the floor brokers and locals who actually execute the transactions. More people in a crowded space can see more other people on the steps of such a pit than if everyone was standing at floor level and was craning to see other traders over the shoulders of those standing in front.

The rules of the Chicago Futures Exchanges require that all business be conducted 'by open outcry': each trader is required to shout out to all other interested parties what quantity of which contract he wishes to sell or to buy, and at what price. The purpose of this requirement is to ensure that no trading takes place surreptitiously, between two individual traders, without others being given an opportunity to participate. However, since there may be well over a hundred people crowded into one pit less than 20 feet across, this obligatory shouting alone would leave some problems of comprehension. Therefore the shouting is accompanied by the use of uniformly understood hand signals, by which each trader indicates whether he is trying to sell or buy and what quantity and at what price. He does not need to use hand signals to express which delivery month is involved, because each step in the pit is for one delivery month only.

One would rather expect in the 1990s that this trading technique of yelling and gesticulating would have been superseded by the use of state-of-the-art computers and electronic dealing screens. Such tools do indeed exist. They are already used on certain futures and options exchanges outside the US. Discussions have been continuing for several years with a view to introducing 'screen trading' in addition to 'open outcry' for certain contracts on the CME and the CBOT. This plan is expected to become reality some time in 1992. However, in the first stage at least, this screen trading is likely to be introduced only outside the currently authorised trading hours for traditional open outcry trading in the Chicago pits. And in all probability this major innovation will be applied only to certain financial futures, which puts the subject outside the scope of the present study.

On the trading floors of the giant Chicago exchanges, there are many people involved other than the floor brokers and locals who are shouting themselves hoarse in the pits. At suitable locations, mostly around the sides of the room where all this organised chaos is actually being conducted, there are hundreds of telephones. There are also hundreds of telephone clerks (and some management personnel) from brokerage companies, whose task is to provide the vital information link between the pits and the world outside. And, as the physical link between the telephone clerks and the actual traders, there are scores of messengers or 'runners', dashing to and fro between the phones and the pits.

For a brokerage house, an error in the execution of a client's order is likely to be very costly. Discipline in following all routine procedures is vital. The client demands extreme speed and extreme precision from his broker, although one could see an inherent contradiction between these two demands.

A grain dealer in New York or a soyabean processor near Rotterdam or a cattle yard operator in Oklahoma will have telephoned to his futures broker to bark an order for immediate execution. The broker, before even finishing his brief conversation with his customer, will have grabbed another telephone and started to give the order to his colleague on the telephone team on the CBOT or the CME. At the same time, the broker in New York or Rotterdam or Oklahoma City will have written down on a special order slip document the essentials of the order. He will (by exchange rules, he must) have a time-stamping machine on his desk, so that he can instantly register the exact moment when he received the order from his client; and also the exact time that he passed on that order to his colleague in Chicago.

Similarly, that colleague in Chicago, as he repeats the order back to the outside broker to ensure that it is understood, will time-stamp his own order slip, of which he will keep a carbon copy. The original is given to a runner, who dashes across the room and hands it to the floor-broker in the actual pit for immediate execution (if the price required by the client is immediately obtainable from another trader in the pit). Amazingly, the whole process, from the moment that a far-away client gives his order until he receives his confirmation that it has been executed in Chicago, often takes only 100 seconds.

The whole scene on the floor of the futures exchanges is made more colourful by the fact that each person (broker, clerk or runner) wears a brightly coloured cotton jacket, whose colour serves to show by which brokerage firm he is employed. Between the yelling and the running and the jostling, the futures trading floors, and especially the pits themselves, are very physical places. The percentage of women in the trading pits is very small. If there were no dress rules, one would expect the preferred uniform of the pit traders to be a T-shirt and jeans. In point of fact, however, the Chicago exchanges rigidly require that each trader wears a jacket (albeit cotton) and a proper shirt and a tie (although the top shirt button is seldom done up and the knot of the tie may be in line with the third buttonhole).

Regulatory surveillance

The US futures exchanges such as the CBOT and the CME are self-regulating in all important aspects of the day-to-day activities of their members. Each has substantial permanent staff; and there are also a number of committees, whose members are employed by member firms but give some of their time every month to the committee meetings of the exchange. Members found to be in violation of any of the rules of the exchange may be ordered to pay a substantial fine and/or may be barred from trading on the exchange for a certain period of time. The offence may be that of 'arranging' a transaction with another member other than by open outcry; or of allowing a client to continue to hold futures positions with the firm, without maintaining the required amount of margins in his account; or of failing to keep complete files of every transaction executed for every client. The exchange staff conduct frequent audits without warning in the offices of the clearing members. However, the exchanges are corporate entities and their officers are ultimately acting in the collective best interests of their members, which may not always be the best interests of the public or of the country.

There is also a governmental agency which in turn regulates and supervises the exchanges themselves, as well as the various market participants, be they large brokerage companies or individual locals. This agency, created by Act of Congress and based in Washington, is called the Commodity Futures Trading Commission or CFTC. They too can take disciplinary action against individuals and/or companies found to be in breach of one or other of the CFTC's detailed regulations covering the trading of futures and options on US exchanges.

These two layers of surveillance over the activities of brokers in the pits, and also of the back-office operations of the brokerage firms, are well-known and highly visible. Something very different burst like a bombshell over the Chicago Futures community in January 1989. This was the announcement, deliberately made with maximum publicity, that the US Federal Bureau of Investigation had for many months been investigating pit trading practices on the Chicago Exchanges. The FBI went so far as to place undercover agents in the pits, where they posed as ordinary traders and gradually became accepted as friends and colleagues by others who had been in the pits before them. As a result of this 'sting' operation, over 40 traders from four Chicago pits were indicted on charges ranging from 'prearranged trading' to the very serious offence of racketeering. Ten soyabean traders went to trial and were found guilty on many but not all of the charges against them. This entire FBI operation aroused great controversy. There are many people in the futures community who feel it was not handled in the way that would have brought the greatest benefit at a reasonable cost.

Be that as it may, the life of a pit trader can never be quite the same again. In future he knows that a breach of the rules and regulations of the exchange can lead, not only to a fine and suspension from trading, but also to a jail sentence and a criminal record. One can safely say that, of the thousands of people trading in the Chicago pits, the overwhelming majority are men of total integrity. Inevitably, among so many individuals, there are a few who break rules from time to time. During the dismay in the early weeks after the explosion of this FBI bombshell, there were prophets of gloom who described this as a blow to the good name of the US futures community from which it would take years to recover. But in fact it was quickly seen to be, not exactly 'much ado about nothing', but a salutary form of shock treatment: it would lead the exchanges to tighten up their own surveillance, but it would not cause lasting loss of confidence among those who use the markets. (In the aftermath of the FBI sting, the CBOT increased the size of its compliance and audit staff by more than one-third. They also committed about one million dollars to improving their Computerised Trade Reconstruction (CTR) system.) The proof of the pudding is in the eating. In spite of all the adverse publicity throughout 1989, total US futures volume was 8.75% higher than the record figures achieved in 1988 (before the news of the FBI investigation reached the public); and the volume in 1990 was even higher than in 1989.

CHAPTER

2

Definitions

This chapter explains some of the jargon terms which are often used by futures traders but which are unfamiliar to the person in the street. These definitions lead into some further exploration of the way in which futures markets work.

Clearing house

The clearing house is the financial backbone of each futures exchange. During the trading hours, the floor brokers and the member firms of the exchange conclude hundreds of deals with other brokers and firms, under the watchful but largely passive surveillance of employees of the exchange. At the close of each day's trading session, however, these member firms must submit details of all their transactions for that day to the clearing house staff, who reconcile all the scribbled records and check for the occasional discrepancies which inevitably occur from time to time in the frenzy of the trading hours. The clearing house then pays out cash balances to and collects cash balances from member firms, on the basis of the day's fluctuations and of the new positions entered. By definition, once discrepancies between members have been resolved, the clearing house will be neither a net gainer nor a net loser on the day. At the end of each day, each member firm deals financially with the clearing house only and not with other member firms. This remarkable feature of the futures exchange system is critically important to the functioning of the market. It enables every market participant to buy and sell futures with no concern whatsoever about the financial standing or the credit-worthiness of the counter-party. A few hours after each transaction, the clearing house has become the seller to every buyer and the buyer to every seller. The clearing house itself is guaranteed collectively by its member firms.

Clearing member firms

There is a paradox in the position of the futures brokerage firms who actually handle transactions for their clients all over the US and indeed all over the world. On the one hand, their role is purely that of agent, acting on behalf of their clients. The clients alone will decide at what price and at what time they wish to buy or sell certain contracts on the futures exchange; and they will give their exact orders to the brokerage firm, which will execute these instructions as an intermediary on behalf of the clients. And yet, at the end of the day, that brokerage firm as a clearing member of the exchange is a principal vis-á-vis the clearing house and has total financial responsibility to the clearing house, even if a client denies a trade or fails to meet his own financial obligation to the broker.

Margin

This is another crucial but unusual feature of futures markets. When any market participant, however large or small, buys a futures contract, he is required to deposit with his broker (who in turn must deposit with the clearing house) a so-called initial margin of a fixed dollar amount per contract. This is usually described as a 'good-faith deposit' and is certainly not a partial payment of the value of what he has bought. This last point is reinforced by the fact that an identical initial margin payment is required when one sells a contract. The initial margin serves as a form of cash float in the books of the executing broker, as long as a given client maintains an open (i.e. not yet offset) futures position. It is a small amount, determined by the exchange, and is subject to change in the event of major price changes and/or abnormal volatility in the price of a given commodity. Under normal market conditions, the initial margin will represent between 3 and 8% of the full value of a contract.

Day by day, the value of each client's open positions is 'marked to the market'. If an open position shows a paper loss, the client must deposit additional funds with his broker, known as variation margin, so as to replenish the cash float, after allowance for the loss which the client would incur if he closed out his position at the new market value. By the same token, if the client's position is showing unrealised profits, he is entitled to draw funds out of his account with his broker, provided that the permanent float of the initial margin remains intact.

Open interest

Open interest means the total number of contracts outstanding and uncovered at the end of each day's business. These figures, which are carried daily in the Wall St Journal for example, serve to show in which deferred delivery months the trading volume has been mainly concentrated. Also, professionals will watch the day-to-day increase or decline of open interest, to monitor whether new participants are entering the market or, conversely, existing positions are on the whole being removed. For corn, as an illustration one could see the following open interest figures for 19 April 1991:

May	54 236
July	91 212
September	19 453
December	58 086
March '92	7 469
May	1 359
July	345

Total open interest 232 160 down 1 944 from previous day

The corresponding figures for 8 May 1991 were:

May	2 895
July	94 851
September	20 815
December	73 775
March '92	9 811
May	2 115
July	923

Total open interest 205 185 down 322 from previous day

It will be noticed that there has been a dramatic decrease in the open interest for the nearby May contracts between these two listings. This is to be expected, since the second list refers to a date in May, i.e. within the month for physical delivery. The other major change is a sharp increase in the open interest for December, which corresponds to the new crop. This is also to be expected at this season, since late April and early May is the season for major planting of the new crop acreage. Many farmers and country grain dealers make forward sales at this time of the year for the new crop delivery period. Hence a rapid increase in the open interest for the December contract. To some extent the liquidation of May contracts between 19 April and 8 May has led to a decline in the absolute open interest figure. And to some extent the former May positions have been moved across by hedgers into the more deferred months.

Carry-over

In grain and soya jargon, carry-over is the quantity from the old crop which remains in storage from the previous crop at the beginning of the new crop-year, i.e. the eve of the new harvest period. When talking of ending stocks, the term 'carry-out' is frequently used. When looking at the new crop-year's supply and demand balance, the old carry-over is referred to as the 'carry-in' or 'beginning stocks'. Among the principal countries competing with the US as exporters to European and Asian markets are Brazil (for soyabeans) and Argentina (for corn). Because of their very high interest rates, these two countries normally ensure that the exportable balance from each year's crop (after domestic needs are satisfied) is in fact exported within ten months and that their carry-over is a very small percentage of each year's production. Consequently the US tends to be the residual supplier to the world; and when the world has a large carry-over situation, the lion's share of the physical stocks are held in the US, where storage facilities are abundant and where the costs of long term storage (including the financing of the inventory) tend to be relatively low. Futures prices are very much influenced by the statistics of supply versus usage ('disappearance') in a given commodity in a given year. As one would expect, weather can have a major impact on the relationship of carry-over to total usage.

For US wheat in 1986, the carry-out was a staggering 97% of usage, meaning hypothetically that the US could have gone through another year with no wheat production at all. And yet, largely as a consequence of the devastating drought of 1988 in the US Midwest, the 1989 wheat carry-out was only 24% and the 1989 soyabean carry-out was below 10% of usage. It is no surprise, therefore, that Chicago May wheat futures were trading during the final months of 1988 above $4.00 per bushel, whereas for many weeks in 1986 they had been trading below $2.50.

Carrying-charge market and inverse market

Carrying-charge market and inverse market are terms used in US futures jargon: their UK counterparts are contango and backwardation respectively. A carrying-charge situation is one in which the forward months have a higher price than the spot or nearby delivery month. An inverse market is one in which the forward has a lower price than the nearby.

For example, the closing prices for 9 May 1991 on the Comex (New York) Gold Futures, were as follow:

June 359.30   Aug 362.00   Oct 365.00   Dec 368.10

This is a classic carrying-charge market. For each sixty days forward, the price is higher by approximately $3.00 per ounce. [The price difference is slightly distorted between the nearest month (June) and the next delivery month (August). This is not unusual, because the nearest month has by far the greatest activity (and open interest). In the very last seconds of the day's trading activity, there is often a flurry of trades in the nearby month, after the last trades in deferred months have been recorded; this can distort the inter-month price relationship.]

The uninitiated could easily suppose, upon reading those gold prices, that the market, i.e. the professional traders, holds the view that gold prices will be higher in December than today; in other words, that the market is bullish. This is an entirely false conclusion. The carrying-charge pattern of prices is caused by the simple fact that there is plenty of gold available in storage vaults today; and mine production is expected to continue at a level sufficient to ensure that no scarcity is feared in the foreseeable future. Thus arbitrageurs will be ready to make combined trades in the nearby and deferred months, to ensure that the price differential remains very close to the real cost of financing gold in storage. To take a naïve scenario, if Mr Goldfinger was convinced that the value of gold next December was going to be no higher than $360.00 and started to offer the Dec futures aggressively, the price of Dec futures relative to August could never narrow by more than (say) 15 cents: dozens of arbitrageurs would always be ready to buy the Dec from Mr Goldfinger and simultaneously sell the August, to maintain the carrying-charge of about $6.00. This is a riskless trade for the arbitrageur, as long as dollar interest rates do not make a sharp move.

On returning to agricultural futures, the story is by no means so simple. In spite of modern technology on the farm, each twelve month crop cycle in wheat, corn and soyabeans is potentially fraught with major problems for the farmers; and each crop-year is different from every other year. In certain years (see under Carry-over above), the US has very large supplies of grain and/or soyabeans in storage on the eve of a new harvest. In such cases the pattern of prices becomes close to that which we have just seen in gold. Traders will then be watching what the jargon calls 'full carry', a shorthand expression for the full cost of physically carrying (storing) grain or soyabeans from one delivery month to another (for example, from May to July). There are three components in the cost of full carry: warehousing charges; interest; and insurance. Traders will know that the premium for July corn futures over May futures can never exceed full carry, since arbitrageurs will always be ready to intervene to prevent this from occurring. In a period of burdensome carry-over, the answer to the question how close the May–July spread, i.e. price differential, gets to full carry will depend on such factors as the availability of Chicago storage space and the relative size of the carry-over between the three principal crops.

In other years, however, such as in 1988, the most recent year of serious drought in the US Midwest, a sharply reduced new crop plus the carry-over from the previous one do not suffice to satisfy all the domestic and export demand which would normally be expected. In such cases price rationing has to occur, i.e. prices for the futures and the related physical goods must rise sufficiently to remove a part of the normally anticipated demand. In such years with a small or 'tight' carry-over, but with expectations of an abundant new crop, a substantial inverse can develop from old crop soyabean futures (nearby months) to the November futures, by which time ample fresh supplies from the new crop will be available.

Let us look again at the consequences for the futures of the 1988 drought. The cycle of the US soyabean crop is for planting to occur between mid-April and mid-May, while harvesting occurs mainly in October. In 1988 the dramatically unfavourable hot weather was experienced in the July-August period, when the soyabean plants are particularly vulnerable to a lack of moisture. In July 1988, when the market was focusing on the implications of the immediate hot, dry weather, trading had already begun all the way forward to the November 1989 contract, that is to say one and a half crop cycles into the future. The following price pattern developed between the July 1989 futures, representing the tail-end of the 1988 crop which was sharply reduced by the drought of July 1988 while the crop was growing in the fields, and the November 1989 futures, representing a crop which would not even be planted until April-May 1989. Thus these two contract months would compare values for one crop which was known to be relatively small; and those for the subsequent crop which traders expected to be relatively large in response to high prices at the time of 1989 plantings, see Table 2.1.

Table 2.1 Prices for July and November soyabean futures

	July 1989 futures, $	**Nov 1989 futures, $**	**Difference (inverse), $**
On 1 July 1988	9.37	7.83	1.54 (16 %)
On 1 December 1988	7.74	6.72	1.02 (13 %)
On 1 February 1989	7.85	7.38	0.47 (6 %)

The same situation can prevail in the livestock sector, whose futures are traded on the CME. Here again the real world of agriculture ensures that there is a period of many months between a farmer's decision to produce additional piglets or calves and the moment when the mature animals are available in the marketplace. In cattle and hogs, as with corn or soyabeans, one can have a market situation, in which there is a relative shortage in the nearby months, but good reason to believe that there will be an abundant supply at some known date in the future: this is the scenario which leads to inverse markets. The closing prices for 22 April 1991 on the CME show the nearby April price for live cattle at 79.92, but the August 1991 price at 74.65 cents per pound. Live hogs on the same date showed an even sharper inverse, with nearby June trading at 58.10 cents per lb and December at 48.25 (17% inverse).

A wry expression in the agricultural markets (which can also be applied to the price of crude oil) says that 'the best cure for high prices is high prices'. A period of (historically) high prices encourages increased production, which in due course leads to lower prices. By the same token, the best cure for low prices is low prices: when US farmers are not able to sell their crops or their livestock for what they consider to be the minimum acceptable price, they will simply produce less. (Their counterparts in France would be more inclined to block the highways with their tractors and organise protests in Brussels.) In the case of field crops in the US, the Federal Government has a whole series of programmes whose purpose is to induce farmers to plant less in times of burdensome carry-over: the farmer is simply paid to leave a certain percentage of his acres fallow, under rather complicated conditions. In the case of livestock, as CIS put it in April 1989: 'The main factor influencing changes in hog numbers is producer profitability. The "hog-corn ratio" has long been a quick and easy standard for assessing profitability. It is simply the price of hogs per cwt divided by the price of cash corn per bushel. The widely accepted break-even ratio has been 20.0. The recent average has been 15.2, with hogs at $39.40/cwt and corn at $2.59 per bushel. Hence producer returns are unfavourable and are not likely to rebound in the coming weeks: hence accelerated liquidation of the breeder herd is likely.' A futures trader must always be alert to fundamental price-influencing factors such as these.

Limit

There are two special uses of the word 'limit' in futures jargon.

(a) *Position limits*. For each agricultural contract, the exchange decides on a limit or ceiling on the number of contracts which any single market participant is permitted to hold, be it on the short or the long side of the

market. The objective of this measure is to ensure that no trader can attempt to control or 'corner' a market and thus be in a position to distort price and to squeeze those who are on the other side from his position.
(b) *Price limit*. The exchange authorities recognise the need to provide a braking effect on any futures market which is subject to a violent price move, as a result of a startling item of news. This may be a political event, such as President Carter's embargo on shipments of US grain to the USSR at the time of the invasion of Afghanistan; or a startling weather forecast; or the publication by the US Department of Agriculture of some important statistics, such as Farmers' Planting Intentions or the Quarterly Report of Hogs and Pigs. For each agricultural futures contract, the exchange determines a daily price limit, i.e. a maximum permitted price movement in one day's trading session above or below the previous market day's 'settlement price', i.e. the officially established closing price. These are permanently established and known to all traders; they are not merely determined at the moment that they are required.

Let us take the example of soyabean meal. The daily limit is $10.00 per short ton. Let us suppose that, on a certain Friday, May soyabean meal (SBM) futures closed at $172.80. On the following Monday, trading in May SBM will only be permitted within the price range from $162.80 to $182.80, namely $10.00 either side of Friday's settlement price. Let us then suppose that a rather unexpected news item has been released in the course of the weekend, for example that a country has made a significant upward revision of the quantity of SBM which it will need to import over the balance of the year. Perhaps the impact of this news is sufficient for the initial trading in May SBM on the Monday to begin at $182.00, i.e. $9.20 higher than the closing transactions on Friday. Then the excitement over the news rapidly feeds on itself; and a flood of buying orders come into the CBOT at $182.40 and then at $182.80. At that point nobody is willing to sell at $182.80. But the limit imposed by the exchange dictates that nobody is permitted to sell on that day at any higher price than $182.80. Trading will simply stop for the balance of that day, unless someone has a change of heart and decides to sell at $182.80.

On the next day, Tuesday, trading on May SBM is permitted up to a price of $192.80. The rationale behind this system of price limits is that panic in the market is given a chance to subside, by the rule which stops trading at the limit price. By the following day's opening of the market, a cooler assessment of the importance of the announcement may lead to a willingness by some traders to sell at or below the Monday ceiling. If, on the other hand, the bullish frenzy continues, it will again be braked on Tuesday after another price advance of \$10.00. If, over three consecutive days, at least three of the available delivery months have moved to the limit, the limit on the fourth market day is 50% greater, e.g. \$15.00 in the case of SBM.

Futures markets are by no means always nervous and volatile. In certain markets, two or three years may go by without the prices ever making a limit move in one day. The livestock sector on the CME tends to be more subject to violent price change than the grains and soya complex on the CBOT. In April 1989, CIS wrote as follows: 'US Department of Agriculture Quarterly Hog and Pig Reports have a substantial impact on all livestock contracts. Limit moves after reports are common. From March 1980 through to December 1988, 36 quarterly reports were issued, with limit moves occurring 17 times in nearby hog contracts. Last month's report showing declines in the breeding herd but large numbers of hogs to be marketed during the summer, led to large (sometimes limit) declines in all livestock and meat contracts for several days.'

CIS made a similar comment on cattle in February of the same year: 'The quarterly USDA January 1st Cattle on Feed Report, released on 26 January, indicated that fed cattle supplies would decline rather dramatically by late winter and early spring. Cattle futures responded by moving 300 points higher (a limit in cattle is 150 points). The market was then torpedoed on 8 February by the release of the annual USDA January 1 Inventory Report, indicating that there were two million more cattle and calves on farms and ranches than the market had expected. Futures responded with a locked-limit-down move the next day. Although some analysts are saying that the Inventory Report is "completely off-base", the track record by the USDA on these estimates is quite good.'

Soyabean crush spreads

A soyabean processor, whether in the US or elsewhere, operates a plant which converts raw soyabeans into two commercial products, meal and oil. The higher the combined value of the meal and oil relative to the cost of the beans, the greater the profit (or, occasionally, the smaller the loss) realised by the crusher. Most crushers would like to buy a year's supply of beans and sell a year's production of meal and oil at an attractive operating profit and well in advance. This is seldom possible in the real world. Since the CBOT has active futures contracts in all these three commodities, it often becomes attractive for a crusher to use futures as a substitute for real or cash transactions. For example, a crusher may have a buying interest for a quantity of soyabean meal four months forward and he may be able to buy beans in the corresponding delivery period, but he may have no customers interested in buying oil at that time. In that case he will sell the cash meal and buy the cash beans and will sell oil futures to complete the operation. In this instance, oil futures are providing him with immediate protection against unfavourable price fluctuation, exactly as in every hedge situation discussed. But crushers also from time to time carry this concept a stage farther and execute all three transactions initially in the futures and only at a later date 'unwind' the futures positions and replace them with real cash trades, perhaps one of the three components at a time. A crusher will do this if he calculates that the price relationship of the three components on 'the board' (i.e. the futures market) gives him a more attractive theoretical operating margin for his plant than the real margin he could obtain by buying beans and selling both products in the cash market at that time.

In June 1986, CIS explained this process as follows: 'When crushed, one sixty-pound bushel of soyabeans yields about 48 pounds of meal and 11 pounds of oil, with the remainder being waste. Allowing for differences in contract size (5000 bushels per soyabean contract, 100 US short tons per meal contract and 60 000 lb per oil contract) the standard "board crush" futures order is in multiples of 10 soyabean contracts (3 million lb) versus 12 meal contracts (2.4 million lb) and 9 oil contracts (540 000 lb). Board crushing margins that are calculated on futures contracts are different from the cash crushing margins realised by the processor, primarily because of varying basis levels at different plant locations.' In the course of one season, one may see very sharp movement in the board crush margin: taking the July 1986 crush as an example, it moved from 50 cents per bushel in December to 36 cents in April and to 12 cents in June. When a crusher (or, indeed, a trader who is not a crusher) considers a board crush margin level to be excessively low, he may elect to put on a 'reverse crush' in the futures, i.e. sell beans and buy the two products.

CHAPTER 3

Hedgers

One cannot understand the workings of the agricultural futures markets, without first understanding how the physical trading in grains and soya products and livestock is conducted. In spite of the sharp increase in recent years in the activity of professional money managers in the agricultural futures markets (see next chapter), the agricultural futures would wither away without the active and large scale participation of those who either produce or handle or consume the commodities in question.

The hedger as middle-man

The farmers are, by definition, the first link in the chain of those who are professionally involved in the movement of grain or cattle from the farm belt to the point of final consumption. The last link in that chain (from a futures point of view) may be an end-user within the US or may be an importer and distributor in Europe or Asia. But in many ways the most important category of hedger in the agricultural futures markets is the middle-man between these two: the large, specialised, often US-based corporation which buys, stores, transports, processes and exports in very large volume the production of America's farmers, be it field crops or livestock or both. Let us create a fictitious multi-national corporation, with its headquarters somewhere in Iowa, and let us call it Khleb Inc (Khleb being the Russian word for grain). One division of Khleb operates small rural grain silos in farming villages, to which farmers can sell and deliver their grain either at harvest time or several months later, depending on the producer's storage possibilities and his need for immediate cash. Another division operates major grain terminal elevators in Chicago and at various seaboard locations through which US exports can flow. A third division operates soyabean crushing plants at strategically chosen locations, producing vegetable oil and the soyabean meal without which the animal feed manufacturer cannot function today. A fourth division is itself a producer of animal feed in certain locations. A fifth operates flour mills, making flour for the bakeries from the wheat produced in the US Great Plains. Another division is involved in the commercial production of broiler chickens and eggs, plus cattle for the stockyards. And yet another is involved purely in the trading of grains and soyabeans, both in domestic and in overseas markets. Such agri-conglomerates do indeed exist; and they play a vital role in the agricultural futures arena.

As stated earlier, a major participant in the physical trading and processing of grain or livestock (such as the hypothetical Khleb group) simply would not be able to operate on a large scale, if it was totally at the mercy of those volatile and seldom predictable price swings in agricultural raw materials, which are a fact of life in the essentially free markets of the US. [The story is very different within the European Economic Community, for example, where prices are largely dictated by governments through price guarantees, which ensure that neither the farmer nor the trader will be subjected to the sort of violent price fluctuations which prevail within the US in the agricultural sector.] Most certainly the system of agricultural futures markets which this book is presenting cannot, and does not purport to, take all the price risks out of dealing in agricultural raw materials. However, the existence of dynamic and viable futures markets does reduce, to a reasonable or at least to a tolerable level, the exposure of the large trader to major unforeseen price swings.

The concept of 'basis'

We must now address ourselves to the concept of 'basis', as that term is used in the US grain and livestock trades. The price basis on a bushel of wheat or on 1000 pounds of live hogs is the market price of a certain lot of physical goods, of a given real quality, in a given real geographical location and for a given real date of availability, relative to the appropriate futures price at the same moment in time. Let us take soyabeans as our first example. Given that most US soyabeans are harvested in October and November, and that somebody has to pay the cost (including interest) of storing them after they have been harvested, it stands to reason that soyabeans in Iowa in March will usually have a higher value than, on a given day, soyabeans in Iowa in January. Now let us look at corn. The greatest part of the commercial US crop of corn (as opposed to the corn which is consumed on the producer's farm) is produced in the heartland states on either side of the middle and upper Mississippi. Consequently, it stands to reason that, on a given day in June and for a given standard quality, corn which is in a barge entering the port of New Orleans on its way to Rotterdam is likely to have a higher commercial value than another barge-load on the same day which has just been loaded from a storage elevator in Minnesota. These differences between one lot and another, reflecting time and place and quality, are known as 'the basis' or 'premium values'. The basis reflects what economists like to call 'time and place utility'.

Price risk

A large agri-business concern, such as our fictitious Khleb Group, will in the course of its business handle millions of dollars' worth of agricultural commodities every hour of the business day. In an ideal and simple world, Khleb could perhaps ensure that the quantities which it bought and the quantities which it sold in any given hour would be more or less the same. Ergo, no major price risk. In the real world of agricultural trade, however, life is not so simple. A trader-dealer-warehouseman-transporter-distributor-processor-exporter (such as Khleb) may well buy, in the eight weeks during and after the US harvest, 40% of all the quantity of that grain which it will originate in the growing areas for a full crop-cycle. Yet its sales are likely to be much more evenly spread over a ten or twelve month period. In a normal year, Khleb will hold substantial stocks of grain and soyabeans in its storage facilities for several months; and it will have paper ownership of even larger quantities through fixed price purchase contracts from others for forward delivery. The total commercial value of the goods in Khleb's inventory, both physical and on paper, will run into billions of dollars during the post-harvest winter period. During those months, between the time when Khleb Group buys the soyabeans and the grain and the time that Khleb Group sells them, the value of those stocks may well increase or decline by 5 or 15 or even 25%. Although it may appear to be in a privileged position of being aware at an early stage of the main events which will influence prices, the Khleb Group simply could not survive if it had to gamble on price swings of this magnitude on huge quantities of goods. What is the alternative? How do things work in reality? The answer is to hedge in the Chicago Futures markets.

Let us for a moment disregard the complexity of the Khleb group's daily activity and look at one typical transaction in isolation. Let us suppose that on 22 April 1991 Khleb sold to a soyabean crusher in Iowa 100 000 bushels (about 2720 tonnes) of physical soyabeans for August delivery at a fixed price of $6.05 per bushel.

Almost automatically, Khleb would then within a few minutes hedge that transaction by buying 100 000 bushels of Chicago July soyabean futures at $6.00 per bushel. As far as Khleb's soyabean merchant is concerned, he has now made a sale at a basis of '5 over July'; and he can sleep soundly at night. In this scenario, let us suppose that, when Khleb bought those July futures, their counter-party was a speculative portfolio manager, whose analysis of the market led him to expect a decline in nearby soyabean futures. (Khleb's soyabean experts might very well share that view at that moment; but their role in the business is such that they routinely hedge their price exposure, to protect themselves against the unforeseen risks which a speculator chooses to assume.)

Now let us suppose that two weeks later, on 9 May, Khleb is able to buy from a country dealer 100 000 bushels of beans which he can use to fulfil his commitment to the crusher; and that Khleb pays the dealer $5.85 for these beans. Within minutes Khleb will sell out his hedge in CBOT July soyabeans at the then prevailing price of $5.82. And let us continue our fairy tale by saying that the counter-party is once again just the same speculative portfolio manager, who is content to take his profit at this level. The portfolio manager has made a profit of 18 cents per bushel ($6.00 less $5.82) or $18 000 in all. This is only 3% on the total value of the beans but 72% in relation to the margin which this portfolio manager had to commit to this risk position at the outset. (Initial margin for a speculator is $1250 per contract of 5000 bushels; and we are talking of a 100 000 bushel transaction.) This is a vivid illustration of the 'leverage factor' inherent to all futures trading: a small profit in terms of contract values can become a large one as a return on committed margin; but the same is painfully true in the case of losses.

What about the Khleb? He has lost 18 cents/bushel on the futures, but he has made 20 cents/bushel on the physical transaction ($6.05-$5.85). In Khleb's thinking, he sold at 5 over July and he bought at 3 over July: hence his 2 cents profit. It is generally believed that, on their futures position, hedgers lose more often than they gain. However, futures are a necessary but secondary part of a hedger's commercial activity, whereas the futures are everything for the speculator.

Hedging and the insurance analogy

Thousands of pages have been written in various learned books about the notion that futures offer to hedgers such as Khleb a form of insurance mechanism, against risks which a large grain dealer cannot carry on his own shoulders. It is true that a conventional underwriter is not in a position to offer to Khleb an insurance policy against unfavourable price movements, in the way that Khleb can insure against a fire or against an explosion at one of his elevators. But those within the business will say that, conceptually, the insurance analogy with a hedger's use of futures has no real validity. In a later chapter, it will be seen that there is a valid analogy between 'insurance' and the buying of futures-related options. But this is another matter. It must be understood that most grain traders, and many livestock dealers, approach all their business from the point of view of the basis. For them it is hardly imaginable to handle large scale business, without systematically offsetting each sale or purchase of physical goods with a simultaneous purchase or sale of the corresponding futures. (The futures position entered is always the reverse of the physical: what is bought in the physical market requires a sale of futures and vice versa. Large hedgers will of course internally offset any purchases and sales which are made within a few minutes of each other; they will use the futures to give them price protection on their net exposure, rather than hedging each and every transaction on both sides of the ledger.) In our over-simplified example above, the only reason for Khleb to be willing to buy those soyabeans on 9 May at the price of $5.85 was his knowledge (a) that July futures at that moment were at $5.82; and (b) that his objective was to buy beans for August at 3 cents over the July, whenever the opportunity presented itself.

Wheat futures

When there is only one US futures market for soyabeans or for corn (excluding the 'mini-contracts' on the MidAm), why should there be three distinct 5000-bushel contracts for wheat futures, in Chicago, Kansas City and Minneapolis? The answer lies in the fact that virtually all corn grown anywhere in the US is more or less interchangeable; and the same could broadly be said of soyabeans and of oats. But this is certainly not the case with wheat, of which three distinct major types or classes are grown in important quantities in the US between the Rocky Mountains and the Atlantic. There are also two minor types of US wheat, which have little importance to the futures markets. One is White Wheat, grown overwhelmingly in Oregon and Washington State: because of geographical considerations, it is almost unthinkable for wheat from these two Pacific states to find its way to the delivery points of the three wheat futures markets. The other is Durum wheat, grown principally in the Dakotas and used only for making pasta rather than bread. The production statistics for these five classes of wheat, as an average over the five crops harvested from 1983 until 1987 (thus excluding the untypical drought year of 1988) and expressed as usual in bushels are as follows:

Hard Red Winter	1144 million	(49%)	(Kansas City)
Hard Red Spring	415 million	(18%)	(Minneapolis)
Soft Red Winter	408 million	(18%)	(Chicago)
White	265 million	(11%)	
Durum	96 million	(4%)	
Total	2328 million, or about 63.3 million tonnes.		

In the last column of the above table will be seen an indication of the futures market to which the production of each of the three leading classes is principally tributary. It is logical that the wheat futures volume in Kansas City is approximately three times that of Minneapolis, in line with the relative production of the two classes of wheat which are tributary to those markets. It is not statistically logical that the wheat futures volume in Chicago is close to double that of the two subsidiary markets put together. The explanation is to be found in the fact that Chicago is the dominant centre for world trade in agricultural futures.

Movement in basis values

Let us now return to the subject of the basis, which was examined earlier in this chapter. It was explained that US grain dealers and processors think and talk basis values rather than flat price values. A trader for our hypothetical Khleb group will say of a particular grain on a given day, FOB the Gulf, i.e. delivered into the hold of a buyer's seagoing vessel in one of the Louisiana export elevators: 'Today I am a buyer at 9 over and a seller at 12 over'. During the course of the morning, the Chicago futures for the grain he is trading may move up four cents a bushel and then down a total of six cents before lunch. But the Khleb trader's view on the value of the 'cash' (i.e. physical) grain remains the same: he would buy at 9 or perhaps 9½ over; and he would sell at 12 or perhaps 11½ over. The Khleb trader himself and most of his customers and many of his suppliers (though probably not the farmers) think in terms of basis. To a very large degree, Khleb makes its profits and its losses in terms of its good or bad judgement of how the basis will move over the coming weeks.

More than half of all the contracts which Khleb makes within the US, and some of those which are made overseas, will actually be expressed in basis terms and will read (for example): 'On 12th July, Khleb sells to XYZ 1 000 000 bushels 2 yellow soyabeans FOB New Orleans, delivery 16–31 December, at 15 over Chicago January beans, futures in exchange.' In due course XYZ will instruct his futures broker to 'give up versus cash' in the pit 1 000 000 bushels of January futures to the broker representing Khleb, at a mutually agreed price, which will normally be within the trading range on the day of the 'give-up'. Khleb will neither know nor care at what price XYZ actually bought those futures. The give-up price establishes a normal fixed flat price per bushel at which Khleb will prepare its invoice and at which XYZ will pay for the soyabeans.

If it should be that Khleb has some uneasiness about the financial standing of XYZ, then Khleb may require that the give-up is not to occur prior to 10 December. As long as the final price has not been established by means of the give-up. Khleb's only risk in event of a default is the movement in the basis, perhaps ten cents per bushel at the most. If on the other hand, XYZ were to give up futures the day after the basis trade had been made, and if soyabean prices steadily declined between July and November, Khleb could well face a loss of $2.00 per bushel, twenty times as much, in the event that XYZ declared bankruptcy in the month of November. This is an indirect, but very significant, form of risk reduction in the agricultural markets which is only made possible by the existence and universal acceptance of the Chicago futures system.

In international markets for grains and soya products, whether they are of US or of other origins, a very large volume of business is conducted between dealers on basis terms also. This may be a cargo of Brazilian soyabeans, bought FOB a Brazilian port, by a Japanese trading company, from a Brazilian agricultural co-operative, at x cents per bushel over Chicago July beans, although the bushel as a unit is unknown within Brazil. An international trader such as Khleb may negotiate over several days to buy a substantial quantity of corn (for export shipment) from the South African Maize Board; or a similar quantity of wheat from the Australian Wheat Board. These negotiations are likely to be carried out on basis terms, so that neither party needs to be distracted by the day-to-day fluctuations of the futures while the cash discussions are being concluded. Needless to say, the willingness of these two governmental boards to make sales at 'such-and-such price per bushel over or under Chicago futures' demonstrates that such far-away boards are perfectly familiar with the mechanism and the concepts of the Chicago markets. Indeed the two Boards mentioned have been taking trading positions in Chicago futures for a number of years, as part of their statutory responsibility to co-ordinate export marketing of these crops and to seek ways to maximise the returns which can finally be paid to their local growers.

As stated, much international agri-business is conducted on 'basis' terms. In recent years, most government agencies which have the task of buying substantial quantities of grains and soyabean meal on the international market have continued to buy on flat price terms without reference to futures. One well-documented example of the potential problems in this area goes back well before 1980. Nevertheless it illustrates in dramatic form the vital difference between so-called 'forward flat-priced cash business', in which one principal-to-principal signed contract stands alone, and 'exchange-traded futures business', in which the clearing house system and the margin requirement provide virtually total protection to all market participants.

The case in point concerns the Ministry of Food in a country which had substantial wheat import requirements. The Ministry decided to plan their forward supplies well in advance. They therefore made purchases from the international grain trading companies for a wide band of delivery periods, some of which ran nine months forward from the date of the purchases. Before the more deferred portions of these contracts were due to be shipped, however, prices declined very sharply in Chicago wheat futures and therefore in the values of physical wheat. By hindsight (which is a very unpopular word among the professionals in these highly volatile agri-markets) those Ministry officials had shown very poor commercial judgement in making their purchases so far in advance. In desperation under the influence of violent abuse and criticism from their domestic political opponents, those responsible for the purchases chose an apparently easy way out: they unilaterally cancelled their purchase contracts without offering any compensation to their suppliers. The difference between the prices of the old purchase contracts, and the price at which similar wheat could be bought at the time of this decision to cancel, amounted in the aggregate to tens of millions of dollars. For the importing country concerned, this appeared to be a bonanza. An ill-informed observer might suppose that the international grain houses, which had made the sales in question, had made enormous profits as a result of the sharp price decline in the meantime. Those who have read and understood the present chapter of this book will be aware that this was not the case. Those who made the sales, to the country which later decided not to honour its purchase commitments, bought futures immediately to offset their deferred sales to that country. They therefore derived no benefit from the subsequent price decline. Needless to say, many lawyers were busy for many years grappling with the consequences of this unilateral decision to cancel a contract which no longer looked attractive to the importing country. This story is a valuable illustration of the whys and the wherefores of the elaborate system of clearing house and daily mark-to-market and the calls for additional margins, which characterise the Agricultural Futures markets.

Wheat - a different story

We have seen that CBOT soyabean futures prices are the point of departure for negotiations over an export cargo of Brazilian soyabeans, for example. The same is true for business in corn from Argentina or Thailand or South Africa. In recent years, however, the same situation has not prevailed in the case of wheat. Why does this distinction exist? The answer lies in the fact that the US dominates the international markets in corn and soyabeans, but encounters much more competition in the case of wheat. The numbers fluctuate considerably from one year to another. But it is not unusual for the US share in the entire international movement of corn to exceed 60% (e.g. US corn exports in the 1988/89 marketing year were about 45 million tonnes, out of total world corn trade of about 70 million tonnes.) Similarly, the US share in world trade in soyabeans often exceeds 70%, with the balance coming almost entirely from South America. With wheat, however, the US share in international trade is usually below 40%, with the European Economic Community in second place. If an importer in Rotterdam or Tokyo wants to buy US corn or US soyabeans, he has to pay the prevailing price for the same item somewhere in the US plus the real shipping and handling costs to get those goods to Europe or to Japan. But in recent years US exporters who made similar calculations in the case of wheat would all too often find that another exporting country, often the EEC, was undercutting the US price to be sure of getting the business. Consequently the US found it necessary to subsidise wheat exports to certain important import markets under a scheme known officially as the Export Enhancement Programme or EEP. In common language, this means 'we will fight for what we consider our rightful share of the international wheat business'.

This battle of nerves and dollars between Washington and (principally) Brussels has had a very unfavourable impact on wheat futures. The whole concept of basis trading, which has been examined in considerable detail, is negated in the case of wheat, when Washington ensures that an increase in domestic US values is *not* promptly reflected in increased values for US wheat overseas, for fear of handing important business on a platter to a competing exporting country. Under such conditions, wheat in the export markets becomes partially, and to an important degree, 'unhedgeable'.

The four CME agri-contracts

The four agri-contracts traded on the CME do not have a broad international application, such as that seen in the case of the CBOT futures. US corn and soyabeans are exported in huge quantitites; live cattle and frozen pork bellies are not. Indeed the US actually imports live hogs and cattle from Canada and also live cattle from Mexico. However, the quantities are not of great statistical significance. (During the five year period 1986–1990, the average US January cattle-and-calf population was about 100 million head, whereas imports were less than 2% of this figure.) Thus the hedgers using agri-futures on the CME are only those in North America. They are not only the large commercial livestock producers and the operators of cattle feeding lots and slaughter facilities, but also those involved in meat marketing on a large scale. In May 1989 CIS wrote as follows: 'With the tighter supplies of cattle and high priced meat products over the past few years, the meat industry has begun to have more interest in hedging meat prices, using livestock futures. Prime candidates for meat hedging are those who are looking to guarantee a price on delivery of a meat product at a later date, such as meat packers, meat processors and even restaurant chains. The goal can be to lock in a finished product price, like a restaurant chain with menus printed every six months with a fixed price for a steak. Another potential user for hedging is the distributor who purchases the meat and stores it while waiting to sell it at a later date. With the product sitting in the freezer with no price protection, the owner is at full risk for each price move.'

CHAPTER

4

Commodity Trading Advisors

In an earlier chapter a brief reference was made to the portfolio managers, who collectively account for a major part of the speculative element in the US futures markets. They are known in the American jargon of this business as Commodity Trading Advisors or CTAs. To an English eye, this is a strange title. Firstly, CTAs as a group trade more in the financial futures than in true commodities, simply because physical commodity futures, combining the animal, the vegetable and the mineral, comprise only about one-third of total futures contract volume these days. Secondly, an 'Advisor' (for which the English spelling would be 'Adviser') is normally deemed in England to be someone who gives advice. In US futures terminology, however, a Commodity Trading Advisor is not someone who gives advice: he is fully empowered to act, i.e. to give trading orders to a broker on behalf of each of his clients. In normal everyday vocabulary, a CTA is a Portfolio Manager in the specific fields of futures and options.

Recent expansion

The past ten years, and especially the years after the famous stock market crash of October 1987, have seen a very rapid growth in this field of professional financial and investment activity. Consequently, its impact on futures markets has grown from a peripheral one to a significant and even disturbing one. Precise figures are not available; but it is probably safe to say that the total amount of clients' capital being traded by professional money managers in the futures markets (overwhelmingly the US futures markets) was under 1.5 billion US dollars in 1983 and was over $25 billion in 1991. A number of people in this futures portfolio 'industry' have recently expressed the view that the total will reach $40 billion by 1995.

There are two principal reasons for this rapid expansion in the futures portfolio sector. One is the continuing ripple effect from the major stock market crash of October 1987; this was followed, in the traditionally 'safe' stock market investment sector, by a second sudden downward lurch in October 1989; and by another after the invasion of Kuwait by Iraq in 1990. These sharp downturns in the values of international equity portfolios encouraged a rather urgent search by individuals, and more particularly by institutional money managers, for a really different asset class, in which portfolio performance could be quite attractive and at the same time would be largely unrelated to the performance of the traditional unit trusts or mutual funds in the equities sector. Apart from this demand side pressure, the late 1980s also saw, on the supply side, a considerable increase in sophistication and in professional quality on the part of the CTAs, i.e. of the specialised futures portfolio managers. This all ties in with the dramatic improvement in the capacity of the individual desktop computer, which is vital for the successful and rapid monitoring of various futures markets by many CTAs.

The move towards speculator-driven markets

What does this have to do with the Chicago agricultural futures markets? It means that these markets, whose origins go back to the nineteenth century and which have long been viewed as primarily a risk-reduction instrument for hedgers, have in the course of two or three years become increasingly speculator-driven, in the sense that the futures community uses that rather sinister word speculator as a catch-all definition for anyone who is not a hedger.

Until 1988, with rare and brief exceptions, the hedgers really dominated the agricultural futures markets, although they were the first to acknowledge that they needed the participation of all three categories of speculators (see Chapter 1). If the markets are to have liquidity, if large hedgers are to feel that they can achieve their hedging objectives without encountering a vacuum, there must be speculators ready to 'take the other side' of the hedgers' orders at reasonable price levels at any hour of every trading day. But when the power and the order volume of the professional large speculators, namely the major CTAs, goes beyond a certain point, the hedgers come to feel that the tail is perhaps wagging the dog.

Technical and fundamental analysis

A long established and major fund manager in the futures sector has explained the two recognised CTA trading strategies as follows: 'There are essentially two ways of attempting to forecast price behaviour in the commodities markets – "technical" and "fundamental" analysis. Technical analysis operates on the theory that market prices at any given point in time reflect all known factors affecting supply and demand for a particular commodity; consequently, only a detailed analysis of (among other things) actual daily, weekly and monthly price fluctuations, volume variations and changes in open interest are of predictive value when determining the future course of price movements. Trading recommendations are generally based on computer-generated signals, chart interpretation, mathematical measurements, or a combination of such items.

'Fundamental analysis, on the other hand, is based upon the study of the external factors that affect the supply and demand for a particular commodity in order to predict future prices. Fundamental analysis assumes that markets are imperfect; information is not instantly assimilated or disseminated; and econometric models can be constructed that generate equilibrium prices that may indicate current prices are unsustainable.'

Each of the larger CTAs in the early 1990s is responsible for the trading decisions for a pool of investor capital in the range from $250 million to one billion dollars. For reasons which are self-evident, every CTA is required to take on identical short or long positions on any given day for all his clients, as a percentage of the total equity in each account. (Of course it will not be possible to obtain exactly the same price for all the clients, since markets would need to stand still to make this possible.) The only exceptions to this statement are the rare cases where a certain client or institution has deliberately restricted the CTA's field of activity. An institutional investor may stipulate that the CTA must trade only in the financial markets and not in agricultural futures. And an Islamic investor may exclude hogs and cattle from the spectrum of futures markets in which a CTA normally seeks his profit opportunities.

The great majority of futures trading by CTAs is based on the technical rather than the fundamental approach, although there are some who use a 'fundamental filter'. This means that the CTA is largely guided by technical buy and sell signals from his computer programs. But, before placing an actual order with his broker, he will ask himself whether there is some very recent item of fundamental news, which should lead him to disregard the computer's latest signal. The computer may generate a signal to sell live cattle, based on price patterns of (say) the past 15 trading days; but the computer cannot take into consideration a USDA quarterly Cattle on Feed Report, released the previous day after the futures close, which may clearly have strong bullish implications. Other CTAs, however, metaphorically refuse to read the newspaper headlines. They feel that they must have faith in their mathematical, computer-based trading discipline; and that, if they permit a human-judgement factor to intervene from time to time, their whole approach is in danger of becoming subjective, whereas its very strength lies in its blind objectivity.

Not only do the majority of CTAs approach the markets from a technical standpoint: equally important is the fact that there is often a lot of common ground between their programs; and therefore on the signals for many CTAs.

In a rather extreme but by no means impossible case, 20 of the leading technical CTAs may trigger selling orders in CBOT corn futures on the same day, since they are seeing and analysing and interpreting essentially the same facts and figures. Successful CTAs generally have severe risk-control and money-management policies to guide their trading. Suppose that their average policy is to commit only 1.5% of the money under their management to any one trading decision and that these 20 CTAs have a total of $3 billion under their collective management. 1.5% of this sum is $45 million. It has been seen that each standardised CBOT corn contract covers a quantity of 5000 bushels. At a price of (say) $2.50 per bushel, then, each contract represents $12 500 in total value. A commitment of $45 million (in terms of underlying value, of course, and not in initial margin actually paid) will require the sale by these hypothetical CTAs of 3600 corn contracts. This may well be more than 15% of the day's total contract volume in the specific delivery months which are of interest to the CTAs. (CTAs will usually not wish to take on new positions in the nearby contract month, where 15 or 20% of the open interest and the daily volume are often concentrated, because they do not want to be either short or long on any contracts when the time for possible physical delivery occurs.) If it is further estimated that locals and small specs may in some cases account for 20% of the total volume in each contract delivery month, the hypothetical selling raid by 20 CTAs looms even larger as a nuisance factor for the traditional large hedgers.

In the financial futures, such as currencies or Eurodollars, a rather sudden buying or selling blitz by a group of technically-guided CTAs does not constitute a problem: those markets are generally so broad, and they offer such cash-versus-futures arbitrage opportunities for the financial institutions involved, that a CTA blitz will hardly cause a ripple. In the Chicago agricultural markets, however, there is a smaller number of large participants; and consequently large CTA orders have sometimes been seen as a matter for considerable concern.

CHAPTER

5

Options on agricultural futures

For nearly 50 years in the US, from 1936 until 1982, the law of the land prohibited the trading of options on any commodities, because of some flagrant fraud in this field which occurred before the Second World War. During the 1980s, however, with cautious step-by-step beginnings, the Commmodity Futures Trading Commission (CFTC) (see end of Chapter 1) began to allow the established futures exchanges, such as the CBOT and CME, to introduce exchange-traded options based directly on their existing futures contracts. Thus the CBOT introduced options on soyabean futures in 1984, on corn in 1985, on wheat in 1986, on meal and oil in 1987 and in oats only in 1990.

However, up to now, the volume of options traded is still far below that in the corresponding futures contracts. If the statistics for the three years 1988-1989-1990 are combined, the total volume of options traded on the six CBOT agri-contracts was between 14 and 15% of the futures volume; and the same is true for the options on the four livestock contracts on the CME over the same three year period.

Entire books have been written in recent years about the concepts of options trading; and about their practical application to both hedging and speculative trading situations. The CBOT and the CME have made available to the public some excellent written material about the use of futures-based options. The present work can only provide an introduction to this subject.

Call and put options

In the mid-1980s, experienced futures traders had to come to grips with some entirely new jargon and some new concepts, new hazards and new opportunities, with the arrival of options on the same trading floors as their futures. A basic definition follows: on the CBOT or the CME, a call option gives its holder the right, but not the obligation, to buy a futures contract, at a predetermined price, at any future date until the option expires (shortly before the delivery month of the futures contract in question). A put option gives its holder a similar right, but this time the right to sell. Both types of option, the calls and the puts, are traded by open outcry in the trading rooms of the futures exchanges; and during the same trading hours as their underlying futures. The term used is 'at a pre-determined price'. In fact the potential buyer of an option has a choice of many different prices at which he may want the right to buy (call) or to sell (put) the futures, at a future date of his choice. Each such price, called a strike price or an exercise price, will of course have a different value on a given day.

A simple example goes back to the concepts and the arguments which were being promoted a few years ago, before these agricultural futures-related options were actually introduced. A farmer in Iowa on 22 April 1991 is about to plant corn on a part of his farm land; he knows that he is likely to harvest it in late October, at which time the nearest CBOT futures contract will be December. He is well aware that the current market price for corn in Chicago in October was as low as \$1.50 per bushel in 1986 and was as high as \$2.80 in 1988. On 22 April the farmer can choose any of four commercial decisions:

(a) He can do nothing about selling his new crop; he can decide he will just wait and see how prices develop nearer to harvest time;
(b) He can sell December futures at that day's price of \$2.57½. He will then have to deposit margin with his broker; and he knows that he will be called for additional margin if or when the price goes above \$2.57½; he

also stands at risk for a change of basis value at his farmgate, relative to Chicago's futures price;
(c) He can make a forward sale of physical corn to a local trader at a price which will be based on the day's futures price of $2.57½. In that case he does not have to pay any margin; nor does he assume the basis risk;
(d) He can buy a put option, giving him the right to sell a corn futures contract, later on, for $2.60 if he chooses to do so.
(We assume here that selling a call is too speculative for most farmers.)

Options and the insurance analogy

This last opportunity, the purchase of an option, can reasonably be likened to paying an insurance premium. We pay in advance a fairly small sum of money to the company which insures us against the theft of our valuables or against a fire destroying our home. At the end of the period for which we were insured, we are pleased that the misfortune has not in fact occurred. The premium money which we paid out is lost to us and has in fact (with hindsight) brought us no benefit; but we know that our decision, at the time, to seek the protection of the insurance policy was a prudent and a sound one. The same is largely true for the buyer of CBOT and CME options.

The idea of taking out a price insurance policy, by buying a put based on a corn price of $2.60, initially looks very attractive to our hypothetical Iowa corn farmer. Under the rules of option trading, the buyer of a put (or a call) pays his premium at the outset, just as with a fire insurance policy, and can never get that payment back. But if in October the price of December corn futures has dropped to (say) $2.18, the farmer is laughing all the way to the bank. On any day which he chooses, between 22 April and late November, he can exercise his rights as the holder of a $2.60 put option. Without further costs, he can declare himself short a December futures contract at the predetermined price of $2.60; and he can immediately buy back that futures contract through his broker at the current price of (say) $2.18. $2.60 minus $2.18 is a gross gain of 42 cents, less the broker's commission of (perhaps) one cent on the option transaction and one cent on the futures operation, leaving a net gain of 40 cents . . . if the futures have indeed moved to $2.18. If, on the other hand, there is a drought once again and the price of December corn futures rises from $2.60 in April to $2.75 in October, the farmer is not too much concerned about his put option based on a price of $2.60. As the holder of a put option, he has the right, but he does not have any obligation, to declare himself short a futures contract at $2.60. With the real market value above $2.60, he will do nothing and will let his option expire worthless. He will sell the corn from his own fields at a better price, since the real market for corn futures has risen above the $2.60 level on which his option was based in the first place. That looks like a very attractive scenario. The farmer buys an insurance policy in April which allows him to 'have his cake and eat it'. If prices go down, his put option protects him. If prices go up, he abandons his option and markets his own corn on the basis of the higher real price pattern in the market.

The cost of buying options

This simple basic overview of the workings of options makes the system look too good to be true, from the point of view of a long-suffering farmer. All the facts presented in the preceding paragraph are true. But the picture is indeed too good to be true, because one crucial factor has been omitted: the cost of obtaining this insurance cover, i.e. the cost of buying the option.

There are no fixed prices for options. Each transaction requires a meeting of two minds between a buyer (perhaps the Iowa farmer in our example above) and a seller (perhaps a local, see Chapter 1). If the current price of December futures were to be at $2.60 on the 23rd of October, with the weather hazards of the growing season already a matter of history, a seller might be willing to grant to a farmer the put option (insurance policy), with a strike (= exercise) price of $2.60, for a premium of only 6 or 7 cents. In late October, the seller can consider his risk of corn futures prices going even 5 cents higher to be rather small, in the remaining time until late November, when the options on December corn futures will automatically expire.

But we have been considering the case of a farmer, who needs to decide what he should do in April. At that moment, the bulk of the new season's crop has not even been planted; and nobody can know the pattern of summer weather conditions. Under these conditions, selling a put option is a highly hazardous matter for the farmer's counter-party on the CBOT, who has to stand behind his one-sided obligation for the best part of seven months. We have seen that the buyer of any option (put or call) has a right, but no obligation; and that he must make an upfront premium payment which will never be reimbursed. The seller of an option, on the other hand, has an obligation without a right; and he receives the premium at the outset, as his inducement to assume an open-ended and theoretically unlimited risk regarding price behaviour over the coming months.

We can see in the Wall St Journal that on 22 April 1991 the farmer would have had to pay 19 cents a bushel for a December $2.60 put option. The buyer of an option (call or put) must pay the agreed price, or premium, immediately to his broker; and so (via the clearing house) to the counter-party who sold it to him. Whatever may subsequently happen to prices, he will never have to pay margin or any form of additional expense. The seller of an option, on the other hand, has the same type of exposure to the impact of unfavourable price moves as a futures trader has. Consequently, sellers of options are required to deposit margins when they make each sale; and, just like futures traders, they must pay further variation margins if and whenever the market moves against their position.

Let us now come back to our earlier illustration of a corn farmer, who (in April) pays 19 cents for a December $2.60 put option, in order to protect himself against a price collapse while his corn crop is in the ground. The price at which he can really begin to 'come out ahead', after buying a $2.60 put option at a cost of 19 cents/bushel, will be $2.41. He may prefer on 22 April to spend a lower 'insurance premium' for less protection. He could on that same date buy a put with a strike price of $2.40 at a premium of only 9½ cents. His cost is half what it would be in the $2.60 example; but his protection only begins at a price of 2.30½ this time, rather than $2.41 in the earlier example. Since the market price is about $2.58 at the time he must make his decision, neither of these option solutions will have much appeal to the farmer.

Risk management

Hedging risk with futures-related options is not a simple matter. In the real world, there are not many farmers who use options. However, to those who understand the mechanism and who carefully study the possibilities, they provide an extraordinarily flexible tool of risk management. The first task is to define carefully what is the risk; what are the exact protection objectives; and what is an acceptable cost of obtaining protection. After the early and exploratory months of trading options in the mid-1980s on the main US futures exchanges, many market participants came to recognise that the simple purchase of a put or a call, for a maturity date half a year forward, was too costly to be seriously viable for a conservative hedger.

It is usually held that there are two components in the price of an option. One is the obvious risk for the seller in insuring the other party on the basis of a price which is already clearly in the option buyer's favour. Let us go back to our example of the farmer who is studying the possibility of buying a put option for December and is looking at the market prices on 22 April 1991. He will see that the December futures closed at \$2.57½. If he decides to buy a put option for December with a strike (= exercise) price of \$2.60, this has an immediate and obvious value of 2½ cents before risk factors are even considered. This obvious value of certain options is known in the jargon of this business as an intrinsic value. Everything else which goes into an option's value is known as time value.

Our Iowa farmer, at planting time in April, is seriously interested in testing the ability of the CBOT options system to give him some price insurance; but he is not prepared to pay more than five cents/bushel (including his broker's commission) to obtain this protection. On 22 April he can take on a double operation to achieve this objective. For each 5000 bushel amount, he will buy a put option, with a strike (exercise) price of \$2.60, at a cost of 19 cents/bushel (as we have seen). But he will simultaneously sell two call options with a strike (exercise) price of \$3.00, well above anyone's current expectations; and for this he will receive 8¼ cents on each or 16½ cents in all. On the day when this decision has to be taken, the chance of December corn futures reaching the strike price of \$3.00 seems rather remote. Should it in fact occur, the farmer would be happy to forget about all his option trades; he would be able to sell his physical corn at a price considerably higher than he anticipated at planting time back in April. Furthermore it is important to emphasise that both the buyer and the seller of an option on the CBOT or the CME are always free to buy back a sold option or to sell out a bought option. In some other markets, options which have once been bought or sold cannot be touched until the maturity date. On the CBOT and CME, every market participant is free to dispose of his option commitments, at the then prevailing price, whenever he chooses to do so. Thus, for example, if the Iowa farmer saw prices moving sharply higher in July because of hot, dry weather conditions, he might choose to buy back his short call options, rather than see a counter-party exercise them against him and so put him short futures in a rapidly advancing market.

Time value and volatility

Apart from the intrinsic value already mentioned, the other element in the price at which an option can be purchased on a given day is known in the jargon as the 'time value'. This is an unfortunate term, since time is in fact only one of the important components in the non-intrinsic part of the cost of any given option. As we have seen in the December corn example, the longer the life of an exchange-traded option, the higher will be the premium which every seller will require for a given strike price. The reason for this statement should by now be clear. But time is only one part of the story. An equally important element, indeed sometimes a more important consideration in the assessment by traders of the appropriate value of any given option (put or call), is the level of volatility in the price pattern of the commodity in question. Steady, stable prices in the futures indicate a low volatility and a moderate risk for the seller of any option. Major, nervous price swings make the selling of options somewhat more hazardous; and sellers will in such an environment increase their minimum premium selling ideas. This volatility is a vital component in the so-called time value of an option, regardless of its time to maturity. Options traders speak of two types of volatility, either or both of which will have an influence on real options prices from day to day. One is historical volatility, which is the known level of price nervousness in the recent past. The other is implied volatility, meaning the traders' collective perception of how volatile prices are likely to be in the near future, as expressed in their willingness or reluctance to sell options at a given price level on a given day.

When markets are calm, a normal range for option volatility in soyabean futures is from 16 to 24%. As a general statement, wheat prices tend to be less volatile than those of soyabeans, partly because soyabeans in the ground are more weather-sensitive than wheat. If we study the historical volatility of Chicago wheat closing prices for the period of 30 months from October 1983 until March 1986, we see that the figure was almost always in the teens, with 10.1% the lowest monthly figure and only two instances of a level higher than 21%, with a peak of 22.6% in August 1985. And yet the volatility in April and May 1986 abruptly jumped to 38.7 and 39.0%. What had happened to explain this dramatic change? The answer is simple. The catastrophic nuclear accident at Chernobyl occurred in late April 1986, which for a few weeks caused panic and confusion in many agricultural commodity markets, leading to nervous and choppy prices. Similarly, volatility in soyabean futures jumped above 50% during the serious drought of the summer months in 1988.

Strike prices

We have mentioned that the potential buyer of an option, whether a put or a call, has a choice of many different strike prices, each with a different value on a given day. The exchange determines what shall be the strike prices at which puts and calls may be traded. In the case of CBOT these are as follows:

- Corn and oats: multiples of 10 cents/bushel, e.g. 2.40, 2.50, 2.60;
- Wheat: also multiples of 10 cents/bushel, e.g. 2.90, 3.00, 3.10;
- Soyabeans: multiples of 25 cents/bushel, e.g. 5.75, 6.00, 6.25;
- Soyabean oil: multiples of one cent/lb, e.g. 19.00, 20.00, 21.00;
- Soyabean meal: multiples of $5 per ton, e.g. 175, 180, 185, 190; (however, when futures are above $200 per ton the interval between strike prices goes to $10.00).

The strike prices on CME agri-options are at intervals of two cents per pound in all four cases: e.g. at 54.00, 56.00 and 58.00 on pork bellies and at 72.00, 74.00 and 76.00 on live cattle.

Exercising of options

We saw in Chapter 1 the paradox that the potential for physical delivery at maturity exists in (almost) all agri-futures contracts; and that this potential plays an important role in the whole functioning of futures markets; and yet in practice physical delivery occurs in less than 2% of the futures contracts traded. Now we come to a somewhat comparable paradox in the world of futures-related options. Conceptually, the whole point of buying an option is to acquire the right (but not the obligation) to exercise that option: and so to become long a futures contract (if it is a call) or short a futures contract (in the case of a put).

And yet only a very small percentage of all the option contracts which are bought on the Chicago futures exchanges are in fact exercised. We shall come on to the figures which illustrate what we mean by the phrase 'only a very small percentage'. But first let us address the question: 'Why?'

First of all, we must recognise that medium term price movements in the underlying futures will leave some options hopelessly out-of-the-money and they can only be abandoned as worthless. This would be the case, for example, with May and July 1988 soyabean puts, with a strike price of \$6.00 or \$6.25 or \$6.50, when the drought had pushed prices well above \$9.00 for a while.

The decision as to whether an option is to be exercised lies of course with the buyer and never with the seller. Many of those who buy options are doing so to obtain some form of price protection; but they may fear the 'margin call' aspect and therefore the 'unlimited risk' aspect of the futures markets. When they buy an option, they stay clear of this alarming world. They know that exercising an option puts them into a futures position, which is something that they specifically want to avoid. That is the first factor. The second one is purely economic. If I exercise an option, I have acquired a futures position, long or short, but I have thrown away or squandered the residual value of that option itself. Even when it is not in-the-money, and especially if it is not too far out-of-the-money, an option has a residual value in the eyes of a local or another professional trader, so long as it is at least (say) more than twenty days from its expiration date. Thus the great majority of holders of CBOT and CME options will either choose to let them expire worthless: or else resell them on the floor of the exchange, either because they are afraid of holding a futures position or because they can earn some money by selling the option or through a combination of these two considerations.

It will be noted in Table 5.1 that, in each of the three years, two points are statistically rather constant. Firstly, in each year the volume of options trading between these five commodities is dominated by corn and soyabeans at 83 and 87% of the total. Secondly, the volume in calls has consistently been 63 to 66% of the total, exceeding the volume of puts by

Table 5.1 Annual volume of options traded on the CBOT agri-futures, '000

	1990			**1989**			**1988**		
	Calls	**Puts**	**Total**	**Calls**	**Puts**	**Total**	**Calls**	**Puts**	**Total**
Wheat	330	153	483	304	181	485	271	174	445
Corn	1308	808	2116	976	543	1519	1034	557	1591
Soyabeans	1317	772	2090	1336	639	1975	2080	1165	3245
SB meal	106	75	181	75	38	113	97	76	173
SB oil	84	54	138	71	30	101	75	50	125
Total	3145	1862	5007	2762	1431	4193	3557	2022	5579
	(63%)	(37%)		(66%)	(34%)		(64%)	(36%)	

almost two to one. It can also be seen that the exceptionally volatile market conditions of 1988, caused by the catastrophic drought, enhanced the use of options (especially in the case of soyabeans), but not to a great extent as a percentage of futures activity. The option volume in 1988 was 15% of the corresponding futures volume, whereas it was 13.5% in 1989 and 14.6% in 1990.

When we turn to the options relating to the agri-futures on the CME, we find that the volume statistics are absolutely dominated by the live cattle options, with 72% of the four-market total, whereas in the case of futures live cattle account for 54% in the period 1988–1990. For these three years and for all four agri-options on the CME, the volume of calls traded was 1 870 000 and the volume of puts was 1 820 000. So the picture was pretty close to 50/50 in the CME options, as against almost two-thirds calls on the CBOT.

Table 5.2 addresses the question: what percentage of the buyers of Chicago agri-options exercise their options, rather than reselling them for their residual value or letting those which are far out-of-the-money expire worthless? The statistics which are presented pertain only to the three most active option markets, namely CBOT soyabeans and CBOT corn and CME live cattle. It will be seen that, overall, only 4 to 6% of all the options purchased are in due course exercised, although the individual percentage figures range from 1.4% to several cases of 7-plus and one extreme instance of over 10% being exercised.

Table 5.2 Percentage of Chicago agri-options buyers exercising these options

	1990		1989		1988	
	Options exercised	**% of trades**	**Options exercised**	**% of trades**	**Options exercised**	**% of trades**
Soyabeans						
Calls	21 290	1.6	23 478	1.8	151 163	7.3
Puts	19 042	2.5	42 542	6.7	32 900	2.8
Total	40 332	1.9	66 020	3.3	183 900	5.7
Corn						
Calls	56 400	4.3	33 282	3.4	69 534	6.7
Puts	62 200	7.7	45 191	8.3	38 306	6.9
Total	118 600	5.6	78 473	5.2	107 840	6.8
Live cattle						
Calls	33 307	10.1	31 190	6.6	39 864	6.8
Puts	5 276	1.4	13 092	3.2	10 441	2.2
Total	38 583	5.4	44 282	5.0	50 305	4.7
Grand total	197 515	4.0	188 775	4.3	342 045	5.8

A speculative option - the long strangle

Let us now look at just one more of the many option trading strategies which are available today on the Chicago agri-futures exchanges. Having previously looked at a hedging situation in corn options on the CBOT, this time we shall look at a speculative situation in live hog options on the CME. Some of the standard option strategies have rather esoteric names, such as the bull call spread or the credit box or the reverse conversion; but they are in fact logical and simple to grasp, if one takes a few minutes to think them through. The example which we are now going to take is called a long strangle. It tends to have a fairly high entry cost, which has to be recouped before the trade can begin to show a profit. But it has merit (in the right circumstances) for a relative beginner in options trading, because it entails no margin requirement; and because it is a trading position with virtually unlimited potential profit, if things go as the trader foresaw, but with a limited maximum cost, which is known in advance, if the market fails to match expectations.

We saw in Chapter 2 (see 'Limits') that 17 out of 36 Quarterly Hog and Pig Reports from the US Department of Agriculture led to a 'limit move' in live hog futures, either a 'limit up' or a 'limit down'. A speculator who is familiar with this past pattern of market volatility in the wake of these statistical reports may decide, a week or two ahead of such a Quarterly Report, that he wants to risk some of his capital on the hunch that the same thing is about to happen again. He does not claim to know whether the sharp move after the report is going to be upwards or downwards. The direction is not important: he believes that there will be a violent move. (This strategy is also known as a volatility spread.)

In these circumstances, he can take on a position known as a long strangle: he buys both a live hogs call and a live hogs put, each with a strike price as close as possible to the current futures price. We have to say 'as close as possible', because live hog futures are traded at intervals of 2½ cents per 100 pounds, i.e. per US hundredweight (cwt), whereas the strike price intervals on options are two cents per pound (equals $2.00 per cwt) apart.

One of the Quarterly Hog and Pig Reports appeared on Friday, 28 June 1991. (The exact dates for the release of these important regular reports by the Department of Agriculture, both on field crops and on livestock, are known many weeks in advance.) On Monday 17 June the August contract for live hogs on the CME closed at 51.25 cents per pound, more or less mid-way between the option strike prices of 50.00 and 52.00. On the same day the closing prices of the relevant August live hog options were at the following levels, also in cents per pound and all related to a CME futures contract for the standard quantity of 40 000 pounds (20 American short tons):

50.00 calls 1.95 ($780 per call); 50.00 puts 0.70 ($280 per put)
52.00 calls 0.85 ($340 per call); 52.00 puts 1.60 ($640 per put)

The futures price which these option premium values reflected was 51.25. It will be noted, then, that the 50.00 call has an intrinsic value of 1.25: the buyer of a 50.00 call can immediately exercise his rights, making him long a futures contract at the strike price of 50.00, which he can promptly sell at the current value of 51.25. The difference between the price of 1.95 (at which the call could be bought) and the intrinsic element in the price (1.25) leaves a time value (or risk value for the seller) of 0.70.

Similarly, on the put side, the 52.00 put has an intrinsic value of 0.75 and a time or risk value of 0.85. An option which has some intrinsic value is described in the trade jargon as being in-the-money; those which have no intrinsic value (the 52.00 call and the 50.00 put in the current example) are said to be out-of-the-money.

We have said that the strike prices selected for a long strangle position are those normally somewhat out-of-the-money, but as close to the current futures price as can be achieved. In our example, that means the 50.00 put and the 52.00 call. (If the current market price happened to be more or less at one of the standard strike price levels, 51.90 for example, some traders would prefer to buy both a call and a put at the same strike price of 52.00. If the put and the call have the same strike price, the strategy is called a long straddle, instead of a long strangle.)

Let us suppose, then, that on 17 June our trader buys one August live hogs 52.00 call at 0.85 cents per lb (× 40 000 lb per contract = $340.00) and one August live hogs 50.00 put at 0.70 (= $280.00). As a buyer of options, he will not have to deposit any margins. However, he will have to pay his broker a commission or transaction charge; this is negotiable, but it may well be $40.00 per option per 'round turn', i.e. for the total operation of first buying and subsequently selling (or exercising) each of his options. $40 per contract of 40 000 lb equates to 10 cents per 100 lb. For each long strangle, then, this trader will have to pay his broker:

- The cost of the call:	85 cents/cwt	=	$340.00;
- The commission on the call:	10 cents/cwt	=	$ 40.00;
- The cost of the put:	70 cents/cwt	=	$280.00;
- The commission on the put:	10 cents/cwt	=	$ 40.00;
Total cost of the operation:	$1.75/cwt	=	$700 per strangle.

This up-front cost of the operation has to be recouped before the trader 'breaks even', let alone makes a profit. In practice this can often, but not always, imply that the impact of the Hogs and Pigs Report has to bring the futures price either to 48.25, namely the put strike price of 50.00 minus the costs of $1.75 incurred up-front, or to 53.75, being the call strike price plus the up-front costs.

We are starting from a futures price of 51.25. And the daily limit, i.e. the most that live hog futures prices can move in one day from the previous closing level, is 1.5 cents/lb, i.e. $1.50 per cwt. Therefore the trader requires a rather substantial market move, after the Department of Agriculture Report is released, to bring him into a profit situation.

However, it should also be noted that, in the event that this trader had been disappointed in his expectation of a sharp price move after the report on 28 June, his loss would by no means have been the full $700.00 which he committed to this risk position. In early July he would always be able to sell out his put and his call, through his futures broker, at whatever prices then prevailed. It is quite likely that he would recover about $300 of the $620 which he had actually paid for the strangle, although he can not avoid the payment of the two commissions totalling $80.

Now let us come back and look at this trader's speculative long strangle position after the event. In reality, the USDA Hogs and Pigs Report did have quite a sharp impact on the market. The August futures had already drifted somewhat lower between the time the trader bought his strangle (17 June) and the time the USDA report was issued, namely after the market closed on Friday 28 June. From 51.25 on 17 June, the August futures price had declined to close on 28 June at 50.575. Then the USDA came out late on Friday with unexpectedly bearish statistics about the hog and pig population. On Monday 1 July, in a classic response, August futures were offered 'down the limit', namely at 49.075 (Friday's closing price minus the maximum permitted daily move of 1.50). But there were no buyers at the limit down price; and no business was done that day in August live hog futures. Options, on the other hand, were trading on that Monday. But our hypothetical speculator decided to keep his head down and see what the next day would bring.

On Tuesday 2 July hog futures continued to decline a little, but were by no means at another limit down level. About an hour after Tuesday's opening bell, everything had stabilised. August futures were trading at 48.775; and the options which we have been watching were at the following levels:

50 calls 0.525 ($210.00 per call);	50 puts 1.70 ($ 680 per put)
52 calls 0.20 ($ 80.00 per call);	52 puts 3.50 ($1400 per put)

What does the speculator do? He decides to take what he can from the market at this point, since he has no valid reason to believe that his situation will improve in the next few days.

He sells his long 52 call at 0.20, collecting only $80.00 for an option which he had bought at $340.00. And he sells out his long 50 put at 1.70 or $680.00, having paid $280 for it. (There are no further transaction costs to reckon with, since the entire commission is paid to the broker at the time the position is entered.) He invested $700 and he comes away from the operation with $760 ($80 on the call and $680 on the put). He has made 8.5% speculative gain in half a month. If he could go on like that even once a month, he would soon be a rich man. But it is easier said than done. A weary old cliché in the futures fraternity says that you never go broke by taking profits on successful trades. Another says that 'Bulls can make money and bears can make money, but hogs (i.e. greedy traders) never do'.

An astute reader of the above long strangle illustration may ask how it could come about that the speculator was able to make a profit on the operation, although the futures price did move down all the way to the theoretical break-even' of 48.25, i.e. the 50.00 strike price of the put minus the up-front cost of 1.75. The answer lies in the increased volatility of the market in the aftermath of the USDA Report. This acted in the speculator's favour for a day or two, but it could well subside a few days later.

For the sake of simplicity, we have followed the example of a long strangle position with only one put and one call, at a total cost of $700 and a total real risk of probably only $400, given that in the first week of July, in a disappointingly quiet market, the two options bought could have been liquidated for at least half of the prices at which they had been bought on 17 June. In the real world, a serious and experienced trader would probably have done exactly the same long strangle with 25 or 50 option units on each side. The percentage gain would have been essentially the same, but the stake would have been much larger and so would have been the sum of money gained. A trader accustomed to trade in units of 50 or 100 lots at a time would probably be able to negotiate with his broker a commission at only half of the rate per option unit which we have used in the single-lot example above.

CHAPTER

6

New York markets

Agricultural futures and options markets in New York are confined to the tropicals, sometimes known as softs, and these are coffee, sugar and cocoa.* These are traded on the New York Coffee, Sugar and Cocoa Exchange (NYCSCE), see Table 6.1.

History of the NYCSCE

The Exchange was originally established purely as a coffee exchange and was founded by a group of coffee merchants anxious to rebuild their trade after uncontrolled speculation coupled with a huge oversupply of coffee caused its collapse in 1880. Set up as a forum for trading coffee for future delivery, it commenced operations as the Coffee Exchange of New York in March 1882, providing a stable marketplace and fixed operating procedures for the trade.

* We have chosen to exclude cotton and orange juice, although also traded in New York, as being too specialised and illiquid for all but those involved directly in the underlying commodities.

Table 6.1 New York Coffee, Sugar and Cocoa Exchange contract specifications

	Coffee	**Sugar**	**Cocoa**
Contract size:	37 500 lb	112 000 lb	10 tonnes
Quoted in:	Cents per lb	Cents per lb	Dollars per tonne
Trading hours:	09.15–14.00	10.00–13.45	09.30–14.15
Delivery months:	Mar, May, July, Sept, Dec	Mar, May, July, Oct	Mar, May, July, Sept, Dec
Minimum fluctuation:	5/100 c/lb ($18.75 per contract	1/100 c/lb ($11.20 per contract)	$1/t ($10 per contract)
Daily price limits:	6 cents (none on two nearby months)	0.50 cents (none on two near months)	$88 (none on first two months)
Position limits:	1000 contracts total. 750 in any one position. 200 on 1st notice day of expiring contract	6000 contracts total. 4000 net in one position	2000 contracts total. 1000 in any one position, 500 on 1st notice day of expiring contract
Delivery points:	Licensed warehouses in New York, New Orleans or San Francisco	Origin port or customary exit port	Licensed warehouses in New York, Hampton Roads or Delaware River District
First notice day:	Seven business days before 1st business day of delivery month	–	Ten business days before 1st business day of delivery month
Last notice day:	Seven business days before last business day of month	First business day after last trading day (only notice day)	Ten business days before last business day of month
Last trading day:	Day before LND	Last day of preceding month	Day before LND

The sugar exchanges of Europe closed down during the First World War, leaving the world without a market, so The Coffee Exchange of New York quickly sought to fill the gap by launching a sugar futures contract in 1916, changing its name to the New York Coffee and Sugar Exchange. This situation lasted until 1979.

Meanwhile, in 1925, the New York Cocoa Exchange was founded, establishing a market for futures trading in cocoa beans, parallel to coffee. It was the world's first cocoa trading exchange. In September 1979 the two exchanges merged and became the New York Coffee Sugar and Cocoa Exchange that we have today. Since the merger, the exchange has kept up with the changing trends of the marketplace, introducing new vehicles for investment for its clients. By the end of the 1980s the Exchange had diversified further, introducing contracts quite unconnected with soft commodities.

The new contracts included, in 1982, traded options for sugar and established the CSCE as the first US exchange to have them. In 1986, coffee and cocoa options were added and they have also proved a great success. Indeed, they played a major part in the CSCE's spectacular growth in the late 1980s and early 1990s. Option strategies are numerous and becoming more plentiful all the time. They can be tailored to meet a wide spectrum of risk profiles and are becoming more and more important in companies' corporate plans, hence their phenomenal growth. Options trading obviates the need to pay margins and limits losses to the premium paid and if the market moves in the right direction, potential profits can be very large indeed.

The Exchange provides a forum for the trading of coffee, sugar and cocoa futures for its membership. Members come from all spheres of the respective industries and include, in addition to the trade, locals, futures commission merchants and floor brokers. There are over 500 membership seats which can be bought or sold on the open market.

Screen-based and open outcry trading

The principles of trading in these markets are the same as for Chicago, but the open outcry method is slowly giving way to screen-based trading in some quarters as it is considered by the regulators to be quicker, safer and fairer than the former. For over a hundred years, the traditional method of trading futures markets has been by open outcry, whereby, as explained previously, any bid or offer is put to the market loud enough for everyone present to hear it, thereby giving all an opportunity to accept it should they so wish. It also provided opportunities for locals - individuals who trade for their own account - to take some of the risk and add much needed volatility and liquidity to markets which would soon die without it. Sugar trading in London is now completely screen-based, but that has yet to reach the CSCE, which at present has no plans to introduce it. The trouble with the screen-based system is that it effectively excludes locals and therefore severely curtails many of the jobbing activities that had, hitherto, enlivened the markets.

Hedgers and speculators

Traders are classified into hedgers and speculators. Hedgers are operators within the respective industries and handle the physical goods, either on the supply or the demand side, or in between. They use the market to take the opposite position to their physical activity, thereby protecting themselves against any adverse price movement. Since these hedging activities are never evenly balanced on both sides of the futures market, the speculator is needed to take the other side and with it the risk involved. The hedger uses the market purely to protect himself from losses, whereas the speculator uses it in the hope and expectation of making a profit. The vast majority of futures contracts do not result in making or taking delivery; nevertheless, the machinery is there should anyone wish to do so and the obligation is implied in the contract which is a binding agreement. It is far commoner, however, that positions are liquidated by making offsetting transactions, thereby removing delivery obligations.

The Exchange acts as a principal to all the trades executed on all three trading floors, thereby guaranteeing their viability. All contracts are cleared through a central clearing association.

New developments in coffee

As stated above, the Exchange keeps in close touch with changing trends and it is constantly reviewing and exploring new product opportunities. In this respect, it achieved two significant developments in the coffee market during 1990. Firstly, it added San Francisco as the third delivery port after New York and New Orleans for the 'C' contract, thereby con-

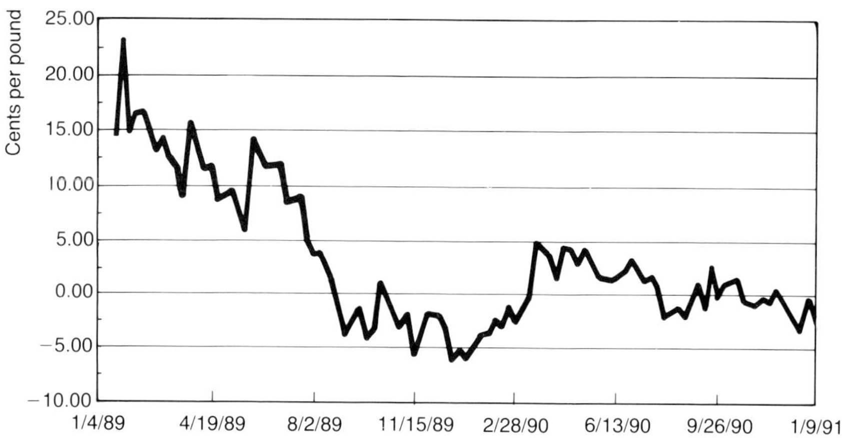

Source: Coffee, Sugar & Cocoa Exchange Inc, New York

6.1 The Euro-Differential (differential between ICO Bremen/Hamburg mild arabicas price and coffee 'C' nearby contract settlement price plotted on weekly prices 5/3/89–1/9/91.

siderably widening its usefulness to the trade. Secondly, it has developed a new contract – the Euro-Differential coffee futures contract. Trading started in April 1991 and, if it proves successful, it could be the forerunner of many more, similar contracts. The Euro-Differential contract is based on the price difference between delivery of coffee in New York and Europe for coffee that meets the quality standards of the 'C' contract (see Table 6.1). It does not reflect the price of coffee – just the price differential that would allow European delivery, see Fig. 6.1. In other words, it measures the premium or discount for making or taking delivery of 'C' coffee in Europe at the following ports: Antwerp, Bremen, Hamburg or Amsterdam/Rotterdam.

The New York CSCE printed the following example of Euro-Differential trading in their brochure.

How does the Euro-Differential contract trade?

Consider the European coffee roaster located in Bremen with profit margins sensitive to the price of coffee. In June, the roaster may contract to sell 2500 bags (375 000 pounds, 170 100 kilograms) of roasted mild arabica coffee for 97.15 cents/pound for October delivery. Suppose the roaster's profits will be maximised if he can obtain the coffee for 87.15 cents/pound or less. This price can be currently locked in with a 'C' contract and/or Euro-Differential contract. Since each coffee 'C' and Euro-Differential contract is equal to 37 500 pounds, the roaster will need 10 of each to hedge his 375 000 pound sale. As the following chronology portrays, by using coffee 'C' and Euro-Differential coffee futures, the roaster is able to lock-in his raw material cost and profit margin.

Roaster's action and results

June 10: contracts to sell 375 000 pounds roasted coffee for 97.15 cents/pound for October delivery, needs to obtain green coffee for 87.15 cents/pound or less;

June 10: buys 10 September 'C' contracts at current price of 85.30 cents/pound;

June 10: buys 10 September Euro-Differential contracts at current price of 410.0185 (410 + 1.85 cents)/pound;

August 31: closes out 'C' futures position, selling 10 September contracts at current price of 90.00 cents/pound, $1762.50 gain/contract [(90.00 − 85.30) × 37 500] = $17 625.00 coffee 'C' futures gain (41 762.50 × 10 contracts);

August 31: closes out Euro-Differential futures position, selling 10 September contracts at current price of 410.0270 (410 + 2.70 cents)/pound, $318.75 gain/contract [(2.70 − 1.85) × 37 500] = $3187.50 Euro-Differential futures gain ($318.75 × 10 contracts);

$20 812.50 or 5.55 cents/pound combined futures gain
($20 812.50 − 375 000 = 5.55 cents/pound);

August 31: purchases coffee in Bremen at 92.70 cents/pound in the cash market,
$20 812.50 or 5.55 cents/pound more expensive than planned
[(92.70 − 87.15 = 5.55) × 375 000];

October 1: delivers roasted coffee to buyer and receives 97.15 cents/pound;

Result: when the combined profits of the 'C' and Euro-Differential futures positions are applied to the cash market coffee price, the roaster has in effect obtained his coffee for 87.15 cents/pound (92.70 cash price paid - 5.55 futures profit = 87.15 net price paid). The roaster has achieved his objective.

The Euro-Differential contract provides a whole new hedging vehicle, taking into consideration the following, increasingly volatile factors: currency fluctuation, freight rates and supply and demand imbalances and provides a valuable risk management tool for the trade. London Fox's new arabica coffee contract has not had a good start and this is seen as fulfilling a need for the European coffee trade.

The new contract trades alongside the 'C' contract and is quoted in cents per lb, Europe minus New York plus $10 to avoid minus figures when European prices fall below New York ones. There are no daily price limits, but position limits are the same as for the 'C' contract.

Coffee futures on the CSCE are traded in the 'C' contract which calls for delivery of washed arabicas produced in several Central and South American, Asian and African countries, or unwashed arabica in Ethiopia.

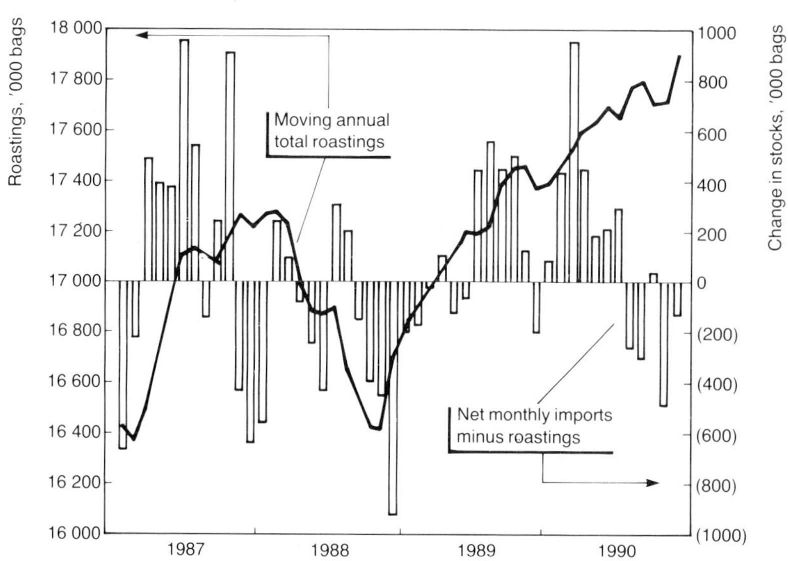

6.2 US coffee market 1987-1990: roastings and monthly stock changes.

Growths tenderable at the basis price are: Mexico, Salvador, Guatemala, Costa Rica, Nicaragua, Kenya, New Guinea, Tanzania and Uganda. Colombians command a premium of 200 points while Honduras, Venezuela, Burundi, India, Rwanda, Dominican Republic, Equador, Peru and Ethiopia have various discounts. A crop of berries from one tree produces about one and a half pounds of ground coffee and eventually becomes about 100 cups of coffee.

Each lot of coffee is sampled and graded by the Exchange and adjustments for inferior parcels are made to the price, according to laid down procedures. If delivery is made at New Orleans or San Francisco warehouses, discounts of 1.25 and 2.25 cents per lb respectively are made.

Figure 6.2 shows roastings and monthly stock changes on the US coffee market in the period 1987–1990.

Sugar contracts

There are three sugar contracts traded on the CSCE, the numbers 11 and 14 contracts and a white sugar contract. The number 11, or world, sugar contract calls for delivery of sound raw centrifugal cane sugar of 96 degrees average polarisation, stowed in bulk, FOB any one of 28 foreign countries as well as the US itself. The number 14, or domestic, contract requires delivery of US origin raw centrifugal cane sugar in bulk, CIF duty paid, at named Atlantic or Gulf ports, while the white refined contract specifies delivery of refined white cane or beet sugar from 19 ports in eight foreign countries and the US. Of these contracts, only the first is a true world contract, the others being far smaller, more specialised and less volatile.

Sugar is probably the most volatile of the soft commodities and the number 11 contract reflects this. With sugar grown and consumed in nearly every country in the world, the price is clearly crucial to the economies of many countries, particularly the poorer, principally producing, ones. With supply and demand rarely in balance in many of them, the futures markets provide a valuable service, enabling producers to minimise much of the risk caused by overproduction and consumers to minimise that caused by shortages. An acre of sugar cane produces about twelve tonnes of raw sugar.

The cocoa contract

The cocoa contract calls for the delivery of ten tonnes of cocoa beans from any origin, including any new or so far unknown ones into licensed warehouses approved and specified by the exchange. The origins fall into three groups: Group A comprises the best growths and commands a premium of $160 per tonne and includes the main crops of Ghana, Nigeria and Ivory Coast. Group B, deliverable at a premium of $80 per tonne includes Bahia, Arriba and Venezuela among others, while Group C comprises the lower grade origins such as Malaysia, Haiti and Sanchez and is deliverable at par.

As is the case for coffee, deliveries are carefully sampled on arrival and graded for imperfection and prices adjusted according to established practices.

Each cocoa pod contains about forty cocoa beans and it takes about ten of them (400 beans) to make one pound of chocolate. This is done by roasting the beans for up to two hours, depending on the variety of bean used. Their thin shells, made brittle by the roasting are then removed; the beans without their shells are known as nibs. The nibs, which contain about 50% cocoa butter are the basis of all chocolate and cocoa products. When the nibs are ground, the cocoa butter liquefies to become what is known as chocolate liquor. This liquor is poured into moulds and left to harden, becoming unsweetened or bitter chocolate. To this is added sugar, flavourings and any other ingredient the manufacturer may want and made into a paste. The paste is refined and kneaded to produce the required texture and flavour, and then tempered to enable the cocoa butter to crystallize. It is then ready for shaping, wrapping and distribution.

CHAPTER

7

The Winnipeg Commodity Exchange

For completeness and comparison this chapter reproduces the volume and open interest figures for all the agricultural futures commodities traded on the Exchange. However, all but canola, and to some extent flaxseed, are largely only serving a domestic need. Flaxseed volume has been diminishing since its record of 338 000 contracts in crop-year 1987/88. Canola (Canadian oil low acid) took over from the rapeseed futures contract in 1988. Canola has become the number one vegetable oil in Canada because it has the lowest saturated fat content of all edible fats and oils. It is therefore well placed to play an important role in improving nutrition and health. As the open interest figures show, canola futures are used very much as a hedging medium, with strong support from the Japanese and North American commercial customers.

Table 7.1 Monthly volume of sales by commodity, 1987–88

1987/88	Wheat	Oats	Barley	Alberta barley	Rye	Canola/ rapeseed	Flaxseed	20 oz gold	20 oz options	200 oz silver	Total
August	13 210	2 746	15 165	---	12 352	71 845	12 789	32	---	1	128 140
September	20 699	5 397	30 841	---	14 529	93 376	40 869	1	---	40	205 752
October	31 257	6 428	26 720	---	9 822	121 599	33 113	1	---	5	228 945
November	31 601	7 401	42 003	---	12 001	102 507	31 931	27	---	1	227 472
December	24 971	3 679	29 686	---	3 241	127 547	17 708	---	---	1	206 833
January	17 648	7 460	39 075	---	6 113	137 387	22 077	---	---	---	229 760
February	19 890	3 200	47 581	---	9 445	131 618	22 854	14	---	---	234 602
March	17 766	3 436	30 838	---	4 242	92 012	18 915	12	---	19	167 240
April	25 537	5 605	70 389	20	6 806	104 171	28 454	---	---	---	240 982
May	27 432	5 067	68 412	---	8 978	170 733	33 336	---	---	---	313 958
June	50 375	11 250	108 355	---	12 889	132 602	49 561	---	---	---	365 032
July	39 717	7 904	90 094	---	5 319	72 880	26 443	---	---	---	242 357
Total	320 103	69 573	599 159	20	105 737	1 358 277	338 050	87	—	67	2 791 073

Table 7.2 Month end open interest, 1987–88

1987/88	Wheat	Oats	Barley	Alberta barley	Rye	Canola/ Rapeseed	Flaxseed	20 oz gold	20 oz options	200 oz silver	Total
August	4 678	1 118	9 086	---	4 139	23 939	6 747	15	---	22	49 744
September	6 259	1 427	11 273	---	3 518	27 953	8 276	14	---	21	58 741
October	7 338	2 055	13 089	---	3 542	23 857	5 690	13	---	22	55 606
November	8 212	2 098	13 030	---	2 876	21 953	5 792	12	---	21	53 994
December	7 471	1 784	12 003	---	2 437	29 265	5 089	12	---	22	58 083
January	9 321	2 077	18 516	---	2 456	30 901	6 179	12	---	22	69 484
February	10 684	2 244	22 409	---	2 833	34 534	6 972	12	---	22	79 710
March	9 395	2 145	22 371	---	2 919	32 538	5 787	---	---	3	75 158
April	10 400	2 331	28 798	---	2 211	34 064	6 920	---	---	---	84 724
May	8 745	2 152	25 665	---	2 738	35 518	6 191	---	---	---	79 009
June	14 024	2 709	33 487	---	3 969	32 020	8 431	---	---	---	94 640
July	13 455	2 648	34 075	---	3 463	29 639	6 101	---	---	---	89 381
Average	9 165	2 066	20 317	—	3 092	29 682	6 514	10	—	15	70 689

Table 7.3 Annual trading volume (contracts)

Year	Wheat	Oats	Barley	Alberta barley	Rye	Canola/ rapeseed	Flaxseed	20 oz gold	20 oz options	200 oz silver	Total
1974/75	128 769	159 315	433 893		153 069	322 848	83 027	108 891			1 396 174[a]
1975/76	37 448	109 609	215 877		155 782	331 570	78 555	30 985			959 917[b]
1976/77	71 082	89 514	225 971		99 929	423 104	102 879	17 513			1 029 992
1977/78	152 224	111 298	325 326		103 311	482 557	152 692	13 618			1 341 026
1978/79	309 653	112 095	722 485		119 174	581 506	198 037	9 250	269		2 052 469
1979/80	263 768	125 622	808 796		149 607	633 880	275 642	2 442	1 001		2 260 758
1980/81	178 484	154 209	620 164		191 454	684 839	425 865	1 851	219	1 281	2 259 229[c]
1981/82	101 131	96 685	361 386		183 296	568 602	268 257	693	24	1 736	1 581 793[d]
1982/83	84 257	61 537	386 156	5 090	177 610	690 612	215 811	604	27	3 437	1 625 141
1983/84	117 022	101 879	620 859	2 372	191 938	743 861	220 207	389	---	3 297	2 001 824
1984/85	97 819	64 422	332 568	433	193 882	929 599	215 780	115	---	891	1 835 509
1985/86	135 757	28 085	297 323	49	144 587	939 610	241 425	187	---	267	1 787 290
1986/87	219 576	43 555	305 260	2	115 989	1 291 290	296 891	157	---	146	2 272 866
1987/88	320 103	69 573	599 159	20	105 737	1 358 277	338 050	87	---	67	2 791 073

a) Includes 6092 corn futures and 270 live beef futures.
b) Includes 91 corn futures.
c) Includes 414 T-bill futures and 449 LT Bond futures.
d) Includes 80 T-bill futures and 3 LT Bond futures.

Table 7.4 Monthly volume of sales by commodity, 1988–89

1989/89	Wheat	Oats	Barley	Alberta barley	Western barley	Rye	Canola	Flaxseed	Total
August	13 677	3 093	29 124			2 141	61 506	16 185	125 726
September	22 031	2 174	57 257			5 582	66 555	27 712	181 311
October	22 891	1 749	20 702			1 922	81 043	15 813	144 120
November	23 141	2 600	46 838			3 486	57 266	21 999	155 330
December	10 195	1 475	17 837			1 643	60 999	10 898	103 047
January	15 984	4 828	20 610	5		2 066	53 322	21 275	118 090
February	12 964	3 723	26 520			2 084	62 513	13 571	121 375
March	10 278	4 181	17 059			2 114	53 926	12 686	100 244
April	12 410	5 720	26 051			1 855	53 143	15 703	114 882
May	10 388	4 302	24 213		521	1 561	80 411	14 630	136 026
June	7 778	7 362	19 084		1 267	2 850	62 378	16 251	116 970
July	6 311	6 384	14 510		747	2 411	52 661	11 905	94 929
Total	168 048	47 591	319 805	5	2 535	29 715	745 723	198 628	1 512 050

Table 7.5 Month end open interest, 1988–89

1988/89	Wheat	Oats	Barley	Alberta barley	Western barley	Rye	Canola	Flaxseed	Total
August	14 171	2 820	34 081			3 650	28 000	7 232	89 954
September	16 595	2 576	34 065			3 533	26 751	8 078	91 598
October	16 924	1 942	29 142			3 231	31 230	9 874	92 343
November	15 026	1 794	23 490			2 500	26 380	10 695	79 885
December	13 891	1 724	22 076			2 189	28 779	7 228	75 887
January	11 736	2 877	20 456	5		2 636	22 024	8 616	68 350
February	10 026	3 897	17 109			2 240	20 428	6 965	60 665
March	7 039	4 192	13 375			1 552	21 336	5 716	53 210
April	7 566	5 610	14 524			1 707	25 419	6 455	61 281
May	5 898	5 560	11 505		252	1 740	21 985	7 296	54 236
June	6 022	7 636	7 753		579	2 224	22 524	8 964	55 702
July	4 725	5 879	9 090		662	1 970	22 268	8 743	53 337
Average	10 802	3 876	19 722	0	498	2 431	24 760	7 989	69 704

Table 7.6 Monthly volume of sales by commodity, 1989–90

1989/90	Wheat	Oats	Barley	Western barley	Rye	Canola	Flaxseed	Total
August	7 923	3 857	20 703	1 331	4 506	51 673	11 313	101 306
September	13 329	6 678	20 887	1 128	3 717	50 701	21 633	118 073
October	10 112	8 319	15 155	1 284	5 031	76 917	18 785	135 603
November	14 360	8 777	28 753	512	4 095	76 173	12 798	145 468
December	4 881	3 574	11 416	351	1 693	50 947	6 082	78 944
January	8 543	4 983	11 236	1 338	2 295	52 473	13 678	94 546
February	6 189	4 000	19 125	202	2 379	66 423	16 180	114 498
March	6 988	7 939	11 564	760	2 512	52 720	13 598	96 081
April	11 168	7 909	18 222	683	2 586	55 158	8 144	103 870
May	8 847	8 643	16 359	573	3 239	82 685	7 174	127 520
June	7 333	4 581	15 754	1 963	3 484	53 085	7 123	93 323
July	9 997	3 511	11 391	1 332	3 007	51 270	7 330	87 838
Total	109 670	72 771	200 565	11 457	38 544	720 225	143 838	1 297 070

Table 7.7 Month end open interest, 1989–90

1989/90	Wheat	Oats	Barley	Western barley	Rye	Canola	Flaxseed	Total
August	5 941	5 747	12 854	724	3 355	20 894	9 600	59 115
September	8 475	5 878	15 178	671	2 753	17 721	6 147	56 823
October	8 653	8 045	13 207	687	3 515	24 718	5 308	64 133
November	6 380	3 997	11 708	596	2 876	21 690	3 734	50 981
December	6 182	2 974	10 230	630	2 618	20 977	3 295	46 906
January	7 519	3 103	10 279	725	3 297	20 892	4 354	50 169
February	7 483	4 013	11 936	607	2 054	17 634	5 435	49 162
March	6 184	4 292	9 330	642	1 996	17 608	5 651	45 703
April	8 847	4 680	10 746	639	2 477	23 920	5 319	56 628
May	8 400	3 501	10 459	632	2 653	23 770	4 882	54 297
June	9 201	2 700	11 487	1 072	2 445	22 251	5 128	54 284
July	10 303	2 308	9 813	1 511	2 772	22 595	4 972	54 274
Average	7 797	4 270	11 436	761	2 734	21 222	5 319	53 539

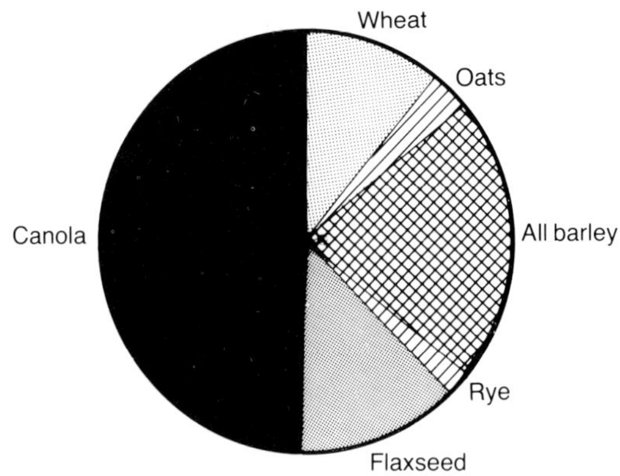

7.1 The Winnipeg Commodity Exchange 1988-89 volume - comparison by commodity.

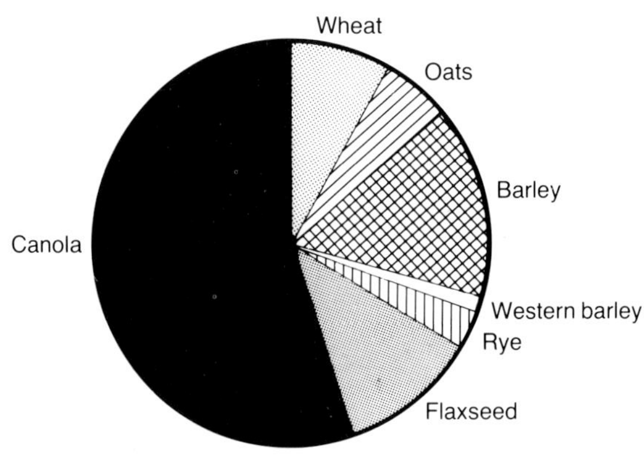

7.2 The Winnipeg Commodity Exchange 1989-90 volume - comparison by commodity.

PART

2

The European markets

Currently there are four cities within Europe providing facilities for agricultural futures markets - London, Paris, Amsterdam and Lille. (Some information on the French markets is provided in Appendix V.) Facilities today can mean the traditional open floor or ring, or even screen trading inter-office. Each has its champions, advantages and disadvantages. In today's environment all futures exchanges must think and behave flexibly as the underlying commodities or instruments, communications, banking and clearing systems evolve. Legislation and regulation also play an important part.

Since the decision to publish this book, what was the Baltic Futures Exchange has merged into London Fox and moved the floor and secretarial operations to Commodity Quay and away from its long-standing connection with the Baltic Exchange. We now have within London Fox what were originally seven separate agricultural futures markets - coffee, cocoa, sugar, grain, soya, meat and potatoes. The various mergings and combinations have been the result of economic and/or regulatory pressures, part of the process mentioned above. Part 2 explores each of the seven markets separately including, where relevant, reference to other European exchanges.

CHAPTER

8

Soft commodities and the London Fox

Trading in commodities in London has been going on since pre-Roman times but it was not until the sixteenth century that any order came to it. In 1571, Queen Elizabeth I opened the Royal Exchange which quickly became a popular meeting place for London's merchant community. The Royal Exchange was the forerunner for many of the exchanges of today; the Stock and Metal Exchanges as well as many individual markets such as coffee and sugar all started around that time.

After The Royal Exchange was burnt down in the Great Fire of 1666, activity switched to the myriad of coffee houses that abounded in the area at that time. During the following 100 years or so, these slowly succumbed to the ravages of time and the careless habits of the population, leaving Garroway's, the most famous of them all, to become the focus of attention until that itself was demolished in 1860.

By this time, auctions of many commodities were frequent and most of them took place at Garroway's and after it was demolished, they were transferred to the London Commercial Salerooms which had opened in 1811. The present exchange owes its origins to these salerooms which flourished until destroyed by bombing in 1941.

During the 130 years of its existence, the London Commercial Salerooms witnessed the evolution of traditional commodity trading into a rough approximation of what it is today.

Four events led the evolution; in chronological order, these were the advent of steamships and railways, the start of international postal services, the opening of the Suez Canal and the invention of the telegraph. These four improvements all had the same end result - they speeded up, and made more reliable, communications over long distances and were the forerunners to the tremendous technological advances of recent years which have bought about the present sophisticated state of the market.

In 1954, the London Commodity Exchange (LCE) was established and a trading floor opened in Plantation House. The advent of post-war futures trading, however, caused the gradual winding down of physical trading on the Exchange and this business gradually moved back into brokers' and merchants' offices, leaving futures trading to take over the available floor space.

The first futures market to be sanctioned by the government after the Second World War was cocoa which began trading in 1952. This was followed by sugar in 1956 and coffee in 1958 and these three commodities with rubber, formed the basis of the LCE at that time.

Throughout the 1960s and 1970s futures operations grew apace and the markets had to move twice to bigger premises. In 1973, they moved to the Corn Exchange in Mark Lane and in May 1987 to their present site at Commodity Quay in St Katherine's Dock. By this time, the three soft commodities had been joined by the recently opened energy markets.

During 1986, the LCE changed from being a trade association into a marketing orientated organisation and, in June 1987, was renamed London Futures and Options Exchange, FOX.

Hitherto, the traditional open outcry method of trading was used on all three markets but, in July 1987, London Fox launched a new white sugar contract where trading takes place on an automated trading system (ATS). This screen-based trading system has since been expanded and in January 1991, raw sugar trading was transferred on to it. The system, known as FAST (Fast Automated Screen Trading) is Fox's own electronic trading operation and seems likely to become the trading method of the future.

The two main advantages of screen-based trading over the open outcry method are the lower costs involved in setting up new contracts and its global reach, enabling it to embrace more overseas traders. It will also lead to continuous 24 hour trading because, as it expands around the world it can overlap different time zones.

Its disadvantages include the demise of face-to-face confrontation where there is more scope for speculation and short term manipulation to trigger a chart point. It also spells the end of the locals which Fox was so keen to introduce just five years ago.

The object of futures markets for all participants in them, in no matter what category, is to contain price risk and reduce operating costs. The best way that this can be done, as explained in Part 1, is by hedging i.e., establishing an opposite position in the futures market to that held in the physical commodity, thereby achieving protection against adverse price movements. Hedging is a prudent tool in day-to-day trading strategies and not doing so, exposes operations to unnecessary risk. A hedging strategy is as vital as any insurance policy.

The soft, or tropical, commodities traded on the London Fox are cocoa, robusta coffee, arabica coffee, raw and white sugar. Of these commodities, only cocoa and robusta coffee continue to be traded by the traditional open outcry system, the remainder are screen-based.

Cocoa

The cocoa tree is an evergreen, known as Theobroma Cacao, whose first name means food of the Gods. It was first discovered in Mexico in the sixteenth century. Cultivation quickly spread to the rest of Latin America and the Caribbean and thence, around 1600, to the Philippines, Java and thence westwards to India and Africa. Originally consumed as a drink prepared by roasting the beans and then grinding them and mixing these with maize meal, vanilla and chilli, it only became popular in Europe when it was mixed with sugar. In the sixteenth and seventeenth centuries, cocoa beans were also used as currency in Central America; this use continued for some time and, as late as 1840, cocoa beans were being used as small change in Mexico and Nicaragua.

In the nineteenth century the drinking of cocoa became popular in Europe; hitherto, it was a heavy drink and was made lighter and more palatable, at this time, by the removal of the cocoa butter. The discoverer of this process was a Dutch manufacturer, Conrad van Houton, who also produced the first solid chocolate bar.

By the middle of the eighteenth century, cocoa was being cultivated in

Brazil and a century later it had reached what is now Ghana and the West African industry was born. In 1900, New World producers were responsible for 75% of world output; that has now fallen to around 27% while West African output has grown to 47%. There have been considerable shifts in the producing areas during this century, one of the most significant being the emergence of Malaysia and Indonesia in the 1980s. During that time, Malaysia's output rose from 48 000 tonnes per year, to 225 000 tonnes while Indonesia's grew from 16 000 to 150 000 tonnes.

Nowadays, Ivory Coast is by far the biggest producer with over 30% of world output, followed by Brazil with 16% and Ghana and Malaysia with just over ten per cent each, Fig. 8.1.

Cocoa's quality varies widely from country to country and can be seriously affected by too much or too little rain. Regular spraying is needed as it is subject to many diseases including black pod and witches broom.

The market has been suffering from a substantial oversupply for the past eight years and this situation does not appear to be about to end. This oversupply has caused the price to drop and the fall has been more or less continuous since early 1985, see Fig. 8.2. However, these low prices are beginning to affect origins as the governments of some of the leading producing countries have been forced to lower prices paid to growers, who, in turn, have consequently been prevented from buying sufficient fertilisers and insecticides. This has been particularly so in Ivory Coast where output hit a record 849 000 tonnes in 1988/89 - over 34% of world output before falling back somewhat. Total world production,

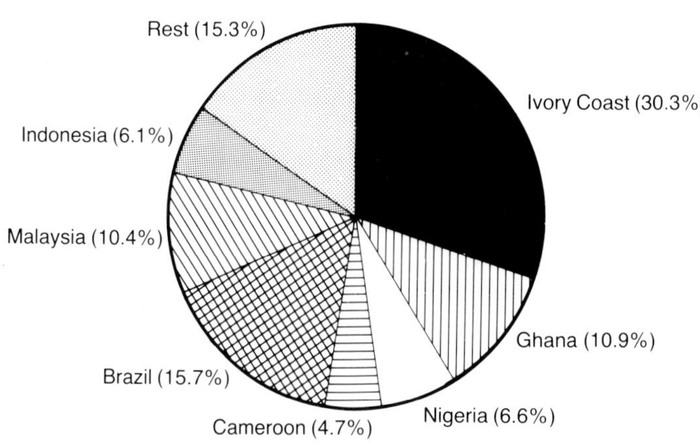

8.1 Cocoa production, 1990/91.

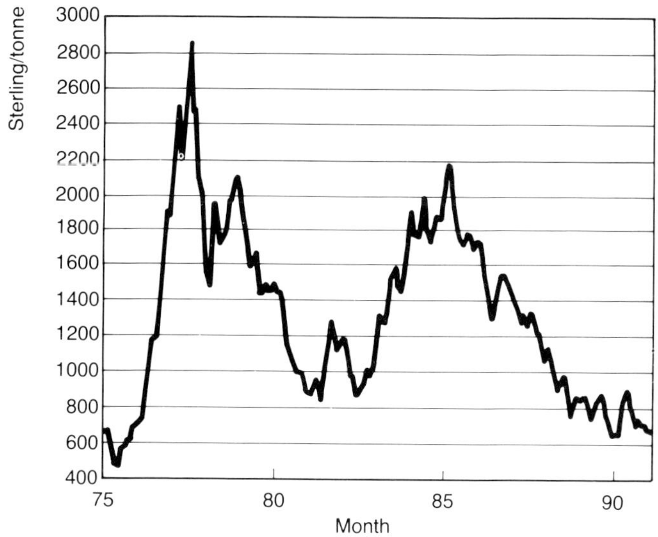

8.2 London second delivery position cocoa prices, 1975–91.

however, has not yet shown any sign of falling. In Ghana, government interference reduced its crop from a peak of over 600 000 tonnes a year in the mid-1960s to below 200 000 twenty years later. Only recently has a modernisation and restructuring programme for the industry resulted in improved output, which is now around 250 to 300 000 tonnes per year.

Another factor contributing to cocoa's oversupply has been the weather; there have been no climatic problems in recent years and this has been significant because the weather plays an important part in production. In the past, adverse weather conditions have caused major problems to crops, damaging them considerably. This has not been the case recently, but, by the law of averages, the situation may change soon.

An advantage of low prices has been a marked improvement in consumption in both the US and Western Europe. Capacity constraints are beginning to tell on the market and there are signs that this could hamper consumption growth somewhat when the 1990/92 recession finally ends. Figure 8.3 shows cocoa grindings during this period. The recession has slowed consumption growth only slightly and in the US, where it grew ten per cent in 1990, further significant growth is expected in 1991/92. However, more capacity is needed if consumption is allowed to grow unhindered.

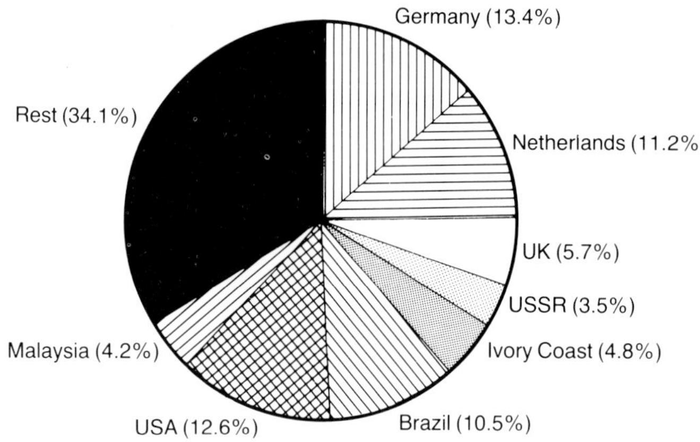

8.3 Cocoa grindings, 1990/91.

Elsewhere in the world there is tremendous scope for long term growth in demand. Eastern Europeans have a sweet tooth and as soon as their economies have picked up and there is money about for luxuries, chocolate will be high on their lists of priorities. In the Far East, cocoa demand is small and little chocolate is consumed; a concentrated marketing campaign in this area could reap dividends.

In 1980, an international cocoa agreement (ICCA) was concluded to defend a price range of about $2250 to about $3500 per tonne; this was to be achieved by the operation of a buffer stock with a maximum capacity of 250 000 tonnes. Financing this stock was through a levy of $22 per tonne paid by both importers and exporters. Unfortunately, neither the largest producer, Ivory Coast, nor the largest consumer, the US, became members. The price band proved to have been set too high and by March 1982, the agreement had ceased to work; by this time the buffer stock had reached 100 000 tonnes.

A new agreement was eventually concluded and came into effect at the beginning of 1987; this time Ivory Coast joined it but the US continued to refuse to take part. The main principals were similar to the previous agreement but the intervention prices were quoted in Special Drawing Rights (SDRs) to get rid of currency distortions, and levies were raised to $45 per tonne. Failure of many countries to pay their dues was a major factor in this agreement's demise after just over a year. Prices continued to fall and the buffer stock reached its maximum 250 000 tonnes by February 1988. Since then, agreement has not been possible either to increase the buffer stock or to operate a 120 000 tonnes withholding scheme, so the ICCA remains a force without economic conditions, fulfilling a statistical role only and it is looking increasingly as though that will remain the position until its expiry in September 1992. Tentative negotiations are already underway, to try to establish a new agreement to start when the current one expires but, so far, no progress in the field of economic provisions has been made. However, there are signs that Malaysia, an increasingly important producer and which has so far resisted all approaches, may at last join the ICCA; possibly Indonesia will also. Reports that Brazil might leave it have been denied by the Brazilian Government.

Should the current agreement be allowed to expire in September 1992 without a replacement, the buffer stock of around 250 000 tonnes will have to be liquidated within four years; not a bright prospect for prices.

Prospects for cocoa beyond 1991 depend on two imponderables, governmental intervention and the weather. Ivory Coast has made several attempts recently to get prices up by negotiating bulk deals; however, these deals do not remove the surplus, they merely shift it to a different location. Political unrest in Ivory Coast in mid-1990 pushed prices to their highest for two years, but they quickly fell back again immediately it

Table 8.1 Contract specifications for futures and options contracts

Futures	
Contract unit:	10 tonnes
Price basis:	Sterling per tonne ex-warehouse UK or in warehouse Amsterdam, Antwerp, Bremen, Hamburg or Rotterdam
Minimum fluctuation:	£1 per tonne
Trading hours:	10.00–12.58 call 14.30–16.45 call
Trading month:	March, May, July, September and December - up to 14 months ahead
Method of trading:	Open outcry
Traded options on futures	
Contract unit:	10 tonnes
Trading months:	As for first seven underlying futures contracts
Trading hours:	Same as underlying futures
Price increments:	£50 per tonne
Expiry date:	Close of business on third Wednesday of month preceding delivery. Instructions to clearing house within one hour of close

had ended. If prices stay low and consumption continues to grow at its present rate, the balance could alter; the annual surplus of supply over demand has fallen for the past two years. After peaking at 340 000 tonnes in 1988/89, it fell to 218 000 the following year, and 140 000 in 1990/91.

Futures trading began in London in 1928 and was suspended during the Second World War. In 1951 all wartime restrictions were removed and the London Cocoa Terminal Market re-opened in early 1952. Activity gradually increased until physical shortages in the mid-1960s led to a price explosion and frenzied activity on the futures market which has continued more or less ever since. Volume reached 11.7 million tonnes in 1976 and after falling away somewhat, touched 13.3 million tonnes in 1983 and 13.5 million in 1988 to peak at 17.2 million in 1989.

Contract specifications for futures and option contracts are as shown in Table 8.1.

Coffee

The traditional story of the discovery of coffee is that of the goatherds in Arabia, who noticed that their charges got frisky after eating certain beans growing wild, and decided to try them themselves. The coffee bean was originally considered to have medicinal qualities. The practice of roasting the beans can be traced back to the thirteenth century and, by the end of the fifteenth, had spread to all parts of the Islamic world.

The first coffee plant to be grown by Europeans was stolen by Dutch traders and planted in the Dutch East Indies; up to then the Arabians jealously guarded the lucrative trade and did not allow strangers anywhere near the plantations – a difficult task with so many travellers to Mecca. Beans were not allowed to be exported without first being steeped in boiling water to destroy their powers of germination.

Coffee was introduced into Europe in the seventeenth century and even then there were drawbacks. In France, attempts were made to discredit it as it threatened the wine trade and Italian priests considered it a Satanic drink, but the Pope liked it and refused to ban it. In London, and elsewhere, numerous coffee houses sprang up and they quickly became fashionable places for meeting both socially and, more importantly, commercially. By the end of the century, plantations had been set up throughout the Dutch sphere of influence all over the East Indies and in Ceylon. Later, a plant was taken to the Caribbean by a French naval officer and from this plant, sprang all the estates of the West Indies and Latin America.

Britain was the last country to cultivate coffee in its colonies, in Jamaica in 1730 and it was introduced into India as late as 1840. It was about this time that newly independent Brazil acquired a plant, from which, helped by a disease that completely wiped out most of Asia's production in the middle of the nineteenth century, it quickly became the world's biggest producer.

Brazil has maintained its position as the world's largest supplier and today accounts for around 27% of world output. The other leading producers are Colombia, Indonesia, Ivory Coast and Mexico.

The coffee bush belongs to the botannical order Rubiaceae; it is an evergreen and is a magnificent sight when in blossom. Its fragrance resembles that of orange and jasmine and is as pleasant but lasts for only two or three days. There are three main species of coffee grown commercially; arabica, which produces the best quality beans, robusta which originated in the Congo and liberica, a native of Liberia.

Arabica flourishes at high altitudes - the higher the plant, the better the quality - of between 3000 and 6500 feet above sea level, but must be free of frost. Arabicas are self-fertilising, prone to disease and infestation and are lower yielding than the others. Robustas, as the name suggests are much hardier and both these and Libericas flourish below 2000 feet and in hotter conditions. Although hard in flavour, as well as inferior in quality, robustas are commonest in Equatorial Africa. The beans are high-yielding and used extensively in the manufacture of instant coffee.

In trade, coffee is divided into four groups; Colombian Milds, Other Milds, Brazil and Ethiopia, and robustas. Colombian Milds comprise the production of Colombia, Kenya and Tanzania while Other Milds cover the rest of South America, apart from Brazil, and the whole of Central America, together with India and Papua New Guinea. Robustas include Angola, Indonesia, Philippines, Uganda, Zaire and Oamcaf, the French speaking African countries.

Since 1962, the coffee trade has been regulated by an International Coffee Agreement (ICA). This agreement has had a somewhat chequered career but survived until 1989 and was successful in keeping prices up through export quotas, see Fig. 8.4. It was frequently held up as an example to other organisations which strove to emulate it. However, negotiations to extend the economic clauses (export quotas) of the agreement beyond September 1989 failed and the International Coffee Organisation, therefore, remains in being purely as a statistical source.

The reasons for the failure of the agreement can be traced to the changing tastes of the world's coffee drinkers. Their desire for better

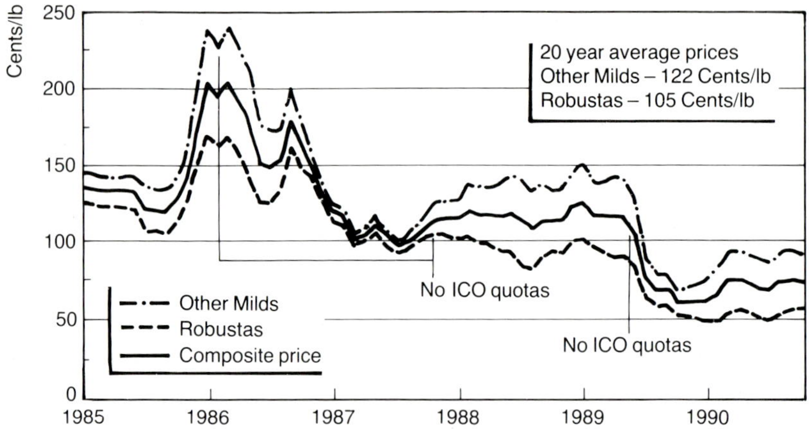

8.4 Coffee prices, 1985–1990 (ICO indicators).

quality coffee has inspired significant technological advances in the manufacture of instant coffee as well as the increased sales of better quality blends of real coffee. This trend slowly eroded Brazil's market share of world coffee consumption and prompted calls for a re-alignment of export quotas with an increase in the share of Other Milds at Brazil's expense and, in robustas, an improvement in Indonesia's quota, since its production had both increased and become more popular. The former was unacceptable to Brazil, which promptly threatened to leave the agreement; the result was deadlock and, lacking any support from the biggest importer, the US, the end of the agreement's economic clauses as Brazil's bluff was called.

Prices began falling in the summer of 1989 in anticipation of problems at the ICO and by the final collapse the arabica indicator price had fallen from 140 cents per lb in May to 60 cents by the end of the year. After recovering somewhat in the spring of 1990, the downward spiral resumed, reaching a low of £548 per tonne in London in July. Since then, the market resolutely ignored any bullish news as Brazil's threat to dump its 27 million bag stock on to the open market effectively extinguished any hopes for any immediate revival.

Since the collapse of the ICA, prices have fallen steadily; the fact that the market is in a huge surplus contributed to the collapse of both. In 1990/91, the surplus was expected to be around two million bags, bringing stocks in producing countries to over 61 million bags. Prices, in early 1991, reached their lowest levels for 15 years as prospects remained gloomy but hopes that they will stimulate demand remain a source of optimism among traders; latest forecasts for 1992 onwards predict a gradual fall in stocks to 56 million bags in four years as demand grows encouragingly.

Trading in robusta futures in London re-started in 1958 after suspension during the Second World War. The restrictions imposed by the ICO's export quotas had no adverse impact on turnover and the market steadily expanded. During and after the great Brazilian frost of 1975, trading

Table 8.2 Specifications for robusta and washed arabica futures

Robusta futures	
Contract unit:	5 tonnes
Price basis:	Sterling per tonne, in warehouse London, Home Counties, Bristol, Hull, Amsterdam, Rotterdam, Le Havre, Hamburg, Bremen or Antwerp
Minimum price fluctuation:	£1 per tonne
Delivery months:	January, March, May, July, September and November up to 14 months ahead
Trading hours:	09.45–12.32 and 14.30–17.00
Method of trading:	Open outcry
Traded options on robusta coffee	
Contract unit:	5 tonnes
Minimum price fluctuation:	£1 per tonne
Exercise and strike price increments:	£50 per tonne
Trading months:	As for first seven underlying futures contracts
Trading hours:	As for underlying futures
Expiry date:	Close of business on third Wednesday of the preceding month. Instructions to clearing house within one hour of close
European washed arabica futures	
Contract unit:	37 500 lb (17 010 kg)
Price basis:	US cents per lb in warehouse London, Felixstowe, Hamburg, Bremen, Amsterdam, Rotterdam, Antwerp, Le Havre, Barcelona or Trieste
Minimum price fluctuation:	0.05 cents per lb
Delivery months:	March, May, July, September and December with seven positions quoted
Trading hours:	08.00–19.00
Method of trading:	Automated trading system

reached its zenith with both volumes and prices spiralling, the latter reaching over £4000 per tonne in 1977.

In March 1991, London Fox introduced a new coffee contract on its fast automated screen trading system; this is a European washed arabica contract, set up to complement the New York 'C' contract. However, this did not prove an instant success and it cannot be said to be doing very well. Its acceptance has been rather blighted by New York's CSCE's introduction of the Euro-Differential coffee contract.

Specifications for the two contracts are shown in Table 8.2.

Sugar

The exact origins of sugar cane are unknown but it is believed to have come from the South Pacific. It was known in India a thousand years before the birth of Christ and in 500 BC it was growing in Persia. After Persia had been conquered and converted to Islam in 640 AD, the plant, known as the 'Persian reed', was taken to other Moslem countries and outposts along the southern littoral of the Mediterranean. Sugar cane was first taken to the New World in 1493, by Christopher Columbus on his second transatlantic voyage, and it quickly flourished throughout the region.

Sugar beet was discovered in Germany in the middle of the eighteenth century, but was not widely used until the beginning of the nineteenth century. The United Kingdom's blockade of Europe during the time of Napolean was the catalyst that forced its acceptance and, by 1813, France and many other European countries had become self-sufficient in sugar.

Today, sugar is consumed in every country of the world and produced in most of them. However, government regulation and interference leaves only 10 to 15% of production available to the trade. As a result, the free market is susceptible to any supply problems and this is reflected in violent price fluctuation from time to time. Sugar has long been considered a political commodity, and most countries operate some sort of regulations to protect domestic industries and availabilities. There have been several attempts to regulate the market through an International Sugar Agreement; however, in five attempts, none of them has succeeded. The latest one was in 1977 and it sought to stabilise prices through export quotas and a withholding scheme within an 11 to 21 cents per lb price band endeavouring to encompass the best parts of the coffee and cocoa agreements. However, it quickly became apparent that the prices could not be defended primarily because the EC, the world's largest exporter, was not bound by the agreement. Like its counterparts in coffee and cocoa, the International Sugar Organisation now exists purely as a statistical forum.

In 1987/88 and 1988/89 sugar consumption exceeded production, resulting in a marked reduction in stocks. The following two seasons, however, saw a return to a surplus which more than replaced the lost stocks. The European Community is the biggest producer with around 17 million tonnes per year followed by India with 12.5 million, USSR with 9 million, Cuba 8 million and Brazil 7.5 million. These countries, together with the US, Mexico, Australia, China and Thailand account for about 69% of world output. These same ten countries also account for around 60% of consumption, see Table 8.3.

Table 8.3 Sugar production and consumption, '000 000 tonnes

	Production	Consumption
EC	17.0	12.5
India	12.5	11.5
USSR	9.0	13.5
Cuba	8.0	-
Brazil	7.5	6.5
USA	6.0	8.0
China	5.5	7.0
Mexico	3.5	4.0
Australia	3.5	1.0
Thailand	3.5	1.0
Total	76.0	65.0
All world	110.0	108.0

Sugar cane is a perennial plant growing to about 15 feet. It has a long growing season and produces several ratoons before having to be replanted. After two or three years, yields tend to fall away but, on average, the canes contain around 15% sugar. Extraction is done by shredding and crushing with the bagasse used as fuel for the mill's boilers. After the impurities have been removed from the juice, it is concentrated into a syrup containing about 70% sugar. The syrup is then boiled several times and crystals are formed by spinning it in centrifuges. The final product, centrifugal raw sugar, is then shipped to refineries and the residue is used for making raw and industrial alcohol. Sugar cane is normally shipped from the country of origin to the country of consumption for refining but the practice of tolling - importing, refining and re-exporting - is growing.

The extraction of sugar from beetroots was discovered in 1747 by a German chemist, Andreas Marggraaf and the first factory was built in Bohemia in 1800. The British blockade of Europe provided the real incentive to production and, from around 1812, factories appeared all over Europe. The first factory in the US was set up in 1838 but a beet factory was not established in the UK until 1912, and that was only because the changing political climate necessitated it. Hitherto, three quarters of the UK's imports came from Europe, almost exclusively from Germany and Austria, countries that were about to become its enemies.

Sugar from beets is produced similarly to cane but the juice is extracted by osmotic diffusion. It is, however, a more delicate plant and prone to disease and infestation and so needs greater care. Sugar beet now comprises just over a third of total world output, the EC being the biggest producer accounting for nearly half.

The world's first sugar exchange opened in Hamburg in 1880 to cope with rising European beet production, London followed eight years later. After the First World War, the contract was altered firstly to a white sugar one and then, when imports of refined sugar virtually stopped, to a raw sugar one to include cane. The market was closed during both world wars. When hostilities ceased at the end of the Second World War, the UK government was reluctant to allow the resumption of free trade, fearing an unacceptable drain on its foreign reserves and it was not until 1956 that it felt confident enough to allow it. The futures contract that started trading on 1 January 1957 was the same as existed before the war and little changed from today's, except that it was then quoted in sterling.

A short-lived white sugar contract was introduced in 1978, but did not last long owing to lack of support. However, a second attempt in 1987 has proved more successful; this is traded on screens to which the raw sugar contract was transferred in 1991.

For over 100 years, sugar was traded in London by open outcry. The transfer of the raw sugar contract on to the screen-based system ended an era of traditional methods where reliance on face-to-face confrontation was an important element of trading. Now that has gone; and gone with it is the participation of the locals who added much needed liquidity to the market when first allowed to operate.

Every day, a special committee, appointed by the market, establishes a London Daily Price (LDP); this price represents the value of prompt physical sugar as reported to the committee with the general tone of the futures market also taken into account. As can be seen in Fig. 8.5, prices can fluctuate violently at times, but the LDP represents a base over which physical contracts can be fixed and it is widely used by the trade, thereby avoiding technical squeezes and speculator induced distortions.

Because sugar is so susceptible to supply problems and prices consequently fluctuate violently at such times, it attracts a large speculative interest. Speculator activity in sugar has always been more popular than for cocoa or coffee and the market is subject to distortions in price on such occasions; for that reason, it is important to have a daily price that can be used as a yardstick for the trade for price-fixing purposes.

The contract specifications for the futures contracts are shown in Table 8.4.

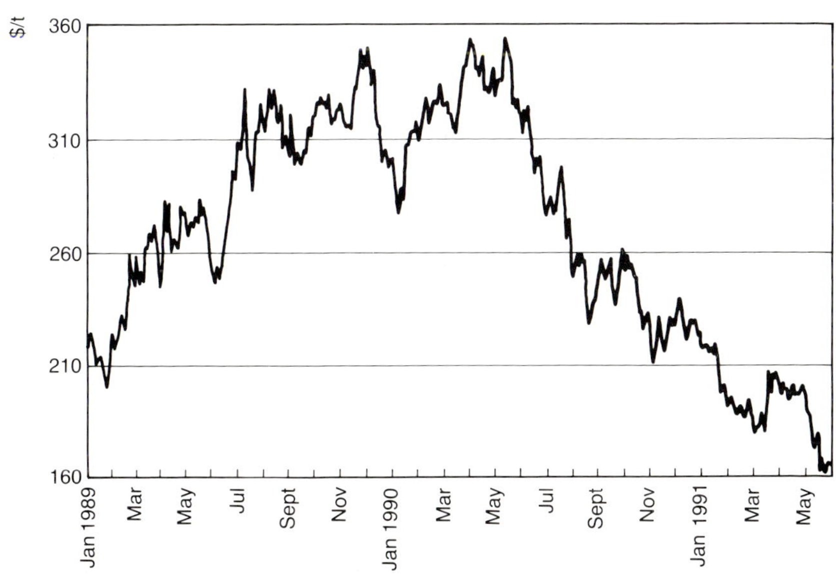

8.5 London daily price of raw sugar, 1989–91

Table 8.4 Contract specifications for sugar futures contracts

	Raws	Whites
Futures		
Contract unit:	50 tonnes	50 tonnes
Price basis:	US currency per tonne FOBS, designated port	US currency per tonne FOBS, designated port
Minimum price fluctuation:	20 cents per tonne	10 cents per tonne
Contract terms:	Raw cane sugar Fair average quality current crop minimum 96 polarisation from specified origins*	White beet or cane crystal or refined sugar of any origin from current crop
Delivery months:	March, May, August, October and September	March, May, August, October, and December
Trading hours:	10.30–12.30 and 14.30–19.00	09.45–19.00
Trading method:	Automated screen trading	Automated screen trading
Options		
Trading months:	March, May, August, October and December	March, May, August, October and December
Trading hours:	As futures	As futures
Contract unit:	50 tonnes	50 tonnes
Minimum price fluctuation:	5 cents per tonne	5 cents per tonne
Exercise and strike price increments:	$10 per tonne	$10 per tonne
Expiry date:	Close of business on 3rd Wednesday of preceding month. Instructions to clearing house within one hour	Close of business on 1st business day of preceding month. Instructions to clearing within one hour house within one hour

*Following origins are tenderable: Argentina, Australia, Barbados, Belize, Brazil, Colombia, Costa Rica, Cuba, Dominican Republic, El Salvador, Equador, Fiji, French Antilles, Guatemala, Guyana, Honduras, India, Jamaica, Malawi, Mauritius, Mexico, Mozambique, Nicaragua, Peru, Philippines, Reunion, South Africa, Swaziland, Taiwan, Thailand, Trinidad, US and Zimbabwe.

CHAPTER 9

The London Grain Futures Market

The London Grain Futures Market (LGFM) is an interesting example of a market that has developed from its own grass roots. It has never been the hunting ground of the screen-based city dealer and yet it has enjoyed considerable success. It is therefore a good example of how futures trading is not, as it may be in the public perception a speculative vehicle to be capitalised on by the wealthy commission houses, but can be born from a very real professional need.

History of the LGFM

The origins of the market go back to well before the war when there was a very active CIF wheat futures market in Liverpool, and a less successful sister market in London. The Liverpool market had dealers standing sometimes four to five deep around the dealing ring, and its participants at the end of the day were frequently as emotionally and physically drained as their Chicago counterparts. At this time there was scarcely any home-grown grain. Consumers, whether millers, compounders or brewers all had water-borne facilities and in most cases no land intake at all. They were clustered in the main ports - London, Liverpool, Leith, Glasgow - where there were substantial storage facilities.

During the war the main users had to adapt to local grain production, and as the home grown production began to flourish in the fifties and early sixties, a need for a home-grown grain futures market to replace the imported wheat market of Liverpool was felt. Accordingly, in 1963 a joint committee was formed consisting of members of the National Association of Corn and Agricultural Markets (NACAM) and the London Corn Trade Association (LCTA) to try and launch the market.

Gordon Wood, who then worked for G M Dower & Co, later to become Dower Wood, was the representative from NACAM and explained in an interview with the author how the new market was submitted to NACAM for their approval at a Council meeting which he was unable to attend. Memories of the depression of the 1930s, where many of their fathers and forebears had lost their entire fortunes on speculations, caused the older members of the Council to reject the idea totally. At the next meeting Gordon Wood attended and challenged the decision on a point of order - it had not been reviewed by the Cereals Committee of NACAM. This put the fledgling market back on the agenda and a sufficient lobby was built up to overcome the resistance of the senior element of the Council.

To get the market off the ground the founder members had to recognise a couple of significant risks. Firstly the only storage available for the tendering process of the physical grain, which is described later, was government leased farm storage. This offered the farm lessor who registered the store for futures grain storage an unfair advantage since he was able to tender directly in his store and avoid the haulage and handling costs of other tenderers. It was also not possible to have the same credit controls in place for a farmer as for a merchant company to minimise the risks of default on the grain. The Committee decided to accept these risks but slowly moved the market away from farms and into commercial stores as they became available.

The second problem the new market had to deal with was one of liquidity. As grain futures slowly took off, it became apparent that any would-be players were inhibited in the volumes they were prepared to trade because of the consistent difficulty in getting out of a futures position once taken. One of the founder members from the LCTA, A A Hooker, decided to stand in and take on this risk. He became the unofficial 'market maker' and in the early days would take on the positions players wished to liquidate, relying on the commissions and the 'buy-sell' spread in the prices to avoid unacceptable losses for his company.

From their experience of the Liverpool market, the founder members of the London 'home-grown market' were well aware of the risk of default by one of the futures trader members and its consequences. They decided to establish a fund, in the care of the LCTA, to enable the market to withstand such events. From these uncertain beginnings the market began to trade.

The UK grain market

To understand what makes the LGFM tick today, and how futures trading in general can be a valuable hedging tool for producer and user alike, it is necessary to survey the UK grain scene.

The UK grain market is one of the liveliest in Europe, and geography is an important contributory factor. A glance at Fig. 9.1 will show the reason. Grain is grown along a line stretching from the North-East of Scotland down through Northumberland and Durham into the intensive producing regions of the Yorkshire Wolds and Lincolnshire, and from there down the East into Cambridgeshire and across into East Anglia, and then West into the Midlands and down to Wiltshire. The main deficit area for grain is in Liverpool with its heavy concentration of flour mills and feed compounders for the poultry and pig industries. The main cattle regions are in the South-West and here due to the high prices of grain set by the Common Agricultural Policy, there is practically no incorporation in feed rations. The compounders rely instead on a blend of NGFI (non-grain feed ingredients), such as soyabean and rape meal, for protein with by-product fillers such as corn-gluten feed pellets, distillers grains, rice-bran and many other materials, some of them exotic imports from third world countries. All the way down the east coast, however, there is a multitude of creeks, gullies and estuaries which accommodate an extraordinary number of ports, some of them very active indeed in grain handling. No grain growing area on the UK mainland is much more than fifty miles from the sea and so even in years when the country was in deficit in grains, exports were a frequent feature. In 1966 the UK exported over

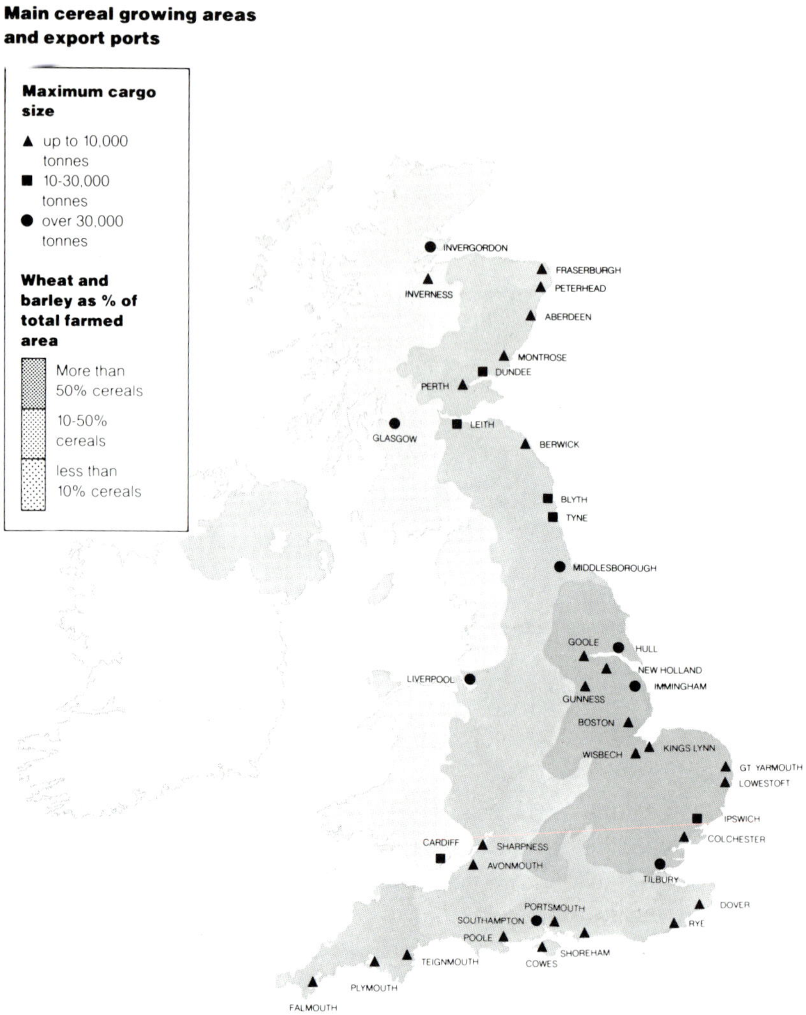

9.1 Main cereal growing areas and export ports.

1 million tonnes of barley, and continued as an exporter for the next two years. However, it was well into the 1970s before the UK farmer reacted to the high grain prices, caused by chronic world shortages (with the USSR as the spectacular importer) coupled with the substantial incentives for production set by the Common Agricultural Policy after the UK entry into the Common Market in 1973 (the dynamic combination of seed technology and intensive farming causing an explosion in output in the

late 1970s) that the UK was able to meet its consumption requirements from domestic production. But even now the UK consumes 18 million tonnes of a 23 million tonne grain production, plus grain imports, excluding maize, of about 1 million tonnes, leaving a surplus of 6 million tonnes for export, or about 25% of production, see Table 9.1. This compares with France where exports account for 55% of production and the US at 33%. Until the mid-1970s an export campaign at the beginning of the season would inevitably lead to imports at the end of the season, producing a hefty swing in price which was derived from our island geography and which our continental counterparts found hard to grasp. If farmers were selling heavily on a bull market caused by foreign demand, the sheer efficiency of the private trade in handling the grain by truck through ports up and down the east coast from nearby farms made it difficult for domestic consumers, many of them independent operators in a county of the UK, to appreciate the scale of the operation and react in time. The business was, and still is, carried out almost entirely by lorries loading an average of 22–25 tonnes of grain. The attraction of the export business for the country market is the fast load (anything from 2400 tonnes a day in a coaster port to 7–8000 tonnes in a deep water facility such as Southampton, Tilbury or Immingham), enabling a snappy lorry turnaround, often permitting four or five trips in a day. In addition, cash-flow is boosted by the receipt of payment for the full cargo on presentation of the shipping documents whilst the custom of trade for paying the farmer is 28 days after delivery. Market prices tend to be led therefore by exports, with the domestic consumer a price follower who will only run ahead of the export market if he fears a supply shortage due to the country over-exporting its surplus, or else sees a substantial forward demand for his product, a rare happening for bread and compounds but not necessarily so for such items as seed or poultry products.

Players in the market

When one considers the market structure in terms of its players against this background, an understanding emerges of what gives the LGFM its vitality and why the UK boasts the only grain futures exchange in Europe. Firstly, the farmer is, for the main part, a fiercely independent and free agent. Less than 20% of the UK cereal crop is marketed by co-operatives, compared with over 80% in France.

Table 9.1 Estimates of annual supplies and consumption of cereals for United Kingdom

(July–June year from 1986/87: August–July years previously) Date: April 1991 *'000 tonnes*

	Wheat (a)					Barley				
	1985/86 1989/90 average	**1988/89 final**	**1989/90 prov**	**1990/91 forecast**	**% change**	**1985/86 1989/90 average**	**1988/89 final**	**1989/90 prov**	**1990/91 forecast**	**% change**
(1) Opening stocks	3818	3025	1895	1365	−28	1753	1580	1550	1380	−11
(2) Production	12735	11750	14030	13890	−1	9164	8770	8070	7895	−2
(3) Imports	1501	1195	805	965	+20	281	305	295	225	−24
(4) Total availability	18055	15970	16730	16215	−3	11198	10660	9915	9500	−4
(5) Human and industrial consumption	5384	5620	5415	5450	+1	1720	1775	1850	1825	−1
(5a) (of which home-grown)	*4075*	*4305*	*4725*	*4630*	*−2*	*1643*	*1710*	*1755*	*1780*	*+1*
(6) Usage as animal feed	5675	5560	5395	4995	−7	4190	3995	4120	4105	0
(6a) (of which home-grown)	*5515*	*5380*	*5270*	*4865*	*−8*	*3986*	*3740*	*3910*	*3925*	*0*
(7) Seed	354	365	355	345	−3	256	240	220	220	0
(8) Other	234	215	260	260	0	162	155	140	130	−7
(9) Total domestic consumption	11645	11755	11425	11050	−3	6330	6165	6330	6285	−1
(10) Balance (4)–(9)	6409	4210	5305	5165	−3	4867	4490	3585	3215	−10
(11) Exports	3378	2315	3940	3840	−4	3158	2940	2205	2410	−37
(12) Intervention stocks	1266	230	40			933	615	575		
(13) Commercial end-season stocks	1765	1665	1325	1330	0	776	935	805	805	0

	Maize					Oats				
	1985/86 1989/90 average	**1988/89 final**	**1989/90 prov**	**1990/91 forecast**	**% change**	**1985/86 1989/90 average**	**1988/89 final**	**1989/90 prov**	**1990/91 forecast**	**% change**
(1) Opening stocks	37	45	30	60	+100	54	45	85	125	+47
(2) Production	0	0	0	0	*	529	545	530	525	−1
(3) Imports	1486	1405	1700	1560	−8	10	5	10	10	0
(4) Total availability	1524	1450	1730	1620	−6	594	600	625	655	+5

(5) Human and industrial consumption	1187	1155	1330	1335	0	185	210	235	235	0
(5a) (of which home-grown)	*0*	*0*	*0*	*0*	*	*183*	*205*	*230*	*230*	*0*
(6) Usage as animal feed	277	250	310	210	−32	300	250	220	245	+11
(6a) (of which home-grown)	*0*	*0*	*0*	*0*	*	*292*	*250*	*215*	*240*	+12
(7) Seed	0	0	0	0	*	22	25	25	25	0
(8) Other	0	0	0	0	*	15	15	15	15	0
(9) Total domestic consumption	1464	1405	1640	1545	−6	521	500	495	520	+5
(10) Balance (4)–(9)	60	45	90	75	−17	73	100	130	135	+4
(11) Exports	17	15	25	15	−40	6	10	10	10	0
(13) Commercial end-season stocks	43	30	60	60	0	67	85	125	125	0

	Other grains					**Total all grains**				
	1985/86 1989/90 average	**1988/89 final**	**1989/90 prov**	**1990/91 forecast**	**% change**	**1985/86 1989/90 average**	**1988/89 final**	**1989/90 prov**	**1990/91 forecast**	**% change**
(1) Opening stocks	5	5	5	5	0	5388	4700	3570	2935	−18
(2) Production	73	85	95	110	+16	22502	21155	22725	22415	−1
(3) Imports	18	20	15	10	−33	3327	2935	2820	2765	−2
(4) Total availability	95	110	115	125	+9	31217	28785	29120	28115	−3
(5) Human and industrial consumption	25	25	30	30	0	8506	8785	8860	8875	0
(5a) (of which home-grown)	*11*	*10*	*15*	*20*	*+33*	*5882*	*6230*	*6725*	*6660*	*−1*
(6) Usage as animal feed	64	75	75	80	+7	10567	10130	10125	9635	−5
(6a) (of which home-grown)	*59*	*75*	*75*	*80*	*+7*	*9907*	*9445*	*9465*	*9115*	*−4*
(7) Seed	0	0	0	0	*	633	630	600	590	−2
(8) Other	0	0	0	0	*	412	385	420	405	−4
(9) Total domestic consumption	90	100	110	110	0	20119	19935	20005	19510	−2
(10) Balance (4)–(9)	5	5	5	10	+100	11099	8855	9115	8605	−6
(11) Exports	0	0	0	5	*	6539	5285	6180	6280	−17
(12) Intervention stocks	0	0	0			2123	845	610		
(13) Commercial end-season stocks	5	5	5	5	0	2435	2725	2320	2325	0

(a) Wheat balance includes wheat flour as wheat equivalent.

★ *Percentage changes not meaningful. For other grains, triticale included for first time in 1989/90.*

Source: HGA

This traditional independence of the farmer has been responsible for the proliferation of country merchant firms who sample and bid for his grain, whilst also counselling him on arable input and selling him fertilizer, agrochemicals and seed. Up until recently a large proportion of these merchants, which numbered 785 on UKASTA's (United Kingdom Agricultural Supply Trade Association) register in 1984, were independent family companies with a long record of service, much of it on the various grain exchanges in Beverley, Leeds, Lincoln, Bury St Edmunds and Mark Lane in London. Sadly, the centralisation in Brussels of much of the price decision making together with the politicisation of the grain markets superseding pure domestic influence has forced a lot of these country market businesses to realise their property assets and hand over to the nationally based merchants, many of them belonging to multinational companies. The UKASTA membership has now dwindled to 505, but the merchant sector still accounts for a large proportion of futures turnover.

The flour millers and animals feed compounders consume between them 9 to 10 million tonnes of grain or 43% of production. They vary in size between the large nationally based companies (such as ABF, Dalgety-Spillers and Ranks) and the smaller independents. They are inevitably substantial influences depending on the timing of their entry into the market, itself usually triggered as with all industrial users, by consumer demand for their product. Seed manufacturers, distillers and integrated poultry producers are also important grain users and will hedge their operations on the futures market.

Finally, the grain shippers, about which much has been written already, are major players. Almost all of them private and multinational, their reading and interpretation of the global supply and demand factors and the politics behind the marketing of the main grain exporting nations (US, Canada, Argentina, Brazil, the European Economic Community and Australia) make them the pace setters. As described earlier, the industrial users, although bigger in terms of volume, are forced into being market followers by the shippers' sudden demand for price cover against their export requirements. It was the international grain shippers who moved in and developed export facilities in the deep water ports in the UK, capable of loading vessels of minimum 25 000 tonnes of grain, and in several cases converting import silos to export. Many of them have now integrated upstream into ownership of country merchant operations to secure a physical supply of grain.

All of the above market players are independent decision takers and have varying needs as to the timing and volume of buying or selling of grain. Occasionally a global influence, such as weather, or sudden large demand from the USSR or China, forces the hand of all the users at once and in the 1970s this happened regularly. In the current situation of grain surplus and politics, there is plenty of room for independent viewpoints on how to approach the market.

The grain futures market

The farmer is not a big user of the futures market at the moment. Indeed the options market might be better suited to his needs, and this is addressed later. However, farmers' selling behaviour has an important impact on the volume traded on the futures market, because as often as not it is out of kilter with the demand. There are times particularly when they are busy harvesting other arable crops such as sugar beet or potatoes, or preparing the land for sowing and then actually sowing, that the farmers are not really sellers of their produce at all. In these instances, the country merchants give the consumers the price cover they need and hedge their risk on the futures. On other occasions, farmers are keen sellers against, perhaps, a dearth of demand. Country merchants do not want to miss out on the chance to gain their share of farm supplies of grain to merchandise, which again they will hedge with futures sales. Prices then have to move to a level where the shipper will accept to act as a price buffer and accumulate long futures positions at an acceptable level of risk, or alternatively to find the backstop of EEC grain intervention stores. In the latter situation the grain futures market becomes redundant. Intervention[1] is a guaranteed outlet for unlimited volume meaning that uncertainty, a vital ingredient of an active futures market, is absent.

[1] Intervention is the mechanism of the Common Agricultural Policy under which grain and other agricultural products if they fall below the intervention price support levels are purchased by member governments funded by the common budget (FEOGA). This system is at the root of the infamous EEC grain mountains, wine lakes, etc.

Trading

Having observed the structure and the price dynamics of the UK grain market, it is time to turn to the technicalities of the grain futures market itself, and hopefully understand more easily how it functions and responds to the multi-facetted demands of its players.

Trading on the LGFM can only be executed via an authorised futures broker, who himself is a trading shareholder of London Fox (the Futures and Options Exchange).[2] The trading unit is 100 tonnes (1 'lot') and the trading months of delivery are shown in Table 9.2.

Table 9.2 Months of delivery on LGFM

Wheat	Barley
January	January
March	March
May	May
June	September
September	November
November	

Trading is carried out by open outcry around a trading ring which, until recently, was always located on the Baltic Exchange. As a result of the merger between London Fox and the Baltic Futures Exchange (BFE), the ring is now with London Fox at Commodity Quay together with the other markets of the old BFE: soyameal, meat, potatoes and Biffex (freight futures). This move to relocate the BFE markets was made to cut down on administrative costs and also to encourage cross participation in the

[2] Exchanges such as the London Fox are now 'recognized' under the Financial Services Act 1986 by the Securities and Investments Board (SIB). Authorised Futures brokers are regulated by the Securities and Futures Authority (SFA) which is a recognized Self-Regulatory Organization under the Financial Services Act regulated by the SIB. The LCTA, who controlled the original grain market merged with another association and became GAFTA (the Grain and Feed Trade Association). When the Financial Services Act came into effect GAFTA was not able to meet the criteria for a Futures Exchange and control of the LGFM passed to the Baltic Futures Exchange (BFE) but GAFTA maintained the clearing of the contracts with BFE by creating the GAFTA Clearing House Co Ltd. BFE subsequently merged with London Fox and the clearing is now handled by the London Clearing House Ltd, itself owned by six of London's largest clearing banks.

different markets. There are two daily trading sessions for grain; between 10.30 and 12.30 in the morning, and 2.30 and 4.00 in the afternoon.

As with all futures markets, the trader on the LGFM enjoys good leverage, for his only consideration for trading is a small deposit margin, details of which are given below, and the maintenance or call margins in the event the market moves against him.

Merchants, shippers, consumers and commission houses all watch the futures prices and look for opportunities to use the market to trade into margins in their own physical marketplace. Once a trade has been concluded it is registered with the Clearing House Ltd (LCH). The trader must pay an original deposit margin of £100 per lot and thereafter he is subject to maintenance or 'call' margins. This system of margins is what offers the trader his so-called leverage i.e. the ability to trade an expensive commodity with relatively little financial outlay. At the same time the Clearing House can offer this facility whilst all the time ensuring the security of the market. If the position a trader has taken goes against him - for example, he may have bought a contract going long on the market only to see the market go down - the trader must pay every day the difference between the previous day's settlement price and the settlement price that day on the futures board. If the trader is small or part of a small company or is an individual, it is likely that his chosen broker will handle the clearing arrangements and charge the trader the cost as part of his brokerage fee. A large company may elect to carry out its own clearing arrangements direct with LCH, which saves the extra administrative cost charged by the broker and also enables that company to trade through several brokers if it chooses and to offset call margins in the event it is long with one broker and short with another.

The Clearing House publishes daily the open interest of the market, which is the sum of all open contracts. The London Clearing House system encourages the trader to close out an open position immediately he decides to liquidate. If he does not do so, keeping an open long with a matching short, he will at a later stage have to match the position by means of a crossed trade on the ring, incurring needless administration fees. The open interest figures enable the trader to analyse the way volumes fluctuate with swings in price, and try to deduce whether a sudden price movement is the result of liquidation of long or short positions or whether, on the other hand, it represents new interests coming into the market and opening up fresh positions.

When a trading month becomes the spot month, there are two options for the grain futures trader who still has an open position. He can either liquidate his position at the going price on the ring, or elect to stay long or short, as the case may be, into the spot month of delivery. This implies that the short will have to deliver the grain into an LGFM registered grain store and tender the grain to the market on settlement of his futures contract, and the long will have to accept a tender. From the moment the long receives a tender, two things happen: firstly as opposed to being a principal to the futures contract with LCH he is now matched up with a physical trading partner selected by the LCH computer at random, as the Clearing House allocates the grain tender to the long on a random principle. The long must then pay the full value of the grain within seven days of the date of the tender in exchange for a warehouse warrant made out by the storekeeper which effectively confers title to the goods in store to the long. Secondly, the long, after a franchise of 14 days free of rent, must start paying a rent of 3.5p per tonne per day to the designated storekeeper until he takes delivery of the grain. Tendering generally starts seven days prior to the month of delivery, and continues throughout that delivery month until the expiration of the contact, about the 20th or 21st of the month. The contract has thus been transformed from a leveraged futures contract with the Clearing House to a physical contract, with the full financial and contractual risks involved.

Delivery

About 10% of the traded volume on the LGFM passes through the tendering process. However, the reader will by now be well aware that the basis is the bedrock to the market, since without some mechanism to ensure the contract is liquidated in an orderly manner, which reflects the fundamentals of the market in question, there will be no confidence in the market to generate the daily turnover. It is worth therefore spending some time analysing the delivery mechanics of the LGFM.

In establishing the basis of physical delivery for the London Grain Futures Market, the founder members took their cue from the success of the Liverpool CIF Wheat Futures Market, of which they had all had experience. Official futures registered warehouses were established. Today these stores number 74 with a capacity of 1 million tonnes from as far north as Invergordon in Scotland down to Exeter. The owners of the stores for the most part are grain merchant companies, who fill in an application form to the Committee and submit the store to inspection by a local Regional Cereals Officer (RCO) employed by the Home Grown Cereals Authority. The store is inspected for the soundness of its construction and its capacity to accept and deliver grain at a reasonable rate. The merchant company is then obliged to provide proof that the store is 'commercially rated' and if it has been the subject of a Government or EEC grant, that there is no restriction on the storage of a third party's grain. This is to ensure fair competition between the merchant companies tendering grain in store. Finally the merchant storekeeper is required to submit his accounts for review by the accountants of Fox.

Since tenders are allocated on a random principle and the acceptor of a tender or 'stopper' has no control or choice over his ultimate trading partner, it is vital that this person has confidence in the list of stores registered by the Exchange under the control of the Grain Market Committee of Fox. The financial standing of the grain merchant dictates the maximum amount of grain which the Fox committee will allow in his particular store at any one point in time, and it is to the credit of the grain futures market committees through all the phases of the market's development, under the control of the LCTA, GAFTA, the BFE and finally London Fox from the beginning of 1991, that there have only been two bankruptcies which have involved registered market storekeepers. When the first one occurred it presented a new set of problems, which will be analysed later.

Having passed all the criteria established in the LGFM rules, the prospective storekeeper's application is put in front of the Stores Sub-Committee of the LGFM who process the application and recommend it, all being well, to the Main Committee. This Committee (12/13 in number) is elected by the Fox floor members and is composed of a mixture of grain futures brokers, merchants and shippers headed by a Chairman (elected by the Committee) and attended by representatives of London Fox and LCH. The Committee, therefore, represents a broad cross-section of the grain trade and a balance between the different sectors of that trade is always sought. This enables the final stage of the screening process to take place. It is highly unlikely that the merchant applicant will be unknown to all members of the Committee. The Committee is not obliged to accept the application, even assuming all previous requirements described have been met, nor is it required to give its reasons if it decides not to register a firm. Past history of good store maintenance and grain quality control, efficient outload and quick attention to any problems are an important requirement of the Committee.

Almost all the grain merchant registered storekeepers use the futures market as a hedging tool and source of income for their store by taking delivery of farm grain themselves into their own stores and then deciding whether or not to tender. There are instances where the storekeeper will lease the store to a third party or else sell the grain in store to a third party and agree to convert the grain into a futures warrant, enabling that party to tender the grain against an open sales, or short, position. In deciding whether to tender or not, the merchant will study the carrying charge available to him on the market from one delivery month to another, whilst scrutinising daily the physical grain markets. If the spread in price between the two delivery months reflects substantially less than the cost of financing the grain plus a reasonable income from the storage, the merchant may well gamble and tender his grain against his short on the first delivery month, cashing the full value within seven days and earning 3.5p per tonne per day after 14 days. The risk he runs is that the narrow carrying charge is due to a physical demand for nearby grain. By tendering the warrants the merchant loses control and is susceptible to having the grain removed from the store by, for example, a shipper with export requirements, thereby depriving the merchant of ongoing storage income from that grain. Depending on the signals he gets from the physical market, the merchant may prefer to roll his short hedge from the nearby month into the deferred month, at albeit a small rental income, in the hope that the situation will improve later. This strategy can bring its rewards. One prominent futures broker relates how a client was able to realize an average of 2.98p per tonne per day by playing the intra-market spreads intelligently. The consistent use of the futures market by a multitude of country merchants hedging their on-farm trading decisions and seeking to maximise profit opportunities afforded by the physical market, imparts to the London Grain Futures Market a reliability which attracts other users, whether millers and compounders, shippers or speculative interests. The LGFM then fulfils its required function of establishing a price on the exchange which is the result of free market dynamics embodying all the known and anticipated price-determining factors in the market.

Regulation

Hopefully the reader now has a more complete idea of how the market works and its relation to physical prices. We should return behind the scene and consider more of the work carried out by the London Grain Futures Market Committee. The founder members of the LGFM had another problem to deal with in the early days apart from the ones of basis and liquidity already mentioned. In every market there will be misbehaviour from time to time and in these early days it was a delicate issue to handle when confidence in futures was so fragile. It was however a 'gentlemanly' trade, and the favoured technique of these pioneers of the market was to bring pressure to bear on any miscreant on a number of fronts, via the trade association, his own company or other colleagues in the trade. It was never necessary to employ legal means to solve a problem. One classic piece of misbehaviour would be a merchant tendering grain before it was actually in store, thus earning storage income to which he was not entitled.

Similar methods are employed today since the grain trade in many ways still functions like a club where any new or outside trading interest is viewed with some suspicion until they have demonstrated their ability to perform in the marketplace, and observe the strict standard of ethics required. However, the Committee has considerable powers to employ such measures as it sees fit in the interests of protecting the market, including suspension or expulsion. As explained earlier, the market went through a considerable period of risk in its early days and it is remarkable that no major problems came to light to interfere with its functions (especially during the inflationary period of the 1970s with some of the enormous price swings caused by the famed world grain shortages).

On February 28th 1989, however, the Committee had to deal with its first major crisis when a merchant storekeeper company went bankrupt with about 350 tonnes already tendered in his registered futures store and with more tenders on the way. Invoking its emergency powers, the Committee immediately met and suspended the company as a futures storekeeper, blocking any new tenders from coming on to the market. This action, prompt and decisive as it was, could not safeguard the warrants which had previously been issued. Since the grain which had been tendered was co-mingled with grain contracted to be delivered to other parties, outside the control of the futures market, the Receivers claimed the grain as their own assets and disposed of it accordingly, leaving the warrant holders empty-handed as unsecured creditors. This affair, which thankfully only involved a small tonnage of grain and was therefore limited in the damage it inflicted, highlighted a legal problem in dealing in bulk commodities. Under the Sales of Goods Act, title to goods can only pass from one principal to another if the goods are identifiable. In the case of grain co-mingled in bulk, it is impossible for the owner of part of the bulk to identify a specific parcel and title, therefore, cannot pass.

The whole question of title to goods in bulk is being reviewed by the Law Commission. Meanwhile, however, the LGFM Committee had to adapt its rules to deal with this problem, and the only solution was to insist that grain tendered on to the grain futures market be kept in one identifiable and segregated bulk of futures grain. This causes the merchants immense difficulties since the segregation practice makes their store less economic to run if it means breaking up the space, whereas devoting an entire store to futures grain hampers their planning of the movement and storage of grain. However, the trade has adapted well to the system, and although the registered warehouse space has declined, the number of tenders has hardly diminished.

An attempt by the Committee to establish a Performance Bond with a leading firm of underwriters to guarantee the market proved unsuccessful, and so the segregation requirement has had to be maintained. This and one or two other less significant incidents have transformed the Committee from the rather clubby and discreet gathering of the earlier days to a more hard-nosed organization who are acutely aware of the responsibilities they carry and are now well blooded in the understanding of the powers they have. The problem of financial failure of a store is now solved by the process of segregation, and meanwhile it is likely that any future malpractices will be subjected immediately to harsh disciplinary procedures, rather than the gentlemanly but persistent persuasive pressures of the early Committees.

Turnover

Considerable accent has been placed to date on the grass roots of the grain market and the basis because it is essential to an understanding of the development of the futures market. However, even the early pioneers were at great pains to point out that the LGFM, like all futures markets, depended on high turnover for its viability and that it was a 'trading' and not a 'procurement' market. The figures in Table 9.3, showing volume turnover and actual grain tendered both on an original and a re-tender basis are a clear indication of this, although it must be noted that the volume figures are on an October/September year basis, and therefore do not correspond exactly to the tonnages traded on an individual contract

Table 9.3 Volume turnover and actual grain tendered, tonnes

	Volume turnover	**Volume original tender and re-tenders**
1987/88	8 716 300	682 600
1988/89	7 754 100	866 800
1989/90	8 112 400	730 200

Note: Years are to 30 September whilst tender volume is volume tendered and re-tendered on the total of all the delivery months in the year in question.
Source: GAFTA Clearing House

month during its life. The figures indicate a range of 7.8 to 11.2% of tenders as a proportion of turnover.

The LGFM has proved remarkably resilient in its capacity to weather all phases of the initial stagnation and then boom-to-bust cycle of the grain markets through the 1970s and early 1980s. This is due to a measure of luck in the way the market overcame some of the early difficulties it had to contend with, the professionalism and expertise of the founder members and subsequent supervision of successive Committees, but above all in the fact that there was a professional requirement for a futures market that sprang from the fundamentals of the UK domestic grain market. The fact that very different and fragmented trading interests take daily independent price decisions has also been the driving force behind the market's turnover.

Developments for the future

There is no reason why the LGFM should not continue to flourish but in concluding it would be worth touching briefly on one or two developments for the future.

In 1988 the traded options market for wheat and barley was launched. An option, as has been described earlier in this book, is the purchase or sale of the right to buy or sell a grain futures contract at a certain price (the strike price) for a negotiated premium. Volume in the options market has been disappointing to date and this may be in some measure due to the comparatively low price volatility of the UK grain markets in recent years. However, the traded option is an extremely useful tool for the farmer above all, since he can hedge any sales decision he has to make at a relatively low cost to cover him in the event he has either drastically misjudged or been unable to anticipate a major market movement. (Example: On today's market a £1 out-of-the-money call option (e.g. a strike price of £111 compared with a current futures price of £110) is available at little more than £1.50–2.00 per tonne. If an unanticipated market event occurs, such as crop failure or large Russian buying interest, after the farmer has made his sale, he can still capitalise on the substantial price swing that may result for a limited outlay.) It is to be hoped that some of the large commission houses will take an interest and assume the role of writing the option – a role reserved for the large, professional risk takers only – so that the product can be marketed by the brokers. The relocation of the markets unifying the old BFE markets and those of London Fox under one roof may help to accomplish this.

More recently a meeting was held under the chairmanship of the London Grain Futures Market to discuss the launch of a European wheat futures contract denominated in US dollars, customs cleared to third-country destinations outside the EEC. London Fox believe that the requirement for such a contract exists, especially with the devolution of the grain markets of Eastern Europe and the subsequent possible privatisation of trade within the Eastern bloc. It is felt that a market closer to home than Chicago and in the same time zone might be an attractive one for large European Community wheat traders and buyers alike. There are considerable technical problems to be overcome since the restrictions in both time validity and destinations applied to EEC subsidies complicate physical delivery as a basis. The discussion continues and should such a market be started, it would need the establishment of a different Committee under London Fox elected mainly from the broker and international shipper trade.

CHAPTER

10

Meat futures

History of the LMFE

The idea for a London Meat Futures Exchange (LMFE) was conceived in 1983 and a meeting of interested parties held at Wye College (agricultural) to discuss it. The proposed meat futures market was to be limited to pigmeat in the initial stages. This was based on the reality that producers in the beef and lamb sectors already had price support mechanisms in place. These were run on a national level and not really approved of by the EEC. Pigmeat therefore was the only meat operating in a free market situation, more or less, if one ignores the financial aid given to freeze and store pigmeat in times of really depressed prices.

The omens for a successful pigmeat market were also enhanced by the widely known and hugely successful pork bellies futures market in Chicago although in effect the LMFE contract was to prove quite different.

The constituent groups within the meetings were definable and distinct. The prime movers were the men from GAFTA (Grain and Food Trade Association). They were the professional organisers and runners of markets. They operated from the Baltic Exchange and already ran the well established grain markets and the more recently added and very successful (in British terms) potato futures markets. They were quite openly desirous to establish and run futures markets where a justification and a good chance of success was present. They felt they had both on offer in the potential pigmeat market.

A second group represented the physical trade. This group was split further into its constituent interests but broadly it divided into producers (farmers), processors (abattoir and cutting plant operators), traders and retailers (supermarkets). This group also included its resident gurus and advisers from the Meat and Livestock Commission (MLC) and the National Farmers Union (NFU). The MLC in particular have been great supporters of futures markets over the years believing they meet a real need for producers to hedge their financial risks, particularly within a political background of declining government assistance. The third group represented the brokers. They had done well out of the potato market and hoped to see the experience repeated with meat.

Discussion largely centred on the viability of the market and the design of the contract. Reservations were expressed about the degree of volatility in the pigmeat price. In general pigmeat prices might vary up to 30% or so. These swings tend to be seasonal, where prices rise in the autumn and decline in the early part of the year with an uplift into Easter and further decline in summer. Underlying all this is a fairly well documented pig cycle where high prices encourage production which in turn produces a glut followed by lowering production and then a return to higher prices. This happened every two to three years. Brokers, however, were looking for rather more volatility as on the potato market where movements doubling or trebling the price were not unknown.

However, despite this shortcoming a contract was put into the design stage and the mechanics of setting up the market set in motion. Eventually the market was established and twenty trading seats were sold. The floor was located within the Baltic Exchange in the City of London. This was an historical and splendid setting with all the grandeur and presence associated with the Baltic trade of the last century.

The contract was to be 50 carcasses with a cold dressed weight of 65 kilos. The delivery months were February, April, June, August, October and November. The price on the futures market was designated in pence per kilo.

The MLC had found a role within the markets and were to be the administrators in the vital delivery process. This was a particularly suitable role as they already had a network of inspectors in place who carried out a similar function within the physical trade. They acted as agents of the EEC in community schemes and ran the Pig Carcass Classification Scheme which formed the basis of payment to the producer in many plants. Trading commenced in April 1984 with the first delivery date in June. The general trend was up and this was to be the initial trend of the prices for some weeks.

The reasons were twofold, firstly the futures market had commenced during one of the periodic tight supply situations on the physical markets, secondly it was becoming clear that the contract would prove particularly difficult to deliver. The contract was for fresh meat from a registered deliverer. The carcass specification called for gilts only (sows), and a certain weight range and fat content. It was clear that such a specification could only be met in large numbers by a limited number of pigmeat specialist companies. Despite the fact that most of these companies had registered as delivery points there was no guarantee that they would be willing to turn over production capacity to make futures deliveries. There was then a distinct nervousness in the market about the delivery procedures. This made for unwilling sellers and the price accordingly moved up some way beyond what would be the normal commercial value of such pigs.

The final moment of truth was reached on the June delivery date. The contract was to close at twelve noon and there remained a large open position right until the end. Large that is in terms of the then LMFE. Some two hundred lots remained to be settled. This represented ten thousand pigs of a particularly tight specification. It was in reality impossible for the shorts to delivery such a number. The longs believed that the shorts would have to pay prices well above the market level to extricate themselves from the position. However, on the shorts side they knew the physical market was in steep decline and only likely to go much lower. This was a normal seasonal trend. They hoped that they would be able to make deliveries at much lower prices than the current futures market level.

In the event the longs cracked right on the dot of twelve. A large position was liquidated and the price collapsed in seconds. The squeeze had been broken, the shorts were jubilant and the market vindicated. However despite the excitement the publicity was not good for the market. The attempted squeeze was repeated many times in subsequent delivery months and serious hedging interests were put off. It was necessary to look again at the contract to improve matters.

The beef market

Before the pigmeat contract was re-examined the market was further extended by the addition of two major developments. The first was the establishment of a similar contract this time for beef carcasses. This contract however never achieved the success that the pig futures market had enjoyed during its early days. The reasons were complex and varied and perhaps one would have expected this market to fare rather better since it had clear role models to follow in successful beef futures markets in the US and Australia. However this was not to be, especially as production methods and marketing arrangements are very different on the three continents.

The main reason however that things did not take off in the beef market was that the initial burst of enthusiasm for meat futures had been used up in the launch of the pigmeat market. The vast majority of throughput in the meat futures markets came from the abattoir and processing sector and was in pursuit of trading profit not necessarily linked to any physical positions. The hedgers, in particular the farmers, were somewhat in the minority in terms of turnover. By the time beef futures arrived, many of the early players had retired from the markets and, since they were essentially not hedgers, had no reason to return if their interest had waned. The farmers had much less interest in beef futures as a hedging medium since the UK already ran a more than adequate price support scheme of its own, backed up by EC buying of beef into intervention if prices were under too much pressure. In addition, a rather complex delivery scheme was developed where the buyer chose the point of delivery. The animals were delivered live and slaughtered at the point of delivery. Final selection took place on the hook. It must be remembered here that futures deliveries, unlike physical deliveries, almost invariably involve an unwilling buyer and an unwilling seller with all the rancour and problems that this implies. Beef deliveries because of the complicated nature of the process accentuated this characteristic. Such deliveries as were made on this ill-fated contract generated such difficulties that it was clear the arrangements could not be sustained.

Cash settlement contract

The combined effect of squeezes and delivery difficulties in both of the meat markets had inevitably led to a decline in turnover. Various methods were tried to stimulate more interest. These included the addition of a live pigs contract, the bolting on of options contracts and the changing of delivery months. However despite some interest, particularly in options, turnover declined to a trickle. Brokers and traders lost interest and it was clear that some radical thought needed to be applied in order to have a market at all.

It was at this point that the LMFE committee began to consider seriously the possibility of turning to a cash settlement contract. The concept of cash settlement always causes difficulty to the uninitiated. It is important to understand that the contract that is traded will not be settled by an actual delivery of the commodity but by reference to a previously agreed index which tracks the price of the commodity. We believe that the LMFE introduced the first commodity contracts to be settled in this way. This method of trading is more common in financial futures where for example the Financial Times Stock Exchange (FTSE) contract is widely traded and used as a hedge against movement in the price of shares. That contract is finally settled out against the FTSE index which derives from the prices of a basket of shares.

The essence of trading such a contract is that the index must be accepted by all interested parties as a sound reflection of price. It must not be open to the possibility of manipulation and it must be produced from a secure source. In the case of the meat market two such indices were available. They were both produced by the MLC and both were widely accepted and already used in the physical trade to fix prices. In the case of pigs this was the Average All Pigs Price (AAPP), produced weekly and derived from private transactions and auction market transactions. As for cattle this was the Medium Steer Price derived from auction market sources and also reported weekly.

The benefits of using such indices are immediately clear. There is of course absolutely no chance of price manipulation by engineering a squeeze on deliveries. The hedger can trade in confidence that his final price will truly reflect the physical market situation at that time. It was however pointed out at the time that no contract in commodities had succeeded using this method of settlement. It was generally felt that the pressure of real deliveries created a great deal of business. Squeezes, actual and feared, often generate a large turnover from traders looking for profit from such situations. However, as a hedging medium, cash settlement clearly has a lot to offer. Finally the old contracts were duly terminated and run down in an orderly fashion and the new contracts introduced in 1987.

The market has traded with these contracts since that time. The beef contract was finally dropped as turnover was not able to produce reasonable levels of liquidity.

Meat futures contracts

The LMFE now offers two contracts. These are both cash settlement contracts and are designed to offer risk management tools for the pork industry and sheepmeat industry, see Table 10.1.

How the meat futures markets can be used

The futures market can be used in a variety of ways. These have been explained previously in this book, but for the benefit of the reader dipping into relevant sections some examples are repeated here.

In very broad terms futures markets can be used to limit risk or to accept risk in the pursuit of profit. The two strategies are clearly complementary in the same way that an insurance company accepts risk in return for a premium. The premium payer limits his risk in the event of unforeseen events causing him loss.

In the case of a futures market, risk limiters trade with risk takers. The bona fide hedger needs the speculator to assume the risk he wishes to avoid. In the classic hedge situation the risk avoider accepts a price on the futures market sufficient to give him a return on his investment. He is in effect insulating himself from an unforeseen drop in the market by offering the chance of any windfall profits to the investor/speculator who takes the other side of the trade.

In effect, the market is a fluid flow of contracts with no limits on the number of contracts that can be raised depending on the interest. However, while the participants are holding their given position they are invariably operating as a hedger or a speculator. They are either avoiding

Table 10.1 Lamb and pigmeat futures contracts

The lamb futures contract	
Unit of trading:	2 000 kg
Contract months:	The current month, and the succeeding nine months excepting December. Starting with the contract month January 1992
Price basis:	Pence per kilogram
Quality specification:	The contract is cash settled against the Meat and Livestock Commission (MLC) GB Standard Quality Quotation Price (SQQ Price) as defined for EC representative price purposes
Last trading day:	The third Friday of the contract month at 12.00
Cash settlement price:	The cash settlement price shall be the MLC GB SQQ Price, which the Exchange shall announce not later than 15.30 on the second market day after trading ceases in the contract month
Minimum price fluctuation:	0.5 pence per kilogram
Trading hours:	10.45–12.30 and 14.00–16.20
The pigmeat futures contract	
Unit of trading:	3 250 kg
Delivery months:	The current month, and the succeeding nine months excepting December
Price basis:	Pence per kilogram
Quality specification:	Cash settled against UK Average All Pigs Price (AAPP)
Last trading day:	Last Tuesday of the delivery month at 12.00
Settlement price:	Announced on the following day
Minimum price fluctuation:	0.1 pence per kilogram
Trading hours:	10.45–12.00 and 14.30–16.30

risk at the cost of potential windfall profits or assuming risk in pursuit of profit. In the case of the two contracts on offer they are clearly designed to appeal to those at risk in the pork and the lamb industries.

The pork industry

The United Kingdom produces around 1000 000 tonnes of pigmeat every year. This is roughly equivalent to consumption although there is a degree of import and export from and to other EC countries as trade patterns dictate.

Around 30% of pigs slaughtered are destined for bacon or bacon related production, the remainder are eaten as pork or in other manufactured goods, e.g. sausages and pies.

The pigmeat industry is very much a European market and, as mentioned previously, is subject to cyclical swings in profitability as production and consumption fluctuate. This scenario is largely unaffected by any EC price support mechanisms apart from aid to private storage schemes. These schemes only encourage traders to store meat, with grant aid, in freezer stores looking for higher prices when the goods re-emerge on the market. This sometimes puts a bottom in the market but has a tendency to depress prices later when stocks re-emerge for sale.

Pork producers therefore are at the mercy of market forces. The producer invests in his breeding sows and mates them at 7–8 months. Piglets are born approximately four months later and sold off several months later depending on the end use. Therefore, the producer is exposed to uncertain returns for some considerable time. Here follows an example of a producer's hedge to show how the futures market can be used to limit this risk.

Producer's hedge

In March a farmer is planning ahead and is drawing up the budget for his pig unit. He has, at that time a batch of sows farrowing, the progeny of which will be at slaughter weight in August. He estimates that his total costs of production, including feed, labour, accommodation, etc, amount to 96 pence per kilo deadweight. August pig futures are currently quoted at 106 pence per kilo.

At the futures price, therefore, he is in a position to lock-in a satisfactory profit of 10 pence/kilo (106 - costs [96p] = 10 p/kg). The farmer contacts his broker to sell August pig futures and has thus hedged his position, see Table 10.2.

In August the price of pigs has fallen due to oversupply of domestic lamb on the market. The farmer sells his pigs to his usual buyer, with whom he has conducted business for years. The price they realise is 92 pence per kilo which would not have covered production costs and resulted in a loss of 4p per kilo.

The farmer closes his futures position by buying August pig futures, which have dropped with the physical price to 92 pence per kilo. The profit made by selling at a high price (106p) and buying back lower

Table 10.2 Producer's hedge

	Physical, p/kg		Futures, p/kg
March			
Sold August pig futures, locking-in profit of 10 p/kg over production costs			106
August			
Pigs sold to usual buyer	92		
Bought August pig futures, closing out his position			92
Cash position	−14		+14
Nett selling price		106	
Costs		96	
Profit		10	

(92p) results in a profit of 14 pence per kilo which compensates for the poor market price of pigs.

There are other businesses active in the pigmeat market, in particular the abattoir operator. The abattoir operator in general trades back to back, he buys live pigs and sells carcasses without exposing himself to the vagaries of the market i.e. he completes both transactions as near as possible simultaneously. However, futures markets can give abattoir operators the confidence to make forward commitments to their customers without undue risk. The following example is one such strategy that could be exploited.

Abattoir operator's hedge

In November the Sales Director of an abattoir is thinking about the Easter trade for pigmeat in the following spring. He cannot decide how the market will behave after Christmas and when pig prices will pick up towards Easter. He notices, however, that the April pig futures prices is 95 pence per kilo. If he based his deadweight contract buying-in price on this figure, the Director calculates that he can offer forward delivery prices for the end of March and beginning of April at 2 pence per kilo above that price (i.e. 97 pence per kilo), see Table 10.3.

Table 10.3 Abattoir operator's hedge

	Physical, p/kg	Futures, p/kg
November		
Quote for spring order based on 95 p/kg (+2 p/kg)	97	
Receives an order and buys April pigmeat futures		95
Prices rise		
March		
Takes delivery of contracted pigs at 117 p/kg from normal supplier	117	
Sells offsetting April pigmeat futures		115
Cash position	−20	+20
Price of input (finished)	117	
Effect of futures profit	−20	
Net price of input (finished)	97	

Accordingly, he quotes at this price and is well satisfied with the response. He therefore makes arrangements to buy April pig futures at 95 pence per kilo which locks in his price and profit.

By February, it is clear that prices have gone against him, a lucrative export market has opened in Germany restricting supplies to the domestic market. The Average All Pigs Price has risen to 117 pence per kilo. The Sales Director has orders for pork dating from November which he is able to fulfil at the agreed price, since the futures price has risen with the physical price. Imaginative use of futures markets could produce many more such opportunities for both abattoirs and other producing units.

The trend as will be seen from Fig. 10.1 is for increasing volatility in the price of pigmeat. The present operators in these markets, whether producers, slaughterers or manufacturers should understand the futures market, should certainly be aware of prices trading and should be familiar enough with the techniques involved to assess and take advantage of opportunities as they arise.

The lamb market

The essentials of hedging on the lamb futures market are very similar to the techniques used and described for the pigmeat market. Lamb production has grown considerably in the UK over the past ten years. Sheep

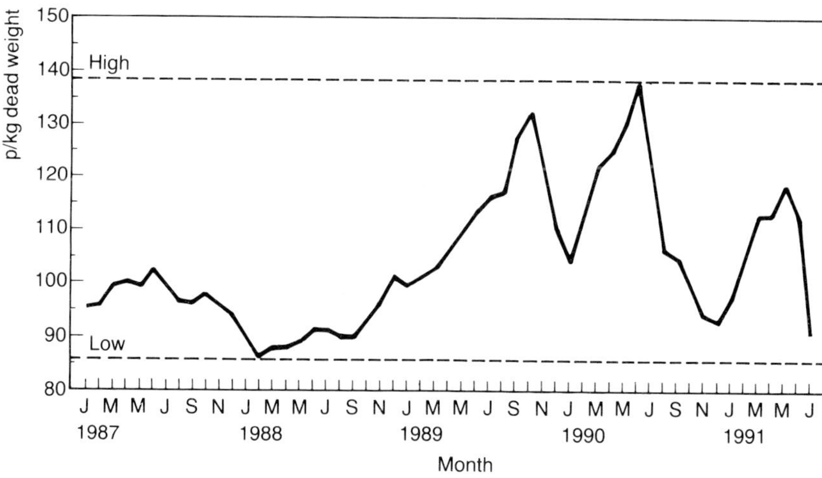

10.1 United Kingdom Average All Pig Price, 1987–1991, showing greatly increased volatility in recent years.

numbers have risen from 31.3 million in 1980 to 42.6 million in 1989. Production of lamb and mutton rose from 276 800 tonnes to 366 800 tonnes during the same period. Britain has now become a major exporter of lamb to its EC neighbours. This growth however flourished under a scheme of price support which was peculiar to Britain and ended in January 1992.

The scheme protected farmers from the volatility of the market by effectively topping up market prices to a predetermined guide price. Figure 10.2 shows monthly movements in the GB average market price which, because of the scheme, had no effect on the producer. The system called for the production of a definite standard of lamb in order to be included in the scheme. Producers were in general able to reach this standard relatively easily and thus were entirely insulated from market forces.

Despite the considerable volatility illustrated by the figure, producers had no need of a hedging medium while the variable premium scheme remained in force. The lamb futures contract has been launched in direct response to this new situation of exposure to market forces. The removal of these schemes is a direct result of EC pressure to rationalise support schemes. There is now a ewe premium scheme to keep down the price of store lambs. It is also in response to EC desire to install market forces as the major factor in agricultural supplies.

Recent innovations have now reintroduced the use of options. Such instruments can be ideal for the farmer who may want to hedge his risk at

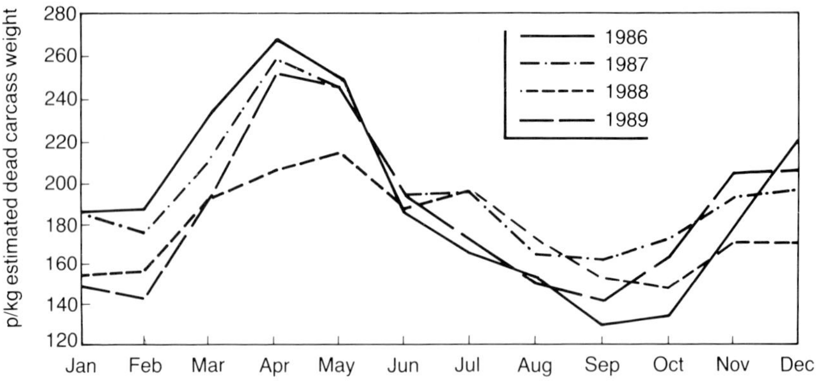

10.2 Monthly movements in GB average market price for lamb.

a fixed price. He can then forget futures markets and rest easy that his profits are locked-in having taken account of the price of his option.

Such contracts work well if liquidity can be found producing competitively priced options. This is the challenge the brokers must meet to develop options successfully.

CHAPTER 11

Potato futures

The humble potato, introduced into Britain during Elizabethan times, is now the staple food of Northern Europe, but because of the crop's total dependence on the weather and its inability to be stored from one year to the next it is one of the most volatile commodities in the world. Each season is seldom like the last and the inelastic balance between supply and demand can lead to physical prices reaching £300 per tonne one year and falling below £50 per tonne the next year. Often it is impossible for growers, merchants and end users to budget for the price of potatoes until the growing cycle is over.

A potato is 80% water and so the crop is at the mercy of the weather during the whole of its growth cycle and at times during its storage period. Moisture, either too little or too much, can mean differences in crop yields from year to year. Although with modern varieties and chemical treatments it is unlikely that we shall see a famine caused by potato blight as witnessed in Ireland during the mid-nineteenth century, a crop reduction caused by drought on the scale of the 1976/77 season cannot be completely ruled out. Hence the potato grower, merchant and processor need as many tools as possible to help minimise the uncertainty of the forward potato price and to help to reduce risk in their forward cash flow. The London Potato Futures Market is one of these tools together with the support of the Potato Marketing Board and fixed price forward contracts. Before we consider these options it is first important to understand the growing season of the potato.

The potato year

1 Planting the crop takes place from March, in the case of 'earlies', until the end of April for the main crop varieties. The principal concern to the trade during this period is excess precipitation which can delay planting. A major delay would cause the growing cycle of the crop to be shortened and so yield potential could be cut and shortages occur.

2 The growing season for the main crop potato is from mid-May to mid-September. Once again weather is the principal factor. With such a high proportion of the tuber being water, precipitation at the right times is very important, as well as warmth to help the plant grow. The crop is most susceptible to drought during July and August when the crop begins to 'bulk up'. It must, however, be remembered that more and more growers, particularly in the drier eastern counties, now possess irrigation which is a major factor in helping potatoes survive drought.

3 The harvest period is from mid-September to early November. Once again weather is the main factor; too much moisture and harvesting may have to stop. In extreme cases, potatoes may have to be left in the ground to over-winter, and high losses occur. An exceptionally dry lifting period can result in damage to the potatoes in the form of internal bruising which is a major quality defect and in particular would make those potatoes impossible to deliver to the London futures market.

4 The storage period is from October to June. With modern storage very little of the crop is at risk during this period and, unless temperatures fall to exceptional lows or reach unseasonable highs during the late spring, any losses during this period are likely to be caused by inefficient handling. As can be seen from the above potato year

the crop at certain times is totally at the mercy of the weather and of course discussing the weather is a British pastime, so some of the reasons for the seasonal volatility of prices can be seen. To this end many growers' co-operatives and marketing groups, as well as brokers, are now developing with various organisations weather forecasting that is producing more and more accurate forecasts for periods of up to a month forward. This enables decisions to be made about planting, irrigating and harvesting with more confidence, and so helps to produce the commodity in the form the public wants.

Earlies

Although the London futures market trades main crop potatoes it is worth mentioning in passing early or new potatoes. These are split into first and second earlies and both types do not store, as they are harvested before their skins are set, and so have to be consumed within a very short period of time. Earlies are the first planted potatoes and have the shortest growing cycle. The first earlies, grown mainly in the warmer coastal areas of Cornwall, Pembrokeshire, and now increasingly Suffolk and Kent, are harvested from late May through to mid-July. Second earlies which are now grown in most areas of the country are harvested from July until the end of August. Three second early varieties Wilja, Estima and Marfona, now tend to be left in the ground to allow the skins to set and are often stored along with traditional main crop varieties. For this reason they are included as tenderable varieties on the London futures market.

The role of the Potato Marketing Board

Unlike the rest of Europe, potato growing is not an uncontrolled 'free-for-all' in the UK. The size of the crop and the potential for surplus or shortage are strictly monitored by the Potato Marketing Board (PMB).

The PMB is funded both by government grant and by a levy on every hectare of potatoes grown by registered producers. It is their job every season to set a total quota hectarage of potatoes which may be grown within the UK and set a target (usually between 95 and 100% of quota) which it expects to be grown. This quota is freely traded between producers. One of the features in the last ten years has been that the quota has changed hands from smaller diversified growers into the hands of the large specialist grower with all the facilities of good land, irrigation and storage. This has led, together with improved plant breeding techniques, to yearly yield increases which has in turn led to the quota hectarage being reduced from 175 000 in 1980 to 155 000 in 1990. The PMB checks that growers plant the correct hectarage allowed under their quota using sophisticated techniques and will fine any grower who oversteps the mark.

The most useful role provided by the PMB to the futures market is that of statistics for the trade. These include an accurate assessment of the total hectarage planted which is formulated from growers returns which have been checked by PMB officials during the growing season.

This provides a guide to total yield which gives traders the total UK production and a comparison with previous seasons. After lifting has taken place and during the remainder of the year an assessment (once again based on returns from growers, merchants and processors) of stocks, together with comparisons of previous years, allows traders to work out consumption trends and wastage levels, and so try to guess whether the end of season will see surplus or shortage.

The London Potato Futures Market

The drought years of 1976/77 led to members of the UK potato trade having to go overseas to look for extra suppliers. Holland has traditionally been an exporter to the UK and the trade over here discovered during these years that it was possible to fix forward prices by using the Amsterdam Potato Futures Market. So the education process began. From initial soundings in the trade in 1978, a potato futures market was opened on the Baltic Exchange in the City of London in 1980. Now just over ten years old, the market has undergone major changes in its contract in keeping with its stated aim of being a trade contract to satisfy the needs of producers, merchants and manufacturers.

The contract traded for the first ten years of the market was of 40 tonnes maincrop ware potatoes, delivered ex-store in 25 kg bags, with a delivery allowance of up to 10% faults within the Potato Marketing Board ware standard. Although initially this contract was most successful, during the 1980s, major changes within the potato trade began to occur which led to the futures contract appealing to a diminishing proportion of the trade. The physical trade was moving into fewer larger hands with growers signing up with large co-operatives or merchanting groups who had the power to get the best deal for their members and this in turn led to the demise of the smaller merchant, one of the traditional users of the futures market. The major change to the trade has been a reduction in the number of potatoes traded in 25 kg bags, the contract specification in London. With this in mind in 1991 the London Potato Futures Market, now part of London Fox, launched a 20 tonnes bulk delivery contract to replace the old bag contract. As in the previous contract the quality specification is based on the PMB ware standard but also includes in the early delivery months tests for the potatoes' dry matters and sugars. These tests are not carried out in the late delivery months, reflecting that the quality criteria of the trade changes as the season progresses, and late potatoes have to be stored at temperatures which affect the sugars if they are to be kept through until the end of the season without quality deteriorating. The main contract specifications are shown in Table 11.1.

The potato trade within Europe

The insular nature of the UK's potato market is currently undergoing many changes as described earlier and in the future this will continue at a greater rate. With the opening up of free trade within the European Community and the barriers between East and West being dismantled, traders will have to expand their horizons and think further afield when making fundamental decisions. Quotas may disappear together with the PMB's ability to hold prices in surplus years by removing over-supply to make for orderly markets. In the future, traders will have to look outside their own backyard to be able to make the correct decisions and realise that potatoes from other countries will not go away. Price risk management will become the necessity for all. The UK's 6 million tonnes of potatoes looks small when compared with the 40 million tonnes grown by the European Community as a whole, but this is then put into perspective when one realises that Poland grows over 50 million tonnes. Admittedly the majority of the Polish production goes into stock-feed, and potato starch manufacturing but, with the cheaper costs associated with Eastern Europe and their need for hard currency, it must be expected that their quality will

Table 11.1 Contract specification on London potato futures market

Size:	20 tonnes
Delivery months:	September, October, November, February, March, April, May, June
Varieties:	PMB recognised maincrop varieties subject to a minimum production area of 1 000 ha with the exception of Record and Russett Burbank, but to include Wilja, Estima, Bintje and Marfona To be of EEC origin
Quality:	PMB ware standard (allowance for delivery of between 5 and 15% faults with allowances of 1% of futures settlement price for each 1% of that deficiency, i.e. 14.5% faults - 10% allowance). Any deliveries with more than 15% faults settled on fixed formula based on futures settlement price
Tuber count:	35–70 tubers per 10 kg sample
Dry matter:	18% minimum dry matter (which may be reduced in exceptional circumstances by the Market Committee). Not applicable to the April, May and June delivery months
Cooking quality:	To fry within three consecutive bands between 00 and 3 on the USDA fry chart. Not applicable to the April, May and June delivery months
Delivery:	Bulk (buyers options to receive in bags at an additional charge) fee on to buyers transport at a time determined by seller from registered grading station in mainland UK

Although the first principle of trading in a futures market is that physical delivery should not take place the ability to make or take delivery of the underlying commodity is important in case prices have been pushed out of line for technical reasons.

The delivery procedure for the 20 tonnes bulk contract is set out below.

The mainland UK is split into four areas and all grading stations are registered within one of these areas. Buyers are able to nominate an area of preference in which they wish to take delivery and the London Clearing House endeavour to try to match them with any sellers in that area. The timetable is as follows:

4th day of delivery month (or following business day)

1230	Trading ceases
1400	Buyer notifies clearing house of his preference for area of delivery. Seller notifies clearing house of area in which grading station is situated from where delivery is to be made

5th day of month	The Buyer receives notice of which area he will receive delivery. He has until 1700 hr to exercise bag option and also if he wishes to ask alternative delivery procedure and so waive right to inspection.
6th day of month until 4th business day before end of month	
Day 1	Seller passes on to clearing house tender
Day 2 or 3	Buyer informs seller and inspector by 1200 hr of transport arrangements and if an am or pm collection
Day 4	Buyer's transport collects potatoes from store in presence of inspector
Grading stations	Grading station to have own weighbridge or be within 5 miles of public or certified weighbridge. A certified weighbridge being a private weighbridge checked by a weights and measures inspector and the owner has given written consent that the grading station has access to the facility

improve and some of this production will be targeted towards Western Europe, probably in processed form.

Traders in Europe have used futures to help manage their forward risk exposure for many years using the Amsterdam Potato Futures Market. This market trades a 25 tonne bulk contract with only one deliverable variety (Bintje the main type of potato grown throughout Holland). The success of this market, together with London's in the early 1980s, led to the French launching a potato futures market in the mid-1980s in Lille in Northern France. This market also trades a Bintje contract but the lot size is 20 tonnes in 25 kg bags delivered on pallets. A majority of the volume in Lille is of an arbitrage nature with Amsterdam. Although it is early days for the new London contract, the switch to bulk together with the testing for dry matters and sugars should produce an increase in arbitrage activity with Amsterdam, as traders will now have a more reliable basis for trade between the two markets. In the future a processor (french fry manufacturer) will be able, with more confidence, to look at prices in the Amsterdam market and trade against his physical stock and forward contract positions. If London were to have gone to an excessive premium over Amsterdam then he will be able to hedge some forward stock by selling London futures contracts but also protect this by buying Amsterdam futures contracts to replace the stock at a more competitive price. As the potato trade becomes more widespread so the use of futures should become more sophisticated and volume and usage should increase significantly.

CHAPTER

12

Soyabean meal futures

History

The idea of a London Soyabean Meal Futures Market was first conceived as a direct result of a soyabean export embargo imposed by the US nearly twenty years ago.

In the early seventies North America was by far the largest producer, exporter and consumer of soyabeans in the world. Therein lies the seeds of a potential global shortage of soyabeans. These seeds began to fertilise when North America had a very poor growing season combined with an annual consumption increase of 10%. Demand was close to out-stripping supply not only in the US but worldwide. The USDA envisaged a situation where the supply of soyabeans in North America would not be enough to satisfy domestic consumption as well as fulfilling export commitments. This was considered a potentially dangerous situation and long discussions took place between the Senate and the Department of Agriculture. Consequently, an export embargo of soyabeans was imposed to guarantee continued supply for domestic consumption.

In Europe, the embargo had a devastating effect, causing soyabean meal prices to rocket from around £100 per tonne to nearly £300 per tonne. As in North America, European demand for soyameal was growing at a rapid pace. Commercial traders were buying North American soyabeans and shipping them to Europe where they were crushed into soyabean meal for European consumption in the hog and poultry industry. These forward soyameal sales were being hedged on the Chicago futures market. Consequently, when the embargo was announced, the Chicago futures prices stabilised in the knowledge that internal supplies would be sufficient. However, prices in Europe surged on the fear of soyabean and meal stocks running out. For anybody who had purchased Chicago futures contracts to hedge forward European sales, this was a financial nightmare.

Following on from this painful experience, there came a clamour from the European trade houses to start up their own futures market. The UK trade took up the idea and a formation committee was set up to investigate the potential of such a market and what type of contract to use. Under the guidance of the UK Grain and Feed Trade Association the committee decided to launch a 100 tonne soyabean meal contract quoted in sterling and deliverable at certain stores around Europe.

Initially, trading was light but volume slowly increased. Although never in the same league as the Chicago soyameal contract, it did provide a hedging vehicle. During its infancy there were several bull markets on the back of droughts in the Mid-West of North America which kept the momentum going. However, a succession of bear markets through the late 1970s/early 1980s because of over-production in both North and South America, caused interest and volume to wane. During the 1980s North America had stiff competition from Brazil, Argentina and other South American countries in marketing their production of soyabeans. Although consumption was still high other ingredients were being used in feed mixes causing over-supply. On the futures markets, consumers became complacent about hedging their forward risk taking volume away from the market. Tight margins, plus a recessionary climate, also caused the major trade houses in Europe to review their trading strategy, consequently trade contracted to a hard core support turning the market into a virtually physical trading market.

The management committee held seminars throughout Europe in the hope of promoting new business. Discussions were taking place on changing the contract quality and size plus its tender stores to encourage more players to use the market. In the physical market a number of companies had gone bankrupt or moved on to other products. As tighter budgets were called for, a number of consumers were going direct to shippers for their supplies, without using a merchant, broker or futures markets.

From the embers that were left a new management committee decided to change the contract to FOB from 100 tonnes to 20 and from low protein to high protein, see Table 12.1. These changes appealed to the UK and European trade (what was left of it). Slowly the new contract is taking shape and the few embers are beginning to glow. The market is now sited at the London Fox which will give it a wider audience and hopefully it will begin to grow again. Only time will tell.

Soyabean meal

The bulk of the world's soyabeans are grown in North and South America. Since soyabean meal is high in protein and energy with the added bonus of being very palatable, it is used to a great extent in the formulation of animal feeds. And because of its higher cost in comparison with the cereal ingredients of feed, the proportion of protein included has an important influence on the price of the feed.

After the US and Brazil, the main areas of production are China, Russia, Argentina, Mexico and Paraguay. Soyabeans are crushed by oilseed processors, producing soyabean meal and soyabean oil as valuable by-products.

Hi Pro

Hi Pro soya earns its name from its high protein and oil content. It is used in the UK and throughout Continental Europe by processors as a major ingredient in their animal feed compounds.

Hedging on the Soyabean Meal Futures Market

Hedging on the Soyabean Meal Futures Market operates in the same way as other commodities described previously. In using futures as a hedge,

Table 12.1 Soyabean meal contract terms

Price:	In £ sterling
Lot size:	20 tonnes of 1000 kg each
Quality:	Minimum 49% protein and oil combined* Maximum 3.5% fibre** Maximum 13.5% moisture Maximum 2.5% sand and/or silica
Origin:	Only meal produced in Europe or the United States shall be deliverable
Delivery months:	February, April, June, August, October and December
Cessation of trading:	Trading for a delivery month shall normally cease at 12.00 on the business day which is two business days prior to the sixteenth calendar day of that delivery month
Delivery free on board (FOB):	In coaster or barge from Amsterdam. Rotterdam of Ghent areas
Minimum fluctuation:	£0.10 per tonne
Trading hours:	10.30-12.00/14.30 16.45
Deposits and margins:	Deposits and margins are required to be paid. It is important to discuss the possibility of margin calls with both your broker and with your bank manager
Commissions:	Commissions payable to your broker are negotiable
Traded options:	Are available

*Denotes that seller may deliver to an absolute minimum of 47.5% with payment to the buyers of an allowance of 1% for 1% of the contract price.
**Denotes that seller may deliver to an absolute maximum of 4.5% with payment to the buyers of an allowance of 1% for 1% of the contract price.

prices and supplies of soyabean meal are assured through the delivery commitment. This enables businesses to plan ahead, and helps them to budget and achieve targeted profits. A shipper, for example, is vulnerable to the price of soyabean meal falling whilst in transit. Similarly, a livestock farmer, perhaps with known product returns faces a risk of the price of soyabean meal rising.

Hedging provides insurance against these price risks by enabling traders to establish a compensating position on futures. So if the trader holds the physical commodity, he sells futures. The futures transaction yields a profit when the physical deal is losing value and vice versa.

Most forward physical transactions are a binding commitment and are difficult to alter should circumstances change. A futures contract, however, can be terminated and reinstated easily to suit individual situations.

In this way the pricing of physical deals - the purchase or sale of soyabean meal, can be timed for when it is convenient to the business concerned.

PART

3

Investing and investor protection

Rather than provide a separate but similar description of how the private or commercial client is handled in the United States this part details how a client is serviced under current United Kingdom and American regulations from a London-based point of view. The client-broker relationship in Europe is naturally international, incorporating North American and European market rules and practices depending on which futures contracts are being discussed and traded at the time.

References to the American regulatory scene and trade practice will be found in Appendix II.

CHAPTER 13

Opening and servicing an account from a United Kingdom viewpoint

A business relationship should never be undertaken without adequate preparation and careful consideration. When opening an account with a futures broker the approach should be the same. Quite simply the most advantageous hedging or trading strategies can be undermined, or indeed even fail, if the client has the wrong broker. This chapter attempts to ask and answer some of the questions prospective users of the futures markets should address before they open an account and hopefully help them choose the right broker.

Who are the brokers?

Futures brokers are described in a number of ways e.g. futures commission merchants, wire houses and brokerage houses. Some will be part of major international companies with interests spanning both commodity and financial markets. Others may be regional in scope and specialise in a particular group of markets and therefore only service clients whose interests mirror their own. However they are described, whatever their size and capabilities, their principal purpose is the same, that is to transact business on behalf of users of futures markets.

How do you find out about the brokers?

Futures commission merchants are registered member firms of futures exchanges so that they can trade on behalf of their clients in the markets housed in the exchange. Without exception these exchanges will provide a list of members to interested companies or individuals. A list of memberships from the exchange may however be too extensive for your requirements and will tell you nothing about a particular broker's capabilities. A better starting point may be the exchange literature on the particular commodity you wish to trade. It is not unusual for a document of this nature to list the brokers actively trading in that market. Alternatively, major agricultural trade fairs are frequently host to the specialised agricultural brokers and the exchanges with agricultural markets. However you begin your search for a broker it is advisable to have a list of at least four brokers, ideally more.

Which one?

Before beginning to assess the merits of each broker it is advisable to establish what type of service you are looking for, what frequency of contact you need, how much market analysis you want and how frequently you need it. Some brokers may not be able to accommodate your basic requirements so avoid spending time with brokers who are not particularly suited to your needs by establishing a basic outline of the service you want. Initiate your search by raising these points at the earliest opportunity.

Next, aim to select two rather than one broker. This is strongly advisable for commercial operations who, for example, are unlikely to be totally reliant upon the services of one bank for all their treasury functions. One broker will become the principal or lead broker transacting the vast majority of business, the other the reserve, less active account.

What should you ask for?

The actual process of selection will be dependent upon a variety of factors, some less scientific than others. You will notice that there are services common to all brokers: placing orders, providing basic accounting records and market analysis. You will, however, find that the accounting systems and quantity and quality of the market analysis vary, so obtain as much material as possible from each broker and evaluate the suitability to your specific needs.

With respect to the accounting practices, it would be advisable to obtain copies of the statements sent out by each broker. It is unlikely that they will be the same and you may find some easier to understand than others. Whatever their clarity ask your prospective broker to explain or confirm your understanding of the statement.

Another aspect of the accounting practices will be the manner in which your prospective broker handles foreign exchange transactions. Major users of the futures markets frequently trade in contracts that are denominated in currencies other than their own. You should find out how each broker manages their clients' foreign exchange. Ask if they have the capability to convert from one currency to another and if so, what method they use.

When evaluating the market analysis you should make sure that you get a good overview of what is available. All futures brokers will provide their clients with daily, weekly and monthly market summaries. Some will also have specialist departments producing articles and reports on specific issues. Make sure you ask what is available and obtain examples.

Finally, find out how your prospective broker sends their statements and analysis to customers. It may be possible to receive the information through a variety of ways. Telex, telefax and transmission direct to a personal computer are some of the methods commonly used.

Perhaps the most important factor affecting your decision will be the people who represent the futures brokers. Like all service industries the brokerage business is relationship orientated and you need to be comfortable with the person or persons with whom you have direct contact. The broker acting on your behalf will be your link to the marketplace so it is crucial that you and your company do not have reason to question their credibility. Furthermore, it is likely that at some point during your initial enquiries the prospective brokers will visit your place of work to assess your business. You should do the same, it will allow you to evaluate their business and the people you are considering dealing with.

What should you have talked about before trading?

Once you have selected the broker or brokers that you wish to do business with, they will discuss with you not only your trading goals but also your ability to withstand the risks inherent in trading futures.

When talking about your trading goals it would be a good opportunity to discuss how you would like to start trading. Without question you should enter the markets slowly and carefully. Not only will it allow you to assess the viability of using the futures markets for your needs but it will demonstrate if you and indeed the broker, have the necessary level of understanding and administrative capability. There should never be an argument that leads you to enter the markets aggressively when you begin trading.

The financial requirements for clients vary from broker to broker but in assessing your suitability to open an account the broker will require an audited financial statement or other documentation giving details of the financial worth of your company. You can, if you want, request similar information from your broker. It is not unreasonable to assess their financial status.

What should you understand before trading?

Once an account is opened and before trading has commenced you will be required to deposit money with your broker to meet margin requirements. It is important that you understand why you have to do this.

A margin is money that futures brokers have to deposit with the clearing houses of the exchanges on which their clients trade. Each futures contract will have a margin requirement and moreover that margin will vary depending upon whether the client is a commercial or individual trader and hedging or speculating. The futures brokers will require their clients to deposit at least the exchange requirements with them so that they can then make the deposit with the clearing house. It would not be unusual for the futures broker to require margins in excess of the requirements of the exchange. In addition, the amount of margins deposited will have to be maintained above a certain level which may require traders to deposit more money with the broker. The first deposit of monies with the exchange for each future contract is called an initial margin. Any additional margin deposits for that contract are called maintenance margins.

Understanding why margins are required is possibly the most difficult part of beginning to trade futures. Make sure you have spent enough time with your broker on this point. Some brokers have the facility to let their prospective clients trade imaginary accounts so that they can understand the mechanics of margins before entering the markets for real (sometimes referred to as paper-trading). If your broker offers this facility you should use it.

Another feature of futures markets that can sometimes result in confusion is the difference between those who look at the markets from a fundamental approach and those who assess the markets from a technical viewpoint, as discussed in a previous chapter. Quite simply a fundamentalist will focus upon the economic forces of supply and demand that cause prices to move. The technical analyst will however evaluate price from market action alone. In reality your futures broker will probably use a combination of both approaches. This is not the place to explore the differences between these two methods. You should, however, be aware of their existence and discuss how you want to view the markets with your prospective broker. If you are interested in these concepts, ask your broker who will be able to provide you with a starting point.

Finally, you can trade the markets using a variety of order entry methods. You do not constantly have to watch the markets until the price level you wish to trade at occurs. Your broker will be able to do that and there are a number of universally accepted methods to describe your needs accurately and accommodate them. It is, for example, possible to trade the market during the closing trading session by placing a market on close order. Alternatively you can leave instructions with your broker to trade a certain amount at a specified level until you instruct them otherwise. In such instances it may be prudent to limit the amount of time that the order is valid. All brokers will be able to discuss the different order entry methods and most will have some explanatory literature on this subject. It would be advisable to discuss this issue before you start trading.

How do you open the account?

Every futures broker has a standard set of account documents which you will be required to complete before trading. These documents require you to disclose your name, address, telephone and banking references. In addition, they contain the following sections although not necessarily in the order detailed below.

- A risk disclosure statement, which will outline in detail the risks inherent in trading futures and options. You will be required to sign that you have read and understood the statement.
- Hedge account certification, which requires you to declare when relevant that trades undertaken by you are bona fide hedging transactions and are not therefore speculative trades. For commercial business this can be important because hedge accounts are subject to lower margin requirements and although unlikely and indeed undesirable for new trades, may allow bigger positions to be taken by the customer.
- For commercial customers Board resolutions passed at a board meeting formally permitting the company to enter into an agreement with the futures broker. Usually this document will also detail a list of authorised traders.
- Client agreement, which is the contractual agreement between you the client and the futures broker. Like the risk disclosure document you will be required to sign that you have read, understood and agree to the terms and conditions.
- For commercial customers there will also be a section on whether you require your margins and any other monies deposited with your broker segregated from the futures broker's accounts by placing them in a separate client bank account. Your broker must determine this under the client money rules of Securities and Futures Authority Ltd, the regulatory authority of futures brokers in the UK. Segregation of clients' money is primarily to protect users of futures markets from any financial misconduct or failure of a broker. Under current legislation, private users of the futures markets are automatically treated as having their monies segregated from the broker's funds although this can be within one overall client account.

Before returning the account documents make a photocopy. The risk disclosure and the client agreement contain information that can act as a useful reference.

Can you start trading?

Before you commence trading you should ensure that you have the names and necessary telephone numbers of the group of people you are dealing with. It is not a good idea to limit your contact to one individual. It is most likely that your broker will cover this point but do make sure you address the issue. Likewise in your absence it may be necessary and prudent to appoint someone to place orders to enter or leave the market.

The futures and options markets are often mentioned in the context of risk management. The markets themselves carry inherent risks such as they can be traded by companies and individuals who do not fully appreciate the concepts, administrative aspects, the language or the alternatives available. With patience, research and the right futures broker for your requirements any prospective user of the markets can overcome these issues and put themselves in a position to add a new dimension to their business.

CHAPTER 14

Regulation

Earlier chapters have made explicit or implicit reference to regulation whether by the Government or its designated authority, by an exchange, or even by the broker with the client. Experience tells us that we must have clear rules and protections to ensure that the markets are open to all who could sensibly want to use them. Any system or weakness in the system which allows an imbalance in opportunity or result is bound to be self-destructive. You will have gathered that the futures and options markets are generally used by people because the markets are reliable as to all but price. Without this consistency there is no confidence, without confidence there is no long term opportunity for any market.

Again, experience sadly tells us that any contractual or operational weakness in the market will quickly be exploited. *Homo sapiens* is generally a greedy fellow, so we need regulations to lay down and enforce rules to protect us against ourselves and others.

The role model, as you would expect, is in the US where the federal government, through the Commodity Exchange Act, deputes its authority to regulate to the Commodity Futures Trading Commission (CFTC). This organisation supervises and regulates the agricultural and much of the financial futures and options industry. The exchange, brokers and trading advisors are all subject to the CFTC, although the latter does consult before introducing new rules or significant regulatory changes. The CFTC remit extends overseas where US owned market participants are involved and, of course, no overseas company or contract can trade in the US without prior clearance.

It is not the intention of this chapter to describe the US, British, or any other regulatory system in great detail, but rather to make the reader aware of the reasons for regulation and what and where to look for it. Who in their right mind goes swimming without the right training, equipment, and environment? A well organised regulatory system provides all of these. Through the National Futures Association (a self-regulatory body representing the futures brokers by size and geographical coverage, professional investors and the individual US futures' exchanges), the CFTC oversees all trading activity, ensures implementation and enforcement of all its regulations. This generally protects the user from unreasonable market practice within the exchange or brokerage house. The CFTC can and does institute investigation into suspect practices or complaints brought before it by any user of the market who can demonstrate possible cause. It has the power to prevent markets, companies or market individuals trading. It has provided the strength and experience necessary for the smooth and secure running of markets which are vital to the well-being of the capitalist and free market systems well beyond the US. (See Apppendix II for further details and brief history.)

The United Kingdom has incorporated much of the American regulatory system but has chosen to rely more on self-regulation and less on direct governmental control. From the early 1980s there was increasing pressure on the government and the financial services industry to introduce investor protection, by which was meant protection of the individual rather than the institution. However the system introduced is basically all encompassing since there is no practical way to define and limit regulation for the private individual investor alone.

The statutory framework was introduced with effect from April 1st 1988. The Secretary of State for the Department of Trade and Industry devolved the authority to oversee, implement and enforce the regulations to the Securities and Investment Board who in turn established basic principles and delegated day-to-day market surveillance and control to the relevant self-regulatory organisation – for the futures industry until recently this was the Association of Future Brokers and Dealers (AFBD) but now is the Securities and Futures Association (SFA). It is sufficient to say here that the investor protection which can extend to all investors, not just private individuals, is similar to that provided in the United States. We do have standardised rules on or off the futures exchange. We have yet to introduce appropriate qualifications for all those dealing with the client but it is only a matter of time. We do require our own definition of client fund segregation. (See Appendix II for further details and some examples of draft client documentation.)

Conclusion

We started by referring to 1992 since, by means of the Investment Services and associated Directives, Brussels is intending to implement the political decision for a community-wide common market in financial services. Agricultural futures and options are not currently included in the Investment Services Directive (along with other 'commodities' such as energy and metals) while financial futures and options are. However, it is hard to see how in practice the futures industry, its customers and regulators can operate those in and those outside the Directive other than in a parallel manner, particularly as 'Europe' now means the former East Germany and, in practice, most of the other Eastern European countries as well.

At the same time, the futures and options industry has its own challenges and problems. We have mentioned examples of markets which have come and gone. The globalisation of communications, the ability of computers to substitute at least in part for brokers on and off the exchange floor, the presence of time zone and commercial competition have all provided their opportunities and headaches. Exchange officials and members need to remain as flexible as possible while satisfying their customers' current needs. Regulators have as big a task balancing between 'too little' and 'too much' within an acceptable cost structure. Customers, whether professional or private, must wonder at the variety and complexity of futures and options contracts, and can get caught out without a full understanding of them.

So we continue to have a dynamic and changing economic and political environment in which financial services and instruments must adapt to survive and develop. We have come a long way since those early beginnings but the basic reasons for the birth of futures and options markets have not changed. Servicing them has become more complex and expensive. We can be sure that there will be plenty to interest and occupy all segments of the industry in any time frame it dares to consider.

APPENDIX

I

Glossary

Actuals: See **Cash commodity**.

Afloat: Physical commodity in harbour or in transit in a vessel.

Against actuals: See **Exchange for physicals**.

Arbitrage: The simultaneous purchase and sale of similar commodities in different markets to take advantage of a price discrepancy.

Arbitration: The procedure of settling disputes between members, or between members and customers.

Assign: To make an option seller perform his obligation to assume a short futures position (as a seller of a call option) or a long future position (as a seller of a put option).

Associated Person (AP): An individual who solicits orders, customers, or customer funds (or who supervises persons performing such duties) on behalf of a Futures Commission Merchant, and Introducing Broker, a Commodity Trading Advisor, or a Commodity Pool Operator.

Associate Membership (CBOT): A Chicago Board of Trade membership that allows an individual to trade financial instrument futures and other designated markets.

At-the-money option: An option with a strike price that is equal, or approximately equal, to the current market price of the underlying futures contract.

Bar chart: A chart that graphs the high, low, and settlement prices for a specific trading session over a given period of time.

Basis: The difference between the current cash price and the futures price of the same commodity. Unless otherwise specified, the price of the nearby futures contract month is generally used to calculate the basis.

Bear: Someone who thinks market prices will decline.

Bear market: A period of declining market prices.

Bear spread: In most commodities and financial instruments, the term refers to selling the nearby contract month, and buying the deferred contract, to profit from a change in the price relationship.

Bid: An expression indicating a desire to buy a commodity at a given price; opposite of offer. (Could also be a GTC or good till cancelled order.)

Broker: A company or individual that executes futures and options orders on behalf of financial and commercial institutions and/or the general public.

Brokerage fee: See **Commission fee**.

Bull: Someone who thinks market prices will rise.

Bull market: A period of rising market prices.

Bull spread: In most commodities and financial instruments, the term refers to buying the nearby month, and selling the deferred month, to profit from the change in the price relationship.

Butterfly spread: The placing of two interdelivery spreads in opposite directions with the centre delivery month common to both spreads.

Buying hedge: See **Purchasing hedge**.

Calendar spread: See **Horizontal spread**.

Call option: An option that gives the buyer the right, but not the obligation, to purchase (go 'long') the underlying futures contract at the strike price on or before the expiration date.

Cancelling order: An order that deletes a customer's previous order.

Carrying charge: For physical commodities such as grains and metals, the cost of storage space, insurance, and finance charges incurred by holding a physical commodity. In interest rate futures markets, it refers to the differential between the yield on a cash instrument and the cost of funds necessary to buy the instrument. Also referred to as **cost of carry** or **carry**.

Carryover: Grain and oilseed commodities not consumed during the marketing year and remaining in storage at year's end. These stocks are 'carried over' into the next marketing year and added to the stocks produced during that crop year.

Cash commodity: An actual physical commodity which someone is buying or selling e.g. soyabeans, corn, gold, silver, Treasury bonds, etc. Also referred to as **actuals**.

Cash contract: A sales agreement for either immediate or future delivery of the actual product.

Cash market: A place where people buy and sell the actual commodities, i.e. grain elevator, bank, etc. See **Spot** and **Forward contract**.

Cash settlement: Transactions generally involving index-based futures contracts that are settled in cash based on the actual value of the index on the last trading day, in contrast to those that specify the delivery of a commodity or financial instrument.

Charting: The use of charts to analyse market behaviour and anticipate future price movements. Those who use charting as a trading method plot such factors as high, low, and settlement prices; average price movements, volume; and open interest. Two basic price charts are bar charts and point-and-figure charts. See **Technical analysis**.

Cheap: Colloquialism implying that a commodity is underpriced.

Clear: The process by which a clearing house maintains records of all trades and settles margin flow on a daily mark-to-market basis for its clearing member.

Clearing house: An agency or separate corporation of a futures exchange that is responsible for settling trading accounts, clearing trades, collecting and maintaining margin monies, regulating delivery and reporting trading data. Clearing houses act as third parties to all futures and options contracts - acting as a buyer to every clearing member seller and a seller to every clearing member buyer.

Clearing margin: Financial safeguards to ensure that clearing members (usually companies or corporations) perform on their customers' open futures and options contracts. Clearing margins are distinct from customer margins that individual buyers and sellers of futures and options contracts are required to deposit with brokers. See **Customer margin**.

Clearing member: A member of an exchange clearing house. Memberships in clearing organisations are usually held by companies. Clearing members are responsible for the financial commitments of customers that clear through their firm.

Closing price: See **Settlement price**.

Closing range: A range of prices at which buy and sell transactions took place during the market close. (The close.)

Commission fee: A fee charged by a broker to executing a transaction. Also referred to as a **brokerage fee**. (Usually charged on a round turn basis covering both the purchase and sale side of the transaction.)

Commission house: See **Futures Commission Merchant (FCM)**.

Commodity: An article of commerce or a product that can be used for commerce. In a narrow sense, products traded on an authorised commodity exchange. The types of commodities include agricultural products, metals, petroleum, foreign currencies, and financial instruments and indexes, to name a few.

Commodity Credit Corporation (CCC): A branch of the US Department of Agriculture, established in 1933, that supervises the government's farm loan and subsidy programmes.

Commodity Futures Trading Commission (CFTC): A federal regulatory agency established under the Commodity Futures Trading Commission Act, as amended in 1974, that oversees futures trading in the United States. The commission comprises five commissioners, one of whom is designated as chairman, all appointed by the President subject to Senate confirmation and is independent of all cabinet departments.

Commodity Pool: An enterprise in which funds contributed by a number of persons are combined for the purpose of trading futures contracts or commodity options.

Commodity Pool Operator (CPO): An individual or organisation that operates or solicits funds for a commodity pool.

Commodity Trading Adviser (CTA): A person who, for compensation or profit, directly or indirectly advises others as to the value or the advisability of buying or selling futures contracts or commodity options. Advising indirectly includes exercising trading authority over a customer's account as well as providing recommendations through written publications or other media.

Contract grades: See **Deliverable grades**.

Controlled account: See **Discretionary account**.

Convergence: A term referring to cash and futures prices tending to come together (i.e the basis approach zero) as the futures contract nears expiration.

Cost of carry: See Carrying charge.

Crop (marketing) year: The time span from harvest to harvest for agricultural commodities. The crop marketing year varies slightly with each agricultural commodity, but it tends to begin at harvest and end before the next year's harvest, e.g. the marketing year for soyabeans begins September 1 and ends August 31. The futures contract month of November represents the first major new crop marketing month, and the contract month of July represents the last major old crop marketing month for soyabeans.

Crop reports: Reports compiled by the US Department of Agriculture on various agricultural commodities that are released throughout the year. Information in the reports includes estimates on planted acreage, yield and expected production, as well as comparison of production from previous years.

Cross-hedging: Hedging a cash commodity using a different but related futures contract when there is no futures contract for the cash commodity being hedged and the cash and futures markets follow similar price trends (e.g. using soyabean meal futures to hedge fish meal).

Crush: The purchase of soyabean futures (or cash soyabeans) and the simultaneous sale of soyabean oil and meal futures (or cash soyabean oil and meal). This spread is used to minimise the financial risks of sudden increases in soyabean costs and/or declining values of finished soyabean oil and meal.

Current yield: The ratio of the coupon to the current market price of the debt instrument.

Customer margin: Within the futures industry, financial guarantees required of both buyers and sellers of futures contracts and sellers of options contracts to ensure fulfilment of contract obligations. Futures Commission Merchants (FCMs) are responsible for overseeing customer margin accounts. Margins are determined on the basis of market risk and contract value. Also referred to as **performance-bond margin**. See **Clearing magin.**

Daily trading limit: The maximum price range set by the exchange each day for a contract.

Day traders: Speculators who take positions in futures or options contracts and liquidate them prior to the close of the same trading day. (**Day order**.)

Deferred (delivery) month: The more distant month(s) in which futures trading is taking place, as distinguished from the nearby (delivery) month.

Deliverable grades: The standard grades of commodities or instruments listed in the rules of the exchanges that must be met when delivering cash commodities against futures contracts. Grades are often accompanied by a schedule of discounts and premiums allowable for delivery of commodities of lesser or greater quality than the standard called for by the exchange. Also referred to as **contract grades**.

Delivery: The transfer of the cash commodity from the seller of a futures contract to the buyer of a futures contract. Each futures exchange has specific procedures for delivery of a cash commodity. Some futures contracts, such as stock index contracts, are cash settled. (The offer for physical delivery is sometimes called **Tendering**.)

Delivery day: The third day in the delivery process at the Chicago Board of Trade, when the buyer's clearing firm presents the delivery notice with a certified check for the amount due at the office of the seller's clearing firm.

Delivery points: The locations and facilities designated by a futures exchange where stocks of a commodity may be delivered in fulfilment of a futures contract, under procedures established by the exchange.

Delta: The measure of how much an option premium changes, given a unit change in the underlying futures price. Delta is often interpreted as the probability that the underlying futures price will move in-the-money by expiration.

Demand, Law of: The relationship between product demand and price.

Differentials: Price differences between classes, grades and delivery locations of various stocks of the same commodity.

Discretionary account: An arrangement by which the holder of the account gives written power of attorney to another person, often his broker, to make trading decisions. Also known as a **controlled** or **managed account**.

Equilibrium price: The market price at which the quantity supplied of a commodity equals the quantity demanded.

Exchange for Physicals (EFP): A transaction used by two hedgers who want to exchange futures for cash positions. Also referred to as **against actuals** or **versus cash**.

Exercise: The action taken by the holder of a call option who wishes to purchase the underlying futures contract or by the holder of a put option who wishes to sell the underlying futures contract.

Exercise price: See **Strike price**.

Expiration date: Options on futures generally expire on a specific date during the month preceding the futures contract delivery month. For example, an option on a March futures contract expires in February but is referred to as a March option because its exercise would result in a March futures contract position.

Extrinsic value: See **Time value**.

Face value: The amount of money printed on the face of the certificate of a security: the original dollar amount of indebtedness incurred.

Feed ratio: A ratio used to express the relationship of feeding costs to the dollar value of livestock. See **Hog/corn ratio** and **Steer/corn ratio**.

Fill-or-kill: A customer order that is a price limit order that must be filled immediately or cancelled.

Financial Analysis Auditing Compliance Trading System (FACTS): The National Futures Association's computerised system of maintaining financial records of its member firms and monitoring their financial conditions.

First notice day: According to Chicago Board of Trade rules, the first day on which a notice of intent to deliver a commodity in fulfilment of a given month's futures contract can be made by the clearing house to a buyer. The clearing house also informs the sellers who they have been matched up with.

Forward (cash) contract: A contract in which a seller agrees to deliver a specific quality, description or grade cash commodity to a buyer sometime in the future. Forward contracts, in contrast to future contracts, are privately negotiated and are not standardised.

Full carrying charge market: A futures market where the price difference between delivery months reflects the total costs of interest, insurance and storage.

Fundamental analysis: A method of anticipating future price movement using supply and demand information.

Futures Commission Merchant (FCM): An individual or organisation that solicits or accepts orders to buy or sell futures contracts or options on futures and accepts money or other assets from customers to support such orders. Also referred to as **commission house** or **wire house**.

Future contract: A legally binding agreement, made on the trading floor of a futures exchange, to buy or sell a commodity or financial instrument sometime in the future. Futures contracts are standardised according to the quality, quantity, and delivery time and location for each commodity. The only variable is price, which is discovered on an exchange trading floor.

Gamma: A measurement of how fast delta changes, given a unit change in the underlying futures price.

Grain terminal: Large grain elevator facility with the capacity to ship grain by rail and/or barge to domestic or foreign markets.

Gross Processing Margin (GPM): The difference between the cost of soyabeans and the combined sales income of the processed soyabean oil and meal.

Hedger: An individual or company owning or planning to own a cash commodity - corn, soyabeans, wheat, US Treasury bonds, notes, bills, etc - and concerned that the cost of the commodity may change before either buying or selling it in the cash market. A hedger achieves protection against the changing cash price by purchasing (selling) futures contracts of the same or similar commodity and later offsetting that position by selling (purchasing) futures contracts of the same quantity and type as the initial transaction.

Hedging: The practice of offsetting the price risk inherent in any cash market position by taking an equal but opposite position in the futures market. Hedgers use the futures markets to protect their business from adverse price changes. See **Selling (short) hedge** and **Purchasing (long) hedge**.

High: The highest price of the day for a particular futures contract.

Hog/corn ratio: The relationship of feeding costs to the dollar value of hogs. It is measured by dividing the price of hogs ($/hundredweight) by the price of corn ($/bushel). When corn prices are high relative to pork prices, fewer units of corn equal the dollar value of 100 lb of pork. Conversely, when corn prices are low in relation to pork prices, more units of corn are required to equal the value of 100 lb of pork. See **Feed ratio**.

Holder: See **Option buyer**.

Horizontal spread: The purchase of either a call or put option and the simultaneous sale of the same type of option with typically the same strike price but with a different expiration month. Also referred to as a **calendar spread**.

Initial margin: The amount a futures market participant must deposit into his margin account at the time he places an order to buy or sell a futures contract. (A deposit.)

Intercommodity spread: The purchase of a given delivery month of one futures market and the simultaneous sale of the same delivery month of a different, but related, futures market.

Interdelivery spread: The purchase of one delivery month of a given futures contract and simultaneous sale of another delivery month of the same commodity on the same exchange. Also referred to as an **intramarket spread**.

Intermarket spread: The sale of a given delivery month of a futures contract on one exchange and the simultaneous purchase of the same delivery month and futures contract on another exchange.

In-the-money option: An option having intrinsic value. A call option is in-the-money if its strike price is below the current price of the underlying futures contract. A put option is in-the-money if its strike price is above the current price of the underlying futures contract. See **Intrinsic value**.

Intramarket spread: See **Interdelivery spread**.

Intrinsic value: The amount by which an option is in-the-money. See **In-the-money option**.

Introducing Broker (IB): A person or organisation that solicits or accepts orders to buy or sell futures contracts or commodity options but does not accept money or other assets from customers to support such orders.

Inverted market: A future market in which the relationship between two delivery months of the same commodity is abnormal.

Invisible supply: Uncounted stocks of a commodity in the hands of wholesalers, manufacturers, and producers that cannot be identified accurately; stocks outside commercial channels but theoretically available to the market.

Last trading day: According to the Chicago Board of Trade rules, the final day when trading may occur in a given futures or options contract month. Futures contracts outstanding at the end of the last trading day must be settled by delivery of the underlying commodity or securities or by agreement for monetary settlement (in some cases by EFPs).

Leverage: The ability to control large dollar amounts of a commodity with a comparatively small amount of capital.

Limit order: An order in which the customer sets a limit on the price and/or time of execution.

Limits: See **Position limit, Price limit, Variable limit**.

Liquid: A characteristic of a security or commodity market with enough units outstanding to allow large transactions without a substantial change in price. Institutional investors are inclined to seek out liquid investments so that their trading activity will not influence the market price.

Liquidate: Selling (or purchasing) futures contracts of the same delivery month purchased (or sold) during an earlier transaction or making (or taking) delivery of the cash commodity represented by the futures contract. See **Offset**.

Loan programme: A federal programme in which the government lends money at preannounced rates to farmers and allows them to use the crops they plant for the upcoming crop year as collateral. Default on these loans is the primary method by which the government acquires stocks of agricultural commodities.

Loan rate: The amount lent per unit of a commodity to farmers.

Long: One who has bought futures contracts or owns a cash commodity.

Long hedge: See **Purchasing hedge**.

Low: The lowest price of the day for a particular futures contract.

Maintenance margin: A set minimum margin (per outstanding futures contract) that a customer must maintain in his margin account.

Managed account: See **Discretionary account**.

Margin: See **Clearing margin** and **Customer margin**.

Margin call: A call from a clearing house to a clearing member, or from a brokerage firm to a customer, to bring margin desposits up to a required minimum level. (Sometimes called cover.)

Market Information Data Inquiry System (MIDAS-Touch): Daily Chicago Board of Trade price, volume and open interest data accessible by telephone.

Market order: An order to buy or sell a futures contract of a given delivery month to be filled at the best possible price and as soon as possible. (At the market.)

Market Price Reporting and Information System (MPRIS): The Chicago Board of Trade's computerised price-reporting system.

Market reporter: A person employed by the exchange and located in or near the trading pit who records prices as they occur during trading.

Mark-to-the-market: To debit or credit on a daily basis a margin account based on the close of that day's trading session. In this way, buyers and sellers are protected against the possibility of contract default.

Minimum price fluctuation: See **Tick**.

Moving-average charts: A statistical price analysis method of recognising different price trends. A moving average is calculated by adding the prices for a predetermined number of days and then dividing by the number of days.

National Futures Association (NFA): An industry-wide, industry-supported, self-regulatory organisation for futures and options markets. The primary responsibilities of the NFA are to enforce ethical standards and customer protection rules, screen futures professionals for membership, audit and monitor professionals for financial and general compliance rules, and provide for arbitration of futures-related disputes.

Nearby (delivery) month: The futures contract month closest to expiration. Also referred to as **spot month**.

Notice day: According to Chicago Board of Trade rules, the second day of the three day delivery process when the clearing corporation matches the buyer with the oldest reported long position to the delivering seller and notifies both parties. See **First notice day**.

Offer: An expression indicating one's desire to sell a commodity at a given price; opposite of bid.

Offset: Taking a second futures or options position opposite to the initial or opening position. See **Liquidate. (Buy in – sell out.**)

Opening range: A range of prices at which buy and sell transactions took place during the opening of the market.

Open interest: The total number of futures or options contracts of a given commodity that have not yet been offset by an opposite futures or option transaction nor fulfilled by delivery of the commodity or option exercise. (Net position.) Each open transaction has a buyer and a seller, but for calculation of open interest, only one side of the contract is counted.

Open market operation: The buying and selling of government securities – Treasury bills, notes and bonds – by the Federal Reserve.

Open outcry: Method of public auction for making verbal bids and offers in the trading pits or rings of futures exchanges.

Option: A contract that conveys the right, but not the obligation, to buy or sell a particular commodity at a certain price for a limited time. Only the seller of the option is obligated to perform.

Option buyer: The purchaser of either a call or put option. Option buyers receive the right, but not the obligation, to assume a futures position. Also referred to as the **holder**.

Option premium: The price of an option - the sum of money that the option buyer pays and the option seller receives for the rights granted by the option.

Option seller: The person who sells an option in return for a premium and is obligated to perform when the holder exercises his right under the option contract. Also referred to as the **writer**.

Option spread: The simultaneous purchase and sale of one or more options contracts, futures and/or cash positions.

Options writer: See **Option seller**.

Out-of-the-money option: An option with no intrinsic value, i.e. a call whose strike price is above the current futures price or a put whose strike price is below the current futures price.

P&S (Purchase and Sale) statement: A statement sent by a commission house to a customer when his futures or options on futures position has changed, showing the number of contracts bought or sold, the price at which the contracts were bought or sold, the gross profit or loss, the commission charges and the net profit or loss on the transactions.

Payment-In-Kind (PIK) programme: A government programme in which farmers who comply with a voluntary acreage-control programme and set aside an additional percentage of acreage specified by the government receive certificates that can be redeemed for government-owned stocks of grain.

Pit: The area on the trading floor where futures and options on futures contracts are bought and sold. Pits are usually raised octagonal platforms with steps descending on the inside that permit buyers and sellers of contracts to see each other.

Point-and figure charts: Charts that show price changes of a minimum amount regardless of the time period involved.

Position: A market commitment. A buyer of a futures contract is said to have a long position and, conversely, a seller of futures contracts is said to have a short position.

Position day: According to the Chicago Board of Trade rules, the first day in the process of making or taking delivery of the actual commodity on a futures contract. The clearing firm representing the seller notifies the Board of Trade Clearing Corporation that its short customers want to deliver on a futures contract.

Position limit: The maximum number of speculative futures contracts one can hold as determined by the Commodity Futures Trading Commission and/or the exchange upon which the contract is traded. Also referred to as **trading limit**.

Position trader: An approach to trading in which the trader either buys or sells contracts and holds them for an extended period of time.

Premium: (1) The additional payment allowed by exchange regulation for delivery of higher-than-required standards or grades of a commodity against a futures contract. (2) In speaking of price relationships between different delivery months of a given commodity, one is said to be 'trading at a premium' over another when its price is greater than that of the other. (3) In financial instruments, the dollar amount by which a security trades above its principal value. See **Option premium**.

Price limit: The maximum advance or decline - from the previous day's settlement price - permitted for a contract in one trading session by the rules of the exchange. See also **Variable limit**.

Price limit order: A customer order that specifies the price at which a trade can be executed.

Pulpit: A raised structure adjacent to, or in the centre of, the pit or ring at a futures exchange where market reporters, employed by the exchange, record price changes as they occur in the trading pit.

Purchasing hedge (or long hedge): Buying futures contracts to protect against a possible price increase of cash commodities that will be purchased in the future. At the time the cash commodities are bought, the open futures position is closed by selling an equal number and type of futures contracts as those that were initially purchased. Also referred to as a **buying hedge**. See **Hedging**.

Put option: An option that vies the option buyer the right but not the obligation to sell (go 'short') the underlying futures contract at the strike price on or before the expiration date.

Rally: An upward movement of prices following a decline.

Range (price): The price span during a given trading session, week, month, year, etc.

Reaction: A decline in prices following an advance.

Resistance: A level above which prices have had difficulty penetrating.

Resumption: The reopening the following day of specific futures and options markets that also trade during the evening session at the Chicago Board of Trade.

Ring method: A method of settlement used by futures markets from the early 1900s until the 1920s, when the first formalised clearing operations were developed. Settlement clerks of brokerage houses maintained daily accounting records of customer transactions in ring notebooks.

Risk disclosure statement: A document enumerating some of the risks involved in trading futures and/or options on futures must sign before opening an account with a brokerage firm.

Runners: Messengers who rush orders received by phone clerks to brokers for execution in the pit.

Scalper: A trader who trades for small, short term profits during the course of a trading session, rarely carrying a position overnight.

Security: Common or preferred stock, a bond of a corporation, government, or quasi-government body.

Selling hedge (or **short hedge**)**:** Selling futures contracts to protect against possible declining prices of commodities that will be sold in the future. At the time the cash commodities are sold, the open futures position is closed by purchasing an equal number and type of futures contracts as those that were initially sold. See **Hedging**.

Settle: See **Settlement price**.

Settlement price: The last price paid for a commodity on any trading day. The exchange clearing house determines a firm's net gains or losses, margin requirements, and the next day's price limits, based on each futures and options contract settlement price. If there is a closing range of prices, the settlement price is determined by averaging those prices. Also referred to as **settle** or **closing price**.

Short: (noun) One who has sold futures contracts or plans to purchase a cash commodity. (verb) Selling futures contracts or initiating a cash forward contract sale without offsetting a particular market position.

Speculator: A market participant who tries to profit from buying and selling futures and options contracts by anticipating future price movements. Speculators assume market price risk and add liquidity and capital to the futures markets.

Spot: Usually refers to a cash market price for a physical commodity that is available for immediate delivery.

Spot month: See **Nearby (delivery) month**.

Spread: The price difference between two related markets or commodities.

Spreading: The simultaneous buying and selling of two related markets in the expectation that a profit will be made when the position is offset. (Otherwise known as switching within the same market.) Examples include: buying one futures contract and selling another futures contract of the same commodity but different delivery month; buying and selling the same delivery month of the same commodity on different futures exchanges; buying a given delivery month of one futures market and selling the same delivery month of a different, but related, futures market. (Otherwise known as a straddle when involving different markets.)

Steer/corn ratio: The relationship of cattle prices to feeding costs. It is measured by dividing the price of cattle ($/hundredweight) by the price of corn ($/bushel). When corn prices are high relative to cattle prices, fewer units of corn equal the dollar value of 100 lb of cattle. Conversely, when corn prices are low in relation to cattle prices, more units of corn are required to equal the value of 100 lb of beef. See **Feed ratio**.

Stop-limit order: A variation of a stop order in which a trade must be executed at the exact price or better. If the order cannot be executed, it is held until the stated price or better is reached again.

Stop order: An order to buy or sell when the market reaches a specified point. A stop order to buy becomes a market order when the commodity or security trades (or is bid) at or above the stop price. A stop order to sell becomes a market order when the commodity or security trades (or is offered) at or below the stop price.

Strike price: The price at which the futures contract underlying a call or put option can be purchased (if a call) or sold (if a put). Also referred to as **exercise price**.

Supply, Law of: The relationship between product supply and its price.

Support: The place on a chart where the buying of futures contracts is sufficient to halt a price decline.

Suspension: The end of the evening session for specific futures and options markets traded at the Chicago Board of Trade.

Technical analysis: Anticipating future price movement using historical prices, trading volume, open interest and other trading data to study price patterns.

Tick: The smallest allowable increment of price movement for a contract. Also referred to as **minimum price fluctuation**.

Time limit order: A customer order that designates the time during which it can be executed.

Time value: The amount of money option buyers are willing to pay for an option in the anticipation that, over time, a change in the underlying futures price will cause the option to increase in value. In general, an option premium is the sum of time value and intrinsic value. Any amount by which an option premium exceeds the option's intrinsic value can be considered time value. Also referred to as **extrinsic value**.

Underlying futures contract: The specific futures contract that is bought or sold by exercising an option.

Variable limit: According to the Chicago Board of Trade rules, an expanded allowable price range set during volatile markets.

Variation margin: During periods of great market volatility or in the case of high-risk accounts, additional margin deposited by a clearing member firm to an exchange clearing house.

Versus cash: See **Exchange for physicals**.

Vertical spread: Buying and selling puts or calls of the same expiration month but different strike prices.

Volatility: A measurement of the change in price over a given time period. It is often expressed as a percentage and computed as the annualised standard deviation of percentage change in daily price.

Volume: The number of purchases or sales of a commodity futures contract made during a specified period of time, often the total transactions for one trading day.

Warehouse receipt: Document guaranteeing the existence and availability of a given quantity and quality of a commodity in storage; commonly used as the instrument of transfer of ownership in both cash and futures transactions.

Wire house: See **Futures Commission Merchant**.

Writer: See **Option seller**.

APPENDIX

11

United States federal and industry regulation

US futures exchanges are required by state and federal laws to regulate the conduct of exchange members, member firms and their employees. The obligations of the exchanges to enforce their own rules and regulations were enhanced in the 1900s with the passing of several federal acts, including the Grain Futures Act of 1922, the Commodity Exchange Act of 1936, the Commodity Futures Trading Commission Act of 1936, the Commodity Futures Trading Commission Act of 1974, and the Futures Trading Acts of 1978, 1982 and 1986.

Grain Futures Act of 1922 and Amendments

The farm depression following World War I generated intense speculation in grain futures. The Futures Trading Act, the first federal law regulating futures trading, was passed in 1921. Shortly thereafter, it was declared unconstitutional by the Supreme Court. In 1922, Congress passed the

Grain Futures Act, based on the interstate commerce clause of the Constitution.

Under the Grain Futures Act, futures trading in specific commodities could take place only on federally licensed exchanges. This legislation focused on exchange responsibility for preventing market manipulation by their members, member firms and employees. If an exchange failed to supervise market activity adequately, its license could be revoked.

Commodity Exchange Act of 1936

US Department of Agriculture (USDA) studies over a period of several years led to the introduction of a number of amendments designed to strengthen the government's regulatory powers. In 1936, these revisions and additions to the law were consolidated in new legislation, the Commodity Exchange Act, which extended regulation from the grains and flaxseed to cotton and other agricultural commodities.

The new act created the Commodity Exchange Commission, which comprised the Secretary of Agriculture, the Secretary of Commerce and the Attorney General, or their designated representatives. The commission was responsible for: (1) licensing futures exchanges, (2) determining procedures for registering Futures Commission Merchants and floor brokers, (3) protecting customer funds, (4) setting position and trading limits for speculative trading, (5) prohibiting price manipulations, false market information and illegal trading, and (6) enforcing the Commodity Exchange Act and dealing with violations.

The Commodity Exchange Act was administered by the Commodity Exchange Commission until 1947 when the Commodity Exchange Authority was established. In addition to administering the act, the Commodity Exchange Authority provided information on futures trading to the general public.

Changing needs for regulation

During the early 1970s, rising affluence in many of the world's industrially developed countries was coupled with declines in crop production in several major production nations. During the same period, two devaluations of the US dollar made imports of US agricultural goods less expensive and stimulated foreign sales. The result was heavy new demand on reduced supplies of feed grains and vegetable protein. In less than three years, previously ample USDA Commodity Credit Corporation holdings of surplus grain shrunk significantly. By late 1974, it was widely estimated that world feed-grain supplies had dwindled to the level of a month's supply.

As supplies continued to shrink and demand and grain prices rose, the public and members of Congress began to question the existing regulation of the futures markets. There were also new pressures to extend regulation to other futures markets not covered by the Commodity Exchange Act, such as metals, lumber and currencies.

In response, the government began a series of hearings in September 1973 on proposed regulatory changes. The result was the Commodity Futures Trading Commission Act of 1974.

CFTC Act of 1974

The new act amended the Commodity Exchange Act and created an independent Commodity Futures Trading Commission (CFTC) to replace the Commodity Exchange Authority of the USDA. Existing Commodity Exchange Authority and Commodity Exchange Commission personnel, records and appropriations were transferred to the new commission. And on 21 April 1975, the CFTC assumed federal regulatory authority over all commodity futures markets.

The agency's five full time commissioners are appointed by the President with Senate confirmation. They serve staggered, five year terms with one designated to serve as chairman. There are three staff divisions - Economic and Analysis, Trading and Markets, and Enforcement. Each division director reports to the commission chairman, who performs the daily administrative duties.

Futures Trading Act of 1978

The legislation creating the CFTC contained a sunset provision under which the commission would have ceased to exist on 30 September 1978, unless it was re-authorised. Extensive hearings were conducted early in 1978, resulting in the Futures Trading Act of 1978, which extended the life of the agency for another four years. CFTC re-authorisation continues on a regular basis. The most recent re-authorisation occurred in 1991 and is subject to renewal in 1992.

The Futures Trading Act of 1978 also expanded the jurisdiction of the CFTC, clarifying some earlier provisions of the Commodity Exchange Act.

Requirements of the CFTC Act

The amended Commodity Exchange Act gave the CFTC the authority to regulate trading in all futures contracts - those currently trading as well as those that will be traded in the future. Prior to 1974, several futures contracts - such as currencies, financial instruments and metals - were not regulated by the federal government.

CFTC regulation of options on financial futures began in 1981 with the initiation of a pilot programme. The success of this programme led to the approval of non-agricultural options in 1982. Then, in 1984, the CFTC extended trading in options to agricultural futures.

Shad/Johnson Accord

During the 1982 re-authorisation of the CFTC, Congress adopted the Shad/Johnson Accord Index Act, developed by CFTC Chairman Johnson and SEC Chairman Shad, to define the jurisdiction of the CFTC and the Securities and Exchange Commission (SEC) over stock indexes.

The amendments gave the CFTC exclusive jurisdiction over stock index futures and options on stock index futures contracts. The SEC, on the other hand, is responsible for the trading of options on any security or index of securities or options on foreign currencies traded on a US securities exchange.

CFTC regulation of exchange actions

The CFTC's regulatory powers extend to exchange actions and to the review and approval of futures contracts proposed by an exchange. Before a new contract is approved for trading, the CFTC must determine that a futures contract is in the public interest. In making that assessment, the commission examines how contracts are used commercially for pricing and hedging to ensure that they serve an economic purpose.

One of the first actions taken by the commission in 1975 was to redefine the term 'hedge'. The definition was broadened to permit anticipatory hedging and cross-hedging within certain limits. Anticipatory hedging allows market users to buy or sell a futures contract before they actually own the cash commodity. Cross-hedging enables market users to hedge a cash commodity using a different but related futures contract when there is no futures contract for the cash commodity being hedged and the two markets follow similar price trends. For example, a hedger could use corn futures to hedge barley, or soyabean meal futures to hedge fish meal.

Exchanges must submit all proposed trading rules and contract terms to the CFTC for approval. When reviewing trading rules, the commission tries to assure that the rule will not restrict competition, and may require the exchange to amend its proposal. Exchange regulations of major economic significance must be made available to the public, and are published in the Federal Register.

Delivery points for commodities that underlie futures contracts also are governed by the CFTC. The commission has the right to require an exchange to add or change delivery locations when necessary.

Review of exchange actions

Review of exchange actions - denying membership, access privileges or disciplining members - is another responsibility of the CFTC. In reviewing actions, the commission may affirm, modify or set aside an exchange's decision. The commission is also authorized to take emergency steps in the markets under certain conditions, such as actual or threatened market manipulation, or some other event that prevents the market from reflecting true supply/demand factors.

Regulation of market participants

The CFTC has broad regulatory powers over floor brokers, Futures Commission Merchants (FCMs), Associated Persons (APs), Commodity Pool Operators (CPOs), Commodity Trading Advisors (CTAs), Introducing Brokers (IBs) and other market participants. For example, the commission is authorised to register APs and office managers, and to establish eligibility requirements which may include proficiency tests.

Federal authority to establish minimum financial requirements for FMs was established in the Commodity Exchange Act of 1936. This same legislation required FCMs to segregate customers' margin deposits from company funds and prohibited the use of one customer's funds to meet the margin requirements of another customer's account. These requirements are enforced today by the CFTC.

Arbitration

Exchanges are required to have arbitration or claims settlement procedures to handle customer claims against members or their employees. The act stipulates that the CFTC establish procedures that can be used as an alternative to exchange arbitration or civil court actions.

Reparations

The CFTC provides a reparation procedure for investors to assert claims based on violations of federal commodities law. Claims are heard by an administrative law judge whose decision can be reviewed by the CFTC. The procedure is flexible depending on the amount of money involved and the consent of the parties.

Powers of injunction

The former Commodity Exchange Authority did not have the power to prohibit an exchange member from violating the Commodity Exchange Act. However, the Commodity Futures Trading Commission has that power and, in addition, may require an exchange or exchange member to perform a specific act. In the case of a violation that is also a criminal offence, criminal penalties may be imposed.

Daily trading record requirements

Exchanges and their clearing houses are required by the CFTC to maintain daily trading records. Also, exchanges must publish daily trading volume before the next day's opening, if practical.

National Futures Association

Under the CFTC Act of 1974, the futures industry was authorised to create registered futures associations. One such organisation is the National Futures Association (NFA) - an industry-wide, industry-supported, self-regulatory organisation for the futures industry.

NFA was formally designated a registered futures association by the CFTC on 22 September 1981, and became operational on 1 October 1982. The primary responsibilities of NFA are to: (1) enforce ethical standards and customer protection rules, (2) screen futures professionals for membership, (3) audit and monitor futures professionals for financial and general compliance rules, (4) provide for arbitration of futures-related disputes, and (5) promote consumer and member education concerning NFA's role in the futures industry.

Customer protection

To protect customers, NFA's ethical standards prohibit fraud, manipulative and deceptive acts and practices, and unfair business dealings. In addition, employees who handle discretionary accounts must follow procedures similar to CFTC requirements.

Membership screening

Membership in NFA and CFTC registration are mandatory for FCMs, CTAs, CPOs and IBs working with customer accounts.

The CFTC requires associate membership in NFA and CFTC registration for most APs. APs solicit orders, customers or customers' funds for FCMs, IBs, CTAs or CPOs. Membership is voluntary for futures exchanges, commercial banks and commodity-related commercial firms.

Regulation of futures professionals begins with applicant screening. In addition to approving applicants for NFA membership, NFA is authorised by the CFTC to screen and approve applications for federal registration. Eligibility requirements are strict and specific, and are designed to ensure high standards of professional conduct and financial responsibility.

NFA staff handle the initial screening process. If an applicant is denied membership or registration, then the final decision is made by the NFA membership committee.

Proficiency testing is another NFA activity and is now required for CFTC registration. FCMs, IBs, CTAs, CPOs and APs applying for registration must pass the National Commodity Futures Exam (Series 3) which tests their knowledge of trading futures and options on futures and understanding of exchange, industry and federal regulations.

Financial and general compliance

One of NFA's major functions is to establish, audit and enforce minimum financial requirements for its FCM and IB members. No such requirements are currently established under NFA rules for other NFA members, such as CPOs, and CTAs.

NFA conducts unannounced audits of all its members except those that are members of an exchange. In those cases, the audits are conducted by the exchange.

NFA audits are all-inclusive and cover every facet of the firm's futures-related business activities. Rule violations may be referred to Regional Business Conduct committees for appropriate disciplinary action.

General compliance rules require members to maintain complete and timely records, and segregate customer funds and accounts. Advertising and sales practices must be clear and honest, and customer orders equitably handled.

NFA financial requirements are patterned after existing financial standards of futures exchanges, as approved by the CFTC. NFA's computerised Financial Analysis Auditing Compliance Tracking System (FACTS) maintains financial records of NFA member firms and assists in monitoring their financial conditions.

Certain financial matters, such as the setting of margin levels, remain exclusively with the exchanges.

NFA has an Office of Compliance responsible for financial auditing and ethical surveillance. If an audit or investigation reveals a possible NFA rule violation, the infraction is reported to one of three regional Business

Conduct committees. Each committee is made up of individuals associated with NFA members in the region where the member under investigation lives. The committee either closes the matter or serves a formal complaint against the member accused of violating a rule. In the latter case, the member must answer the complaint and is entitled to a hearing before the committee. If the committee decides against the member, he may appeal the decision to the Appeals Committee (a subcommittee of the NFA Board of Directors). The decision of the Appeals Committee is final, following a review by the CFTC.

NFA has authority to discipline any member (other than floor brokers or traders). NFA may expel, suspend, prohibit contact with members, censure, reprimand, or impose fines of up to $100 000. In emergency cases, when there is imminent danger to the markets, customers or other members, NFA's president with the agreement of the Executive Committee or board can require the firm to stop doing business immediately. This action may be issued with or without a hearing. If a hearing is not held before the action is taken, a hearing will be scheduled as soon as possible before the appropriate Business Conduct Committee.

Arbitration

Another important function of NFA is to provide a centralised, uniform arbitration system. In most cases, when requested by a customer, arbitration is mandatory for all NFA member firms and their employees including FCMs, IBs, CPOs, CTAs and APs. Counterclaims made by members and disputes between NFA members also may be heard by NFA arbitrators. Decisions of the arbitrators are generally final and may not be appealed to NFA. Alternatives to NFA arbitration include the CFTC's reparation procedure, exchange arbitration or any other arbitration system mutually agreed to by the member and customer. After a particular method is chosen, no other may be used unless both parties agree.

Under NFA compliance rules, any NFA member or employee of a member is subject to disciplinary action for failure to comply with an arbitration decision.

Education

NFA educational efforts are directed to both members and the investing public. Members are assisted in complying with NFA rules and CFTC registration. For the investing public, NFA produces materials concerning such topics as the fundamentals of futures trading and identifying fraud.

Structure

NFA is governed by a 42-member board of directors. This board makes decisions concerning priorities, policies, plans, funding, budget and bylaws. It represents all sectors of NFA membership as follows: fourteen directors represent FCMs; three directors represent CTAs; two represent CPOs; two directors represent IBs; three represent commodity-related commercial firms; two represent commercial banks; and thirteen represent futures exchanges. The remaining three are public directors, that is, individuals with no present direct affiliation with the futures industry. All, except for the public directors, are selected by NFA members during the annual election held in January. Public directors are chosen by the board; all directors serve three year terms.

Executive committee

Although the full NFA board makes all major decisions, the direction and supervision of day-to-day operations are provided by an Executive Committee. The Executive Committee comprises ten members including the NFA president, the chairman of the board of directors, plus eight other members of the board. Of the eight directors, three represent FCMs, plus IBs, two represent exchanges, two represent industry participants (CTAs, CPOs, commercial firms and banks), and there is one public director.

Both the board and the Executive Committee are designed to provide balanced representation by membership category and geographic location. Thus, the number of directors allowed from the same NFA geographic region (Eastern, Central or Western) is limited for each category.

APPENDIX

III

United Kingdom industry regulation

The Security and Investment Board's principles

1 Integrity.
2 Skill, care and diligence.
3 Market practice.
4 Information about customers.
5 Information for customers.
6 Conflicts of interest.
7 Customer assets.
8 Financial resources.
9 Internal organisation.
10 Relations and regulators.

Securities and Futures Authority rules for dealing with clients

Objectives of SFA rules:

1.1 The objective of these rules is to ensure that a member firm will at all times:

(a) observe high standards of integrity and fair dealing in the conduct of investment business and comply with best market practice;

(b) act with due skill, care and diligence in providing any service which it provides or holds itself out as willing to provide either in connection with or in the course of carrying on investment business;

(c) act in the best interests of its customers in the provision of advice and in any transaction entered into or arranged to be entered into with them or on their behalf; and

(d) observe proper standards of disclosure and accountability.

Customer agreement and risk disclosure statements

5.37 General

5.37.1 A member firm shall not in the course of carrying on investment business provide any service otherwise than in pursuance of the terms of a written instrument ('a Customer Agreement') which is effective or which the member firm may, under rule 5.44.1 take to be effective when the services are provided and which satisfies the requirements relevant to it in this part of these rules unless:

(a) the service constitutes the effecting of a transaction with or for a person who is a market counterparty or an execution-only customer of the member firm;

(b) the service is by way of advice given in the course of and for the purposes of preparing a Customer Agreement;

(c) the service is in pursuance of a Customer Agreement which has ceased to be effective, but only for the purposes of fulfilling any obligation outstanding when it ceased to be effective;

(d) the service consists of the issue of any tip sheet, brokers circular or other publication pursuant to the rules under 6.4 of these rules;

(e) in the case of the customers eligible to receive a Customer Agreement other than a terms of business letter, the following conditions are fulfilled:

   (i) where the terms of that agreement which are required by rule 5.38.1 to be included in every Customer Agreement have been agreed;

   (ii) the member firm reasonably believes that the customer understands them; and

      (aa) is not the purchase of an investment, which is not a readily realisable investment,

      (bb) if the transaction is a margined transaction, is one which does and was intended to close out an open position of the customer acquired under a previous margined transaction,

      (cc) is the first or only transaction contemplated under the proposed agreement or the reversal of that transaction, and

      (dd) is not a transaction effected by the member firm as a discretionary portfolio manager; or

(f) in the case of a customer eligible to receive a terms of business letter, the member firm has finalised provisions thereof and those terms would satisfy the requirements of these rules as to the matters to be contained in a Customer Agreement with that customer; and either,

   (i) the service is the first service to be provided under the provisions of the proposed terms of the business letter and the member firm reasonably believes that the customer knows and understands those terms, and a terms of business letter is given or sent to him forthwith upon the service being provided; or

(ii) the service is provided for him within a period of three months after the terms of business letter has been given or sent to him, and when it is provided negotiations between the member firm and the customer are proceeding with a view to the settlement of an agreed terms of business letter.

5.37.2 A Customer Agreement shall be in the form of:

(a) a full Customer Agreement containing at least the matters specified in the rules under paragraphs 5.38 and 5.40;

(b) an occasional Customer Agreement containing at least the matters specified in the rules under paragraphs 5.38 and 5.41; or

(c) in the case of a business, professional or experienced investor, a terms of business letter, containing at least the matters specified in the rules under paragraphs 5.38 and 5.42.

5.38 Matters to be contained in every Customer Agreement

5.38.1 Every Customer Agreement shall:

(a) state that the member firm is regulated in the conduct of its investment business by the Association;

(b) specify the nature of the services to be provided by the member firm under the agreement which, in the case of a terms of business letter for a customer, who is an experienced investor or a professional investor should be confined to services in relation to which the customer is an experienced or professional investor, as the case may be;

(c) (i) specify whether the services provided by the member firm will include advising on or effecting:

(aa) margined transactions, or

(bb) units in collective investment schemes which are not regulated collective investment schemes; and

(ii) in the case of paragraph (aa) above, specify:

(A) the circumstances in which the customer will be

required to pay a deposit or margin in support of such transaction, or supplement that payment after the transaction has been effected,

(B) the form in which such payment or supplement is to be paid, and

(C) the rights exercisable by the member firm if the customer fails to make any such payment;

(d) contain where relevant a warning as to the circumstances in which the member firm may close out the customer's existing contracts without reference to him pursuant to the rules under 7.7 of these rules or otherwise;

(e) if the member firm has the authority of the customer to effect margined transactions with or for the customer in other than marketable investments, state that fact;

(f) state, where relevant, the arrangements by which the member firm may hold, use or transfer client money for the purposes of effecting transactions outside the United Kingdom;

(g) subject to rule 5.41.1, specify the circumstances, if any, in which the member firm may make unsolicited calls upon a customer and contain a warning that the customer may, in relation to any investment agreement entered into in the course of or in consequence of such a call, forfeit the right conferred upon him by s.56 of the Act to treat such an agreement as unenforceable;

(h) state fully and intelligibly the basis on which any commissions or charges payable to the member firm by the customer are to be calculated, how they are to be paid or collected and how frequently, specifying:

(i) whether the member firm may benefit from any price difference or remuneration paid by another party;

(ii) where any fee, charge or commission is to be shared by the member firm with a third party as a reward for the introduction of business to the member firm, that fact and either the amount of his share or stating that the amount will be given to the customer on request; and

(iii) where the basis for any fee, charge or commission may be separately negotiated, that fact and the general circumstances in which it may be so negotiated;

(i) state how a customer should give instructions, how the member firm is to confirm receipt of those instructions, the scope of its right (if any) to refuse those instructions and how any authority of the member firm to act for the customer may be terminated; and

(j) state how the agreement may be terminated, that it may be terminated on an immediate written notice given by the customer to the member firm or, *in the case of an investment in a collective investment scheme, in accordance with the rules of that scheme*, and that such termination shall be without payment by way of a penalty by the customer of any additional payment in respect of that termination, other than the realisation of dealing losses or the incurring of dealing expenses.

PRACTICE NOTE

This rule would not preclude the negotiation by the member firm of an additional payment on the termination of a Customer Agreement of a customer eligible to receive a terms of business letter.

5.39 Discretionary managed portfolios

5.39.1 Where the service to be provided by the member firm or by any associate of the member firm includes the management of a discretionary managed portfolio, a Customer Agreement shall, in addition to the requirements under rule 5.38.1 and, where applicable, 5.40.1:

(a) specify the customer's investment objectives and any restrictions on the categories of investment or the markets in or on which funds may be invested;

(b) specify whether and to whom the member firm is authorised to delegate the whole or any part of the exercise of its discretion in managing a customer's portfolio;

(c) state whether the member firm is authorised to invest in a collective investment scheme operated by or on the advice of the member firm or one of its associates;

(d) state whether the member firm is authorised to commit the customer to a financial obligation to supplement the funds in his portfolio, either by borrowing on his behalf or committing him to a contract, the performance of which may not be possible without such a supplement, specifying the limits thereupon or that it is unlimited;

(e) where there is a limit to the amount which may be committed by way of margin out of the funds in the customer's portfolio (with or without any supplement thereto) the amount of each limit, stating clearly whether and in what circumstances (if any) the client may be required to pay margin in excess of that specified limit;

(f) state the frequency with which the customer is to be provided with a statement of the money and investments comprised in his portfolio, the value thereof and the basis of such valuation; and whether or not the statement will include a measure of portfolio performance, and if so, the basis on which that performance is to be measured; and

(g) state whether the member firm has a commercial arrangement with a third party under which the member firm will receive investment advice from that third party as to how the funds of the customer ought or might be invested and giving particulars of that arrangement.

5.39.2 A member firm shall provide a statement pursuant to rule 5.39.1 (f) at least once in every 6 months or, if the customer has on his own initiative expressly requested it, once in every year, and, in either case, send it to the customer within 10 business days of the date as at which the statement was made up.

5.39.3 If a discretionary managed portfolio may include uncovered open positions or if money may be borrowed from a third party against the security of investments in such a portfolio or any of those investments may be lent to a third party, the member firm shall supply to the customer, not later than 2 weeks after each calendar month in which there are uncovered open positions, borrowings or loans of investments, as the case may be, a statement of:

(a) the uncovered open positions in the portfolio during the month and a valuation thereof at the end of the month;

(b) the investments which have been on loan to third parties at any time during the month and the income which has accrued to the portfolio during the month in respect thereof; and

(c) the amount borrowed for the portfolio and outstanding during the month and the interest charged to the portfolio in respect thereof.

5.40 Contents of a full customer agreement

5.40.1 In addition to the matters required to be contained in every Customer Agreement under rule 5.38.1 a full customer agreement shall:

(a) specify the customer's investment objectives, and state whether or not there are any restrictions on the categories of investment or the markets on which funds may be invested and, if there are, specifying them;

(b) if the member firm is authorised to invest the customer's funds in investments not readily realisable, contain a warning that such investments may be difficult to realise, that market makers may not be prepared to deal in them and that proper information for determining their current value may not be available;

(c) where the member firm does not have standing authority to act for the customer, state how the customer is to give instructions to the member firm, how the member firm confirms those instructions and the circumstances (if any) in which they may be refused by the member firm;

(d) state the manner in which the member firm's advice (if any) is to be conveyed to the customer and the extent (if at all) to which it is to communicate the basis for such advice;

(e) state where relevant the arrangements for accounting to the customer in respect of transactions arranged on his behalf;

(f) state whether and, if it be the case, the extent to which and how and in whose name the customer's investments and money is to be held by someone other than the member firm, specifying whether that person is an associate of the member firm and the fact and nature of that connection; whether or not the member firm accepts liability for any default in respect thereof; and the arrangements for accounting to the customer for income received and rights conferred in respect of such investments;

PRACTICE NOTE

The reference to money being 'held' by someone other than the member firm does not include money deposited by the member firm with a bank or other person, such as a building society, acting in the capacity of a deposit taking institution.

(g) if documents of title or documents evidencing title to investments belonging to a customer are to be held by or on behalf of the member firm, specify whether or not those documents can be lent to a third party and whether or not money can be borrowed on the customer's behalf against the security of those documents; and

(h) in the case of a managed portfolio, state the initial value of the portfolio, giving the date on which either the member firm assumed responsibility for managing the portfolio or on which the investments in the portfolio were acquired, the initial composition of the portfolio and the periods of account for which statements are provided pursuant to the rules under 5.20 of these rules.

5.40.2 Before a member firm can provide an investment service pursuant to a full customer agreement, a copy of the agreement signed by or on behalf of the member firm must be sent by post to the customer and either:

(a) the member firm must have received:

(i) a copy of the agreement signed by or on behalf of the customer, or

(ii) a letter, fax, telex, or similar written communication signed by or on behalf of the customer which clearly indicates unqualified assent to the terms of the Customer Agreement; or

(b) if the customer is not resident in the United Kingdom and has declined an opportunity to sign a copy of the agreement, the member firm must reasonably believe that he has consented to the terms of the agreement.

5.41 Occasional customer agreement

5.41.1 In addition to the matters required to be contained in every Customer Agreement under rule 5.38.1 an occasional customer agreement shall not provide that a member firm may make unsolicited calls upon a customer and shall contain statements of the advice which the member firm has given the customer and of the instructions which the customer has given the member firm to effect transactions on his behalf.

5.41.2 Before a member firm can provide an investment service in pursuance of an occasional customer agreement, a copy of the agreement signed by or on behalf of the member firm must be sent by post to the customer and the customer must have received a copy and confirmed the instructions stated in it:

SAVE THAT such copy may be delivered otherwise than by post where the customer's instructions are to dispose of investments or to close out open positions and the member firm reasonably believes a delay in carrying out those instructions will expose the customer to the risk of loss.

5.42 Terms of business letter

5.42.1 In addition to the matters required to be contained in every Customer Agreement under rule 5.38.1 a terms of business letter shall, where services are to be provided on the basis that the customer is a business investor state that fact or in the case of an experienced investor, identify the descriptions of investment in connection with which services are to be provided and state that the member firm regards him as an experienced investor in relation to them or, in the case of a professional investor, identify such services and declare the customer to be a professional investor in relation to them.

5.42.2 A terms of business letter may provide that the member firm does not owe the customer a duty to secure best execution of any transaction in an investment of any description which is effected with the customer by the member firm as a principal and which the customer has requested the member firm so to effect:

BUT a terms of business letter shall not contain such a statement, in relation to transactions which are to be effected with the customer on the basis that he is an experienced investor, unless the member firm reasonably believes either:

(a) the customer (being an individual) has such competence in financial matters generally and knowledge of the investments in question and of markets in them as to enable him:

(i) to make on his own behalf a judgement of professional quality as to the merits of any advice he may be given in relation to those investments or possible transactions in them, and

(ii) competently to protect his own interests in effecting transactions in those investments on his own behalf; or

(b) that the customer (being a body of persons carrying on a business) has as a member, officer or employee of the body such an individual as is described in sub-paragraph (a) above and who will be responsible for dealings between the member firm and the customer.

PRACTICE NOTE

Member firms are reminded that the definition of 'discretionary portfolio manager' does not release a member firm acting in that capacity from a duty to secure best execution.

5.42.3 A member firm shall not provide an investment service in pursuance of a terms of business letter, unless a copy of the letter signed by or on behalf of the member firm has been given or sent to the customer and:

(a) the member firm must not have been notified by the customer either:

(i) that he does not accept any of the terms of business set out in the letter, or

(ii) before the letter was sent to him, that services were not to be provided until he had confirmed to the member firm his acceptance of the letter (in which case no such services may be provided until the customer has notified his acceptance accordingly); and

(b) in the case of transactions to be effected with a customer who is an experienced investor and the letter provides either that:

(i) the member firm does not owe a duty to secure best execution of such transactions; or

(ii) money held or received by the member firm for the customer shall not be treated as client money subject to the Client Money Rules, the member firm reasonably believes that the customer understands that provision and has consented to it and to the other terms of business set out in that letter.

5.42.4 In this rule and in rule 5.40 and rule 5.41, references to sending by post include references to sending by telex, fax or other methods of electronic transfer and a telex is deemed to have been signed by the person sending it if the recipient has satisfactorily tested its authenticity.

5.43 Customer Agreement ceasing to be effective

5.43.1 A Customer Agreement shall cease to be effective for the purpose of these rules on the earliest of the following:

(a) the time specified in the agreement for its termination;

(b) the time notified by the customer to the member firm, or by the member firm to the customer, as the time at which the agreement is to cease to have effect; or

(c) in the case of an occasional customer agreement where no such notification has been given, when the instructions which the customer has given to the member firm have been carried out.

5.44 A customer who is more than one person

5.44.1 Where the customer is more than one person, all of whom are acting as trustees and the relevant requirements of this part of these rules as to signature, consent or confirmation have been fulfilled by one or more but not all of the trustees, those requirements may, in the period of 6 months from the time when they are first so fulfilled, be taken as fulfilled by all of the trustees, unless the member firm has reason to believe that any of the other trustees has refused to provide his signature or give his consent or confirmation, as the case may be.

5.45 Risk warning statements

5.45.1 Subject to rule 5.45.3, a member firm shall not effect with or on behalf of a customer or advise or procure a customer to enter into a transaction relating to an investment of a description referred to in paragraphs 8 or 9 of Schedule 1 to the Act (or to any right or interest therein including any such right or interest which falls within paragraph 7 of that Schedule) unless:

(a) (i) except where the transaction is a bet placed with the member firm as a bookmaker, the member firm has, before the transaction is effected or the advice given, delivered to the customer a written Risk Disclosure Statement containing the matters set out in Appendix 3 to these rules, and:

(aa) if the transaction in question is a limited liability transaction, the member firm shall have delivered to the customer an additional Risk Disclosure Statement containing the matters set out in Appendix 4 to these rules,

(bb) if the transaction in question is undertaken or proposed to be undertaken otherwise than on a recognised or designated investment exchange or otherwise than in a contract of a type traded thereon, the member firm shall have delivered to the customer an additional Risk Disclosure Statement containing the matters set out in Appendix 5 to these rules, or

(ii) if the transaction is a bet placed with the member firm as a bookmaker, the member firm shall have delivered to the customer an additional Risk Disclosure Statement containing the matters set out in Appendix 6 to these rules and if the transaction in question is a limited liability transaction, and additional Risk Disclosure Statement containing the matters set out in Appendix 7 to these rules; and

(b) subject to rule 5.45.2, the member firm has received:

(i) a copy of such statement or statements, signed by the customer in the appropriate places, or

(ii) a letter, fax, telex or similar communication signed by the customer stating that he has read and understood the risk disclosure statement or statements.

PRACTICE NOTE

A risk warning statement is effective for each transaction of the type referred to in the risk warning statement and does not have to be given on the occasion of each transaction.

5.45.2 The requirements under rule 5.45.1(b) shall not apply in the case of any such statement where the member firm (not being an execution-only dealer) reasonably believes that the customer is a business investor, or an experienced investor or a professional investor in relation to the relevant transaction and that he has read and understood the statement or statements.

5.45.3 The requirements under rule 5.45.1 shall not apply in the case of a transaction which is to be effected or proposed to be effected by a member firm:

General risk disclosure statement

This statement is made pursuant to rule 5.45.1 of the rules of the Association of Futures Brokers and Dealers Limited.

The risk of loss in investing in commodity, financial or other futures, options or contracts for differences can be substantial. You should carefully consider whether such investments are suitable for you in light of your circumstances and financial resources. You should be aware of the following points:

1 If the market moves against your position, you may, in a relatively

short time, sustain a total loss of the funds placed by way of margin or deposit with your broker. Alternatively, you may be called upon to deposit a substantial additional margin, at short notice, to maintain your position. If you do not provide such additional funds within the time required, your position may be liquidated at a loss and you will be liable for any resulting deficit.

2 If you deposit collateral as security for calls made upon you by your broker, it will not receive the same protection as if it were a cash deposit held on trust in a segregated client bank account and, once dealings on your behalf are undertaken, that collateral will cease to be your property and may be passed on to an exchange, clearing house or other brokers. Even if your dealings should ultimately prove profitable, you may have to accept payment in cash and not get back the actual assets which you have deposited.

3 Under certain market conditions it may be difficult or impossible to liquidate a position. This may occur, for example, where trading is suspended or restricted at times of rapid price movement.

4 Where permitted, placing a stop-loss order will not necessarily limit your losses to the intended amounts, for market conditions may make it impossible to execute such orders at the stipulated price.

5 A spread or straddle position may be as risky as a simple long or short position and can be more complex.

6 Markets in futures, options and contracts for differences can be highly volatile and investment in them carries a substantial risk of loss. The high degree of 'gearing' or 'leverage' which is often obtainable in trading these contracts stems from the payment of what is a comparatively modest deposit or margin when compared with the overall contract value. As a result, a relatively small market movement can, in addition to achieving substantial gains, where the market moves in your favour, result in substantial loss which may exceed your original investment where there is an equally small movement against you.

7 If you take (buy) an option, your risk in most cases will be less than trading in futures since you should not lose more than the premium you paid plus any commission or other transaction charges.

If you grant (sell) an option, your risk of loss may be as great as your exposure in trading futures, since you carry the risk of unlimited potential loss which, following a relatively small adverse market movement, can exceed the premium payment received by you for granting (selling) the option. Moreover, you have no control over when you might be required to exercise the option. Only experienced traders with substantial capital should contemplate granting options.

There are many different types of options and you should discuss with your broker, your investment requirements and the risks involved in entering such contracts, before committing yourself.

8 Unless you have effectively agreed otherwise in circumstances where this is permitted under the rules of the Association, when your broker deals for you, you should do so only in contracts of the types dealt with on one of the recognised or designated exchanges. If you instruct your broker on foreign markets, he will probably instruct a broker in the country concerned. Normally that broker will not be subject to the rules or regulations of the Association and the exchange on which he effects the transaction may not be subject to as strict regulations as a recognised investment exchange in the United Kingdom. Hence, the degree of protection afforded to you may be less than if you restrict your transactions to the United Kingdom markets. You should ensure that your broker explains the protections which will operate and ascertain whether he accepts liability if the foreign broker defaults.

9 Prior to the commencement of trading, you should require from your broker written confirmation of all commission and other transaction charges for which you will be liable. If the charges are not expressed in specific money terms (but, for example, as a percentage of contract value), you should obtain a clear written explanation, including appropriate examples, to establish what such charges are likely to mean to you in specific money terms. You should realise that when commission is charged as a percentage it would normally be as a percentage of the total contract value and not simply a percentage of your deposit.

10 Brokers may also be dealers trading for their own account in the same markets as you, in which case their own account involvement could be contrary to your interests. Your broker is required to inform you in advance if he deals on his own behalf in relevant markets. The guarantee of performance by the exchanges' clearing house applies only to their contracts with members. They do not guarantee performance of your broker's contracts with you.

11 Your broker's insolvency or that of any other brokers involved in your contracts may lead to your positions being closed out without your consent.

12 Your broker is required to hold your money in segregated trust accounts in accordance with the regulations of the Securities and Investments Board and the Association, but this may not afford complete protection.*

13 You have agreed that your money held by your broker need not be segregated in a client bank account and you will lack that protection should your broker become insolvent.**

This brief statement cannot disclose all risks of investments in futures, options and contracts for differences. They are not suitable for many members of the public and you should carefully study such investments before you commit funds to them. They may also have tax consequences and on this you should consult your lawyer, accountant or other tax adviser.

*Delete if statement given to business, professional or experienced investor who has opted out of segregation.
**Delete unless statement given to business, professional or experienced investor who has opted out of segregation.

....

(Name of Firm)

....

(On duplicate for signature by customer)

I have read and understood the risk disclosure statement set out above.

Date ....

(Signature of customer)

APPENDIX IV

An independent and central clearing house

Since it was founded in 1888 as the London Produce Clearing House to clear sugar and coffee trading in London, the International Commodities Clearing House Limited (ICCH) has played a leading part in the development of commodity and financial futures and options trading in London and elsewhere.

ICCH Limited is owned by six of London's largest clearing banks: Barclays Bank plc, Lloyds Bank plc, Midland Bank plc, National Westminster Bank plc, The Royal Bank of Scotland plc and Standard Chartered Bank plc. As the Clearing House to the London futures exchanges, it is able to provide a centralised service to clearing members across the different contracts and markets with particular regard to banking systems and delivery administration.

As independent guarantor to four London markets the Clearing House has a wide diversification of risk. The Clearing House's effective internal risk management incorporates data on clearing members' trading across a range of different contracts, providing the Clearing House with an overall view of financial, metal and soft commodity futures and options activity in London. Being independent the Clearing House is able to balance the financial integrity of the markets with the commercial pressures on the exchanges and their members.

While owing no allegiance to any one exchange, the Clearing House is dedicated to the promotion and growth of London's derivative markets both in the UK and in the international arena. In providing a centralised service across markets, the Clearing House benefits from significant economies of scale. Clearing members benefit directly from more standardised back-office trade processing procedures across different markets and centralised margin payment and receipt routines.

In funding its own guarantee backing of £150 million, the Clearing House enables clearing members to control their own risk without the additional uncertainty of the risk associated with a mutual guarantee.

A recognised clearing house

Under the regulatory regime in London governed by the Financial Services Act 1986, a clearing house may only retain recognised status if several stringent criteria are met to the satisfaction of the Securities and Investments Board (SIB), the lead regulator in the UK. Those criteria are:

Sufficient financial resources;
Adequate monitoring and compliance arrangements;
The provision to exchanges of the clearing services necessary for their own recognition;
The maintenance of high standards of integrity and fair dealing;
Willingness to co-operate in the sharing of information with the Secretary of State and other relevant regulatory agencies.

In addition to meeting these specific requirements of the legislation the Clearing House has developed over many years a system of risk management to handle the counterparty, market price and delivery risks arising.

A principals' market

The London exchanges provide facilities for their members to trade; members may execute trades with one another across a trading floor by open outcry or, for certain contracts, through automated screen-based trading systems or inter-office dealing. All transactions executed by members are on a principal basis.

All trades must be routed to the Clearing House through a clearing member. Any non-clearing member wishing to trade on an exchange floor must be guaranteed by a clearing member through the establishment of a formal standardised clearing agreement, to which the Clearing House is a party. The Clearing House clears exclusively for the clearing members of the exchanges it supports. All non-clearing member trades must be cleared through a specific clearing member.

Clearing members do not necessarily execute all the transactions they clear, but may instead be allocated such business from executing brokers in accordance with their clients' instructions. Indeed some clearing members do not maintain a physical presence on the exchange floor.

Once a trade has been matched and registered in the name of a clearing member, the Clearing House is substituted by novation as the seller to every buyer and buyer to every seller on a principal to principal basis. Thus as the counterparty to every clearing member the Clearing House minimises counterparty risk. The Clearing House is legally responsible for the financial performance of the contract.

As principals to the contracts with their clients, clearing members are able to control their own risk. The service provided to a client by a broker and the commission paid are completely negotiable.

Membership requirements

The system employed for vetting applicants to membership forms an integral part of counterparty risk management. Membership is open to companies and partnerships who can fulfil certain criteria concerning financial integrity and probity, trading history, net worth, management reputation, parentage, type of business, administrative efficiency and relevant exchange and regulatory body membership.

The financial requirements for clearing members measure both liquidity (in terms of net current assets) and permanent capital base. The level of requirement varies depending on which markets are to be cleared by the member and on the category of membership. The standards required for each market are determined in consultation with the relevant exchange. Each exchange also has its own established membership requirements and application procedures.

In addition to these safeguards, the Clearing House clearing and settlement systems are designed to ensure that reliance is not placed solely on a member's net worth to make good any market losses, as in most circumstances the amount required will already be held as initial margin within the clearing system.

Application for membership

To be considered for membership of the Clearing House an applicant must provide the following background information and documentation:

Latest audited accounts;
Memorandum and articles of Association, Certificate of Incorporation;
Details of group structure, including the audited accounts of the parent company (if any);
Identity of any major shareholders;
Names of directors and relevant senior executives.

All clearing members must sign a standard Clearing Member Agreement with the Clearing House which establishes the legal nature of the relationship between the two parties.

Segregation of customer funds

One of the cornerstones of the regime of investor protection under the Financial Services Act is the requirement placed on brokers to segregate their clients' money into client bank accounts which are held on trust for the clients. At clearing house/exchange level, however, the rules require the members' money paid to the clearing house/exchange to be dealt with according to their own regulations.

Under UK legislation private investors funds must be segregated by their brokers. Other (business and professional) clients may choose in negotiation with their broker whether or not to request segregation. These arrangements are governed by the Client Money Rules of the SIB.

Under its regulations and procedures, the Clearing House has provided facilities for each clearing member to use two separate clearing accounts: one account in respect of the trades and positions of any member's segregated clients and one account in respect of all house and non-segregated client business.

Both clearing accounts are margined separately on a net basis with separate margin calls, payments and receipts. Neither the Clearing House nor the clearing member has any right of offset or netting across these two accounts.

In addition, for certain exchanges, the Clearing House has established further subdivisions of clearing members' non-segregated business (e.g. a split of house and non-segregated client trading) for position maintenance and regulatory purposes.

Customer protection

In order that a firm may execute and clear trades on behalf of customers in any of London's futures markets it must satisfy the membership requirements of the appropriate Self-Regulatory Organisation (SRO), the Clearing House and the relevant exchange(s).

Dealings in futures and options contracts are regulated by one of two SROs: the Association of Futures Brokers and Dealers Ltd (AFBD) or The Securities Association (TSA), depending on the firm's mix of investment business. Having achieved membership of the appropriate bodies the firm must subsequently ensure its strict compliance with the various rules, regulations and reporting requirements, or risk disciplinary action and possible curtailment of its investment activities.

The Clearing House, exchange and AFBD/TSA membership screening procedures form the first line of defence for clients, in conjunction with the rules for the segregation of clients' money, against the event of a default by a member.

The provision of segregated accounts at clearing house level and the prohibition of client/house account set-off provide further safeguards for the client.

A compensation scheme designed specifically for smaller clients in the event of a broker's insolvency is administered by the SIB. Under this scheme the SIB is empowered to compensate such an investor up to

100% of the first £30 000 loss suffered by the client and up to 90% of the next £20 000 making a maximum sum of £48 000 per claim.

The system of margining

As the ultimate counterparty to every trade and guarantor to the markets the Clearing House is at risk to the default of a clearing member. The extent of this risk is related to the size of each clearing member's net open position in each of the different markets. All open positions are revalued on a daily basis and any profits/losses arising are paid/received by the Clearing House by way of variation margin (see below). To cover its risk exposure the Clearing House requires collateral or margin deposits on all net open positions held by clearing members; this requirement is referred to as initial margin.

Initial margin

The Clearing House, in conjunction with the exchanges, sets rates of initial margin for all contracts which it clears. These rates are set to cover one day's price risk with reference to the volatility of each contract and hence may vary from time to time. Initial margin is intended to provide the Clearing House with sufficient funds to make good any losses following a forced close-out. Clearing members may impose more stringent requirements on their customers in accordance with the rules of the relevant exchange(s). All clearing members must provide the full initial margin daily; the Clearing House may, at its discretion, require additional margin buffers in special circumstances.

Initial margin requirements are set with primary reference to daily price moves, and are usually set to cover 90–98% of observed daily price movements. Reference is also made to other market data e.g. the spread of open interest and implied (option) volatility. Initial margin deposits are normally set at between 0.1 and 10% of contract value. Rates are set to cover outright positions; separate rates for spreads (straddles) are determined in the same way. Options are margined with reference to the underlying instrument taking account of offsetting risks.

Clearing members' margin liabilities are assessed throughout the day and recalculated at the end of each day. If a member does not have sufficient cover lodged with the Clearing House a Protected Payment System (PPS) call is issued to his bank by 8.30 am. Initial margins must be covered in one of the forms of approved collateral which are currently cash (normally sterling, dollars, deutschmark, ECU or yen), certain Government Securities or Bank Guarantees from Clearing House approved banks.

Margining is on a 'net' basis. Net margining ensures that the margin held is directly proportional to the risk inherent in a member's position. The Clearing House does not monitor its members' relationships with clients but works closely with the exchanges and appropriate regulatory authorities to ensure the financial viability of its members.

Variation margin

London's financial and commodity futures markets operate on a daily settlement (or mark) to market basis. This means that at the end of each day's trading all open contracts are registered or revalued anew at that day's closing price. This is, in practice, determined by the relevant exchange but the Clearing House reserves the right to determine its own official quotations, if necessary.

Debits and credits arising from the settlement (or mark) to market process are posted daily to members' accounts. These procedures are also applied to traded options. If there is any shortfall a call to the member's bank will be made through the PPS by 8.30 am. During periods of extreme volatility the Clearing House may call for additional variation margins to be paid during the day to supplement the initial margin cover already held but now eroded to the extent of the adverse price move. Additional margins must be paid within an hour of such a call being issued.

The only exception to the daily settlement process is the London Metal Exchange (LME). LME futures contracts cannot be settled before the prompt day. However, each open contract is compared with that day's closing price and a contingent variation margin is calculated. If this is a credit (e.g. current market prices are above that when the contract was bought), this may be used to offset contingent debits. Net debits must be covered in the same way as initial margins. These procedures are also applied to contracts that are to be fulfilled by physical tender (of bonds, cocoa, etc).

Delivery and banking administration

A key element of the Clearing House operations is the provision to clearing members of centralised delivery and banking facilities.

Delivery

As the counterparty to all clearing members' open positions, the Clearing House undertakes a central role in the final settlement of futures and options contracts at maturity, in effect guaranteeing the financial performance of the contract by both parties. The range of products cleared by the Clearing House includes those contracts involving the physical delivery of a soft commodity, metal or financial instrument in addition to a number of cash settlement contracts. In respect of physical deliveries, the Clearing House administers the allocation of sellers to buyers, although in many instances neither party will know of the other's identity. In all cases, to ensure the integrity of the market, the seller must deliver to the Clearing House prior to receiving payment and the buyer must pay the Clearing House prior to receiving delivery. Wherever the underlying cash or physical market allows, same-day delivery versus payment is achieved.

Banking

The daily recalculation of margin liabilities (see separate section) generates daily payments and receipts between the Clearing House and each of the clearing members. As far as possible, payments and receipts within the same currency are netted for each clearing member account. This practice considerably reduces the number of monetary transactions for those members trading across several different contracts and exchanges. In addition, the Clearing House allows members the flexibility to cover their initial margin liabilities with cash or collateral of a different denomination. The Clearing House operates a centralised treasury function, enabling it to pay members a reasonable rate of interest on the bulk of their margin deposits. This central system is also utilised by the Clearing House for the collection of exchange and Clearing House fees from clearing members.

Risk management and surveillance

The Clearing House's central role in the London markets and the real time systems available (which cover trade matching, allocation, confirmation, clearing, risk management and banking) provide a continuous and progressive monitoring and amalgamation of liabilities. This facilitates overall market monitoring which the Clearing House can undertake either independently or in conjunction with the exchanges and regulatory bodies such as the SIB, AFBD and TSA. The mutual interchange of information on matters of crucial importance to the efficient and orderly functioning of the markets is a requirement of the Financial Services Act.

Further controls exist in the requirement on members to provide regular balance sheet and other financial information and the carrying out of specific trading reviews if the circumstances require.

The Clearing House makes its own independent assessment of members' resources and monitors the ratio of members' initial margin liabilities to their resources.

The Clearing House maintains comprehensive statistical information to enable its risk analysis team to survey and monitor historical volatilities, implied volatilities, seasonal price movements and correlations between delivery months or different contracts. This statistical information is essential to a full analysis of market conditions, liquidity, positions and deliveries.

The Risk Management Department within the Clearing House has specific responsibility for financial and market surveillance, margin requirements and membership applications and monitoring.

The financial resources of the Clearing House

As the Clearing House is an independent clearing house there is no mutual guarantee or common bond liability placed on members who are insulated from the effects of a default by another member.

The Clearing House may itself call upon the following resources:

The margin deposits of the defaulting firm;
Surplus capital of the Clearing House;
Discrete backing of £150 million provided by the consortium banks and the insurance market, financed independently by the Clearing House.

Default of a clearing member

Under the General Regulations of the Clearing House a clearing member is deemed to be in default in a number of circumstances, which include the following:

Where a member is in breach of relevant Clearing House, exchange or regulatory body rules or procedures;
Where a member fails to make any payment due or fails to perform any tender or delivery obligation;
Where, in respect of a member, there is a bankruptcy or winding up or where an administrator or receiver is appointed.

In the event of a member default the Clearing House has the power to act in a variety of ways, including the following:

To close out and settle open contracts;
To transfer open contracts to another member with the recipient's agreement;
To call in any relevant bank guarantees;
To realise any relevant securities being held as collateral.

While seeking to limit its own liability, the Clearing House would keep all the relevant exchanges and regulatory authorities fully informed of the situation regarding a member's default and seek to act in the best interests of the market, the clients and the member involved.

All default procedures must take account of the segregation provisions so that collateral held for a member's segregated client account may only be realised in respect of a default involving a member's segregated client account. In addition there can be no set-off between a member's house and segregated client accounts.

In taking any of the actions described above, the Clearing House has been granted protection by the 1989 Companies Act against challenges under the existing UK insolvency rules.

Summary of the benefits of central clearing

1 The diversity of the markets cleared by the Clearing House means lower overall risk, with enhanced risk management through accurate assessments of intermarket exposure.

2 The Clearing House's independent status enables maximum attention to be paid to the paramount objective of market security.
3 The lack of a mutual guarantee reduces the costs and liabilities of all clearing members in the event of a default by a clearing member.
4 Central banking allows single settlement payments for multiple markets and the lodgement of a single unit of collateral or currency for use against liabilities across multiple markets, thus reducing back-office costs.
5 Similarly, a central accounting system simplifies the process of fee collection from, and interest payments to, clearing members.
6 The central overview created by multi-market clearing has allowed the Clearing House to develop a central risk management research and development capability.
7 Against a background of exchange development, growth, diversification and competition in both products and systems, the London Clearing House is uniquely placed in providing a secure platform and common link for the London exchanges to the benefit of all London market participants.

APPENDIX

V

The French markets

Contract specifications - French markets

	White sugar	Cocoa beans	Robusta coffee	Potatoes
Contract size	50 tonnes in bags	10 tonnes in bags	5 tonnes in bags	20 tonnes in bags on pallets
Delivery months	Mar/May/Aug/ Oct/Dec	Mar/May/July/ Sept/Dec	Jan/Mar/May/ July/Sept/Nov	Nov/Feb/Apr/ May
Price basis	USD/t	FF/100 kilos	FF/100 kilos	0.25FF/100 kg (50FF)
Delivery point	Approved port	Authorised warehouses in Amsterdam or Dunkirk	Authorised warehouses Approved ports	
Contract basis	Any origin	Ivory Coast*	Ivory Coast*	
Trading hours	1045–1330 1500–1900	1030–1300 1455–1755	1015–1300 1500–1830	1100–1245 1500–1630

* Other origins are deliverable with allowances laid down by the technical committee

MATIF (Marché à Terme d'Instruments Financiers)
Commodities - Traded volume from January 1991 to January 1992

		Contracts			
Month	**Sessions**	**SCD US white sugar**	**SCR FRF white sugar**	**P50 Potato 50mm**	**CAF Coffee**
January '91	22	20 897	35	1 358	30
February	20	16 023	10	2 355	110
March	20	18 595	-	5 994	33
April	21	17 961	-	5 324	105
May	19	14 986	-	3 445	0
June	20	16 083	-	745	15
July	23	18 600	-	1 505	0
August	20	10 803	-	1 720	163
September	21	21 806	-	1 033	12
October	23	23 178	-	1 955	0
November	19	11 691	-	824	20
December	21	8 745	-	529	0
January '92	22	24 975	-	1 062	0
Total	271	224 343	45	27 849	488

Index